Preface

Like all Schaum's Outline Series books, this is intended to be used primarily for self study, preferably in conjunction with a regular course in the fundamentals of computer science using the Java programming language.

The book includes over 200 examples and problems. The author firmly believes that programming is learned best by practice, following a well-constructed collection of examples with complete explanations. This book is designed to provide that support.

Source code for all the examples and solved problems in this book may be downloaded from the author's website http://www.mathcs.richmond.edu/~hubbard/schaums, or at his sites http://jhubbard.net/schaums or http://www.projectEuclid.net/schaums. These sites also contain any corrections and addenda for the book.

I wish to thank all my friends, colleagues, students, and the McGraw-Hill staff who have helped me with the critical review of this manuscript, including Eric Ciampa, David le Roux, Andrew Somers, Michael Somers, Maureen Walker, and Stefan Wentzig. Special thanks to Anita Hubbard for her advice, encouragement, and supply of creative problems for this book.

JOHN R. HUBBARD
Richmond, Virginia

Dedicated to our next generation:

Sara, John, Andrew, and Michael

Contents

Chapter 1

Getting Started

1.1 THE JAVA PROGRAMMING LANGUAGE

The Java programming language was developed by James Gosling at Sun Microsystems in 1991. Its name is a slang term for coffee. When the World Wide Web appeared on the Internet in 1993, the language was enhanced to facilitate programming on the web. Since then it has become one of the most popular languages, especially for network programming.

To see why Java is the language of choice among network programmers, imagine a network of different computers like this:

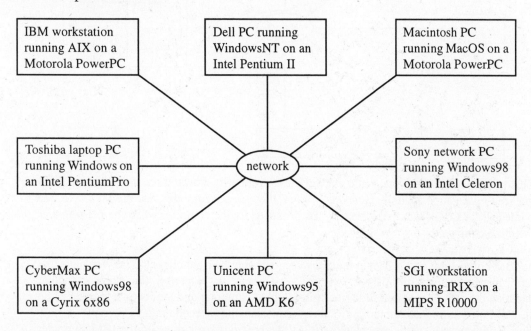

These might be eight computers in the same room connected within a local area network, or they could be in eight different cities on four continents connected by the Internet. The point is that they are running different operating systems (AIX, WindowsNT, *etc.*) on different processors (PowerPC, Pentium II, *etc.*). Suppose that you want to write a program on the IBM workstation that can be run on all eight computers.

Before a computer program can be run, it has to be translated into the machine language that the computer's processor understands. In programming languages such as Pascal and C++, this translation is done by a *compiler*, and the resulting machine language version of the program is called the *executable image*. But different processors have different machine languages. So, for example, an executable image produced on the IBM workstation would not run on any of the other computers in the network shown above. To have his or her program run on all the computers in the network, the programmer would have to compile it separately on each one!

To solve this problem, Java provides both a compiler and a software system called the Java Virtual Machine (JVM) for each computer system. The Java compiler, `javac`, translates Java source code into an intermediate level language, called *bytecodes*. Like the source code itself, bytecodes are independent of the type of computer system. The same bytecode file can be used by any computer. When one computer wants to run a Java program written on another computer, it downloads that program's bytecode file and delivers it to its own JVM. The JVM then translates the bytecodes into its own system's machine language and runs the result.

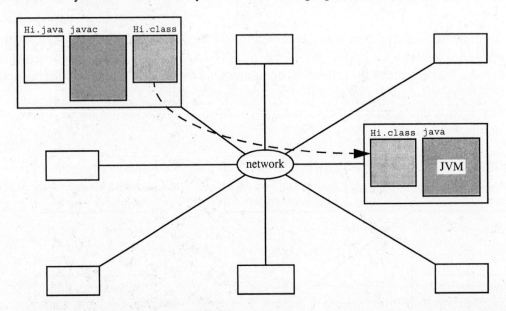

This picture represents the same network as before. It shows three files on the IBM computer: a Java source code file named `Hi.java`, the `javac` compiler, and the Java bytecode file named `Hi.class`. That bytecode file was produced by the compiler when the programmer executed the command

```
javac Hi.java
```

on the IBM computer. Later, a user at the Sony computer on the right clicked on a Web page that includes instructions to run the `Hi.class` program. In response, the Sony computer downloaded the `Hi.class` bytecode file from the IBM computer and ran its own local JVM on it. The JVM on the Sony computer knows how to translate the bytecode into its own processor's machine language so it can be executed there. All the previous work done on the IBM computer is completely independent of the Sony computer. In fact, the `Hi.class` bytecode file could have been produced long before the Sony computer or its Intel Celeron processor were ever invented!

Most Web browsers (Netscape's Communicator, Microsoft's Internet Explorer, *etc.*) come bundled with the JVM. So when you load a web page that includes instructions to run a Java program, the browser automatically downloads the bytecode file and runs the JVM on it. All you see are the results on your web page: animated images, data entry forms, buttons, scroll panes, check boxes, *etc.*

The JVM system is an *interpreter*. That means that it translates and runs each bytecode instruction separately, whenever it is needed by the complete program. For some programs, this can be quite slow. As an alternative, Java also provides local compilers for each system that will compile a bytecode file into an executable image for faster running. Java calls these compilers "Just-In-Time" (JIT) compilers. They come bundled with some web browsers (*e.g.*, Netscape).

1.2 DOWNLOADING THE JAVA DEVELOPMENT KIT

The process of designing, coding, testing, debugging, documenting, maintaining, and upgrading computer programs is called *software development*. An Integrated Development Environment (IDE) is a collection of integrated programs that facilitates software development. If you have access to an IDE (*e.g.*, Metrowerks's CodeWarrior, Enprise's JBuilder, Microsoft's Visual J++, Symantec's Visual Cafe, or IBM's Visual Age) skip to Section 1.6 on page 11.

The Java Development Kit (JDK) is a collection of programs to help developers compile, run, and debug Java programs. It is not as good as an IDE, but it is quite adequate for developing Java programs. Sun Microsystems provides it free of charge. This section describes how to download it from Sun's `javasoft` website.

To download the JDK to your computer, open your web browser (*e.g.*, Netscape Navigator) and enter the following URL in your browser's Location or Address field:

```
http://www.javasoft.com
```

This brings up the Java home page which should look something like this:

Click on the link labeled **Products & APIs** (the third item on the left side of the page shown here). This brings up the PRODUCTS & APIs page. Use the pull-down menu labelled ***Product Quick Pick*** to select the most recent version of the Java Development Kit. In the window shown below, that was **Java Development Kit 1.2 Platform -- JDK**.

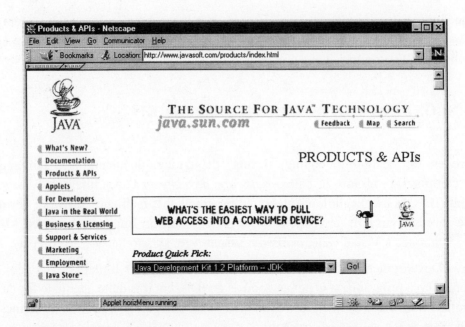

Then click on the Go! button and follow the directions given on the next page that comes up to download the JDK. You may be asked to become a member of the Java Developer Connection, requiring you to submit a User ID and Password that you select yourself.

Eventually, you should get to another pull-down menu labelled **Download JDK**:

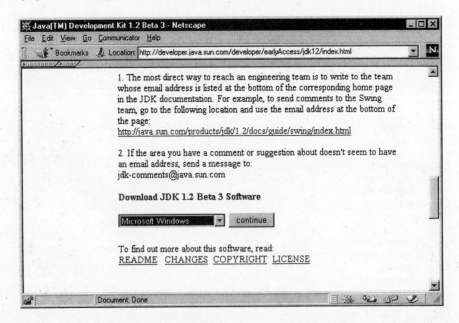

Select your computer's operating system and click on the continue button. You will then be asked to accept Sun's License & Export agreement.

When you finally get to the actual download button, it will probably be labelled with the name of the executable file that will downloaded, something like `jdk12-beta3-win32.exe`. Click on that button to begin the download.

If you are running Microsoft Windows, the system will bring up a panel like this:

Navigate up to the Desktop (as shown here) so that the file will appear there when it has finished downloading. Then press the Save button.

The JDK download is a large file. The one shown here (beta Release 1.2) is over 15 megabytes. So it may take well over an hour to download, depending upon the current traffic level at your site on the web.

1.3 INSTALLING THE JDK

After you have downloaded the JDK you can install it simply by running the executable program that you downloaded. To do that, double-click on the icon that was placed on your Desktop.

This only takes about a minute to install. Confirm all the suggested alternatives during the installation. During the installation process, the 15 megabytes gets decompressed into about 25 megabytes. The normal installation (in Microsoft Windows) would be into a new folder on your C: drive. When finished, it should look like this:

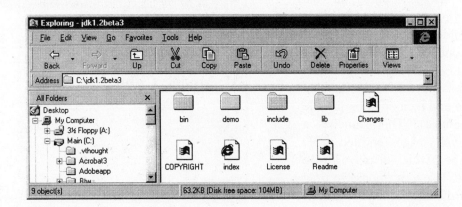

The `Readme` file is a text file that gives current information about the JDK and summarizes the contents of your `jdk` directory. The `index` file is a hypertext (web browser) file that outlines the JDK and provides browser-type access to its documentation, examples, and the JavaSoft web site. The `bin` directory contains the executable programs (binary files) that make up the JDK. The `lib` directory contains the library files for the Java language. The `include` directory contains the source code files that define the standard classes of the Java language. The `demo` directory contains over 20 demonstration programs.

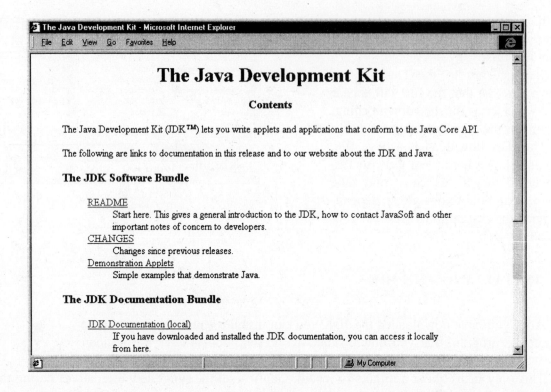

Double-click on the index file. This launches your web browser, displaying a web page entitled **The Java Development Kit**, as shown below.

To get an idea of what Java programs can do, click on the <u>Demonstration Applets</u> link. That opens a folder window that shows the contents of your `C:\jdk1.2beta3\demo\applets\` folder. Click on the folder labeled Wire Frame and then click on the file named example1. This launches a separate web page entitled "3D Model: Cube," which displays a wire frame cube. Use your mouse to drag a corner of the cube around within its picture frame and watch it rotate.

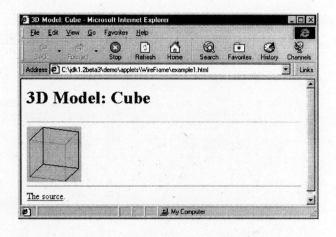

1.4 CREATING AND RUNNING A PROGRAM IN MICROSOFT WINDOWS

To create a Java program, you need to use an editor. You can use a word processor, such as Microsoft Word, but you have to be careful that the files you create are pure text files and that their file type is ".java". This section shows how to create a Java program using the simple Windows editor Notepad.

Start up the Notepad editor by selecting Programs > Accessories > Notepad from the Windows Start key. Then type the following four lines of Java code exactly as it is shown here:

```
public class HelloWorld
{ public static void main(String[] args)
  { System.out.println("Hello, World!");
  }
}
```

Type capital letters as capital letters and lowercase letters as lowercase letters. (Java is *case-sensitive*.) Type the parentheses, brackets, and braces exactly as shown here, and don't miss the semicolon at the end of the third line. Your Notepad window should look like this:

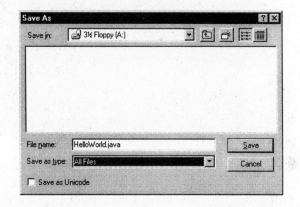

Save your file with the name `HelloWorld.java` as shown here.

Select All Files in the Save as type: field so that you can save the file with the correct file type. Notebook's default file type is `.txt`. But Java programs must have the file type `.java`.

Open a DOS command window by selecting Programs > Command Prompt from the Windows Start key. Use the DOS `cd` command to navigate to the folder that contains your Java program and then use the `dir` command to check that it is there and that it has the correct name.

```
Microsoft(R) Windows NT(TM)
(C) Copyright 1985-1996 Microsoft Corp.

C:\>a:

A:\>dir
 Volume in drive A has no label.
 Volume Serial Number is 0000-0000

 Directory of A:\

05/14/98  03:20p                    117 HelloWorld.java
               1 File(s)            117 bytes
                          1,457,152 bytes free

A:\>
```

(In this demonstration, we are storing our Java programs on a floppy disk on the `A:\` drive.)

Execute the following DOS command to view the contents of your file:

```
type HelloWorld.java
```

It should appear exactly as you typed it in the Notepad editor.

Now compile your program in the DOS window by executing the command

```
javac HelloWorld.java
```

If all goes well, the system should respond with another DOS prompt within a few seconds, thereby indicating that your program compiled successfully. If it did, then check your directory again to see that the compiler has produced a new file named HelloWorld.class.

```
Command Prompt
05/14/98  03:20p                    117 HelloWorld.java
             1 File(s)              117 bytes
                              1,457,152 bytes free

A:\>type HelloWorld.java
public class HelloWorld
{ public static void main(String args[])
   { System.out.println("Hello, World!");
   }
}

A:\>javac HelloWorld.java

A:\>dir
 Volume in drive A has no label.
 Volume Serial Number is 0000-0000

 Directory of A:\

05/14/98  03:20p                    117 HelloWorld.java
05/14/98  03:34p                    473 HelloWorld.class
             2 File(s)              590 bytes
                              1,456,640 bytes free

A:\>
```

This is the bytecode file that the JVM system uses to run your program. (Notice that it is more than four times the size of your source code file.)

Finally, execute the following command to run your program:

```
java HelloWorld
```

The system should respond by displaying the "Hello, World!" message:

```
Command Prompt
A:\>javac HelloWorld.java

A:\>dir
 Volume in drive A has no label.
 Volume Serial Number is 0000-0000

 Directory of A:\

05/14/98  03:20p                    117 HelloWorld.java
05/14/98  03:34p                    473 HelloWorld.class
             2 File(s)              590 bytes
                              1,456,640 bytes free

A:\>java HelloWorld
Hello, World!

A:\>
```

1.5 TROUBLESHOOTING

If you were able to get your program to run, skip to Section 1.6.

If your `HelloWorld.java` file did not show up in your folder when you executed the `dir` command, re-save it from the Notepad window.

If your `HelloWorld.java` file did show up in your folder but with the wrong name, re-save it from the Notepad window.

If your `HelloWorld.java` file did show up in your folder with the right name but its contents did not come out right when you executed the type HelloWorld.java command, go back to your Notepad window, correct the errors, and then re-save the file.

If the `javac HelloWorld.java` compile command did not work, try it again. Be sure you type "javac" (for "java compiler").

If the system does not know what the `javac` command is, then either the JDK is not installed correctly or the system does not know where it is installed. Use your Windows Explorer browser to find the folder where the JDK is installed. It should have a name like `jdk1.2` and be located on your `C:\` disk. Find the correct name for this folder, and then try executing the compile command with its path as a prefix, like this:

```
c:\jdk1.2\javac HelloWorld.java
```

If that works, then all you have to do is change the system PATH variable. If that does not work, then the JDK is probably not installed correctly. In that case, run the installation program again. If that doesn't work, start over again with a new download.

To determine whether the problem is with your system PATH variable, execute the following DOS command:

```
path
```

The system should respond like this:

```
 Command Prompt
 Volume Serial Number is 0000-0000

 Directory of A:\

05/14/98   03:20p                     117 HelloWorld.java
05/14/98   03:34p                     473 HelloWorld.class
              2 File(s)               590 bytes
                              1,456,640 bytes free

A:\>java HelloWorld
Hello, World!

A:\>path
PATH=C:\WINNT\system32;C:\WINNT;C:\Program Files\Kawa30;C:\jdk1.1.5\bin;C:
\system32;C:\WINNT;C:\Program Files\Kawa30;C:\jdk1.1.6\bin

A:\>_
```

The code that begins PATH=C:\WIN... is a listing of all the paths that the operating system checks to find the commands that you want to execute. The paths are separated by semicolons. One of them should include the name "jdk". If one does, then that is where the system is looking for the instructions on how to execute the `javac` command. If none of the paths includes the name "jdk", then you'll have to amend your system PATH variable.

To amend your system `PATH` variable so that it includes the path to the JDK, execute the following DOS command:

```
set path=c:\jdk1.2\bin;%path%
```

and then execute the plain

```
path
```

command again to see if the PATH variable was amended correctly:

```
  Command Prompt
                    2 File(s)              590 bytes
                               1,456,640 bytes free

A:\>java HelloWorld
Hello, World!

A:\>path
PATH=C:\WINNT\system32;C:\WINNT;C:\Program Files\Kawa30;C:\jdk1.1.5\bin;C:
\system32;C:\WINNT;C:\Program Files\Kawa30;C:\jdk1.1.6\bin

A:\>set path=c:\jdk1.2\bin;%path%

A:\>path
PATH=c:\jdk1.2\bin;C:\WINNT\system32;C:\WINNT;C:\Program Files\Kawa30;C:\j
5\bin;C:\WINNT\system32;C:\WINNT;C:\Program Files\Kawa30;C:\jdk1.1.6\bin

A:\>
```

If it was, then you should now be able to execute the `javac` command successfully without using the prefix.

The instructions in the previous paragraph assume that the JDK is successfully installed in the folder named `jdk1.2`. If your JDK folder has a different name, then use that instead.

If it was necessary to amend your `PATH` variable, then you should add the same set path command to your `c:\autoexec.bat` file so that that system variable will be set correctly each time to restart your computer.

If the compiler displays error messages when you execute the `javac` command, then you have to go back into the editor and fix the errors. For example, if you omitted the semicolon at the end of the third line, then the compiler would respond like this:

```
  Command Prompt
A:\>javac HelloWorld.java
HelloWorld.java:3: ';' expected.
   { System.out.println("Hello, World!")
                                         ^
1 error

A:\>
```

The Java compiler is pretty good about locating and describing syntax errors like this.

If you see an error message like this

```
  Command Prompt
A:\>javac HelloWorld.java
HelloWorld.java:1: Public class HelloWorl must be defined in a file called
oWorl.java".
public class HelloWorl
             ^
1 error

A:\>
```

then the problem is that the file name of our source code program does not match the name that follows the keyword `class` on the second line. These two names must be identical, even with the same capital and lowercase letters. In this example, the programmer omitted the "d" at the end of the `class` name.

Another common compile-time error is omitting one of a pair of quotation marks:

```
Command Prompt
A:\>javac HelloWorld.java
HelloWorld.java:3: String not terminated at end of line.
  { System.out.println("Hello, World!);
                      ^
HelloWorld.java:4: ')' expected.
  }
  ^
2 errors

A:\>
```

Like parentheses `()` and braces `{}`, quotation marks must always come in pairs.

1.6 ANALYSIS OF THE `HelloWorld` PROGRAM

Here is the text of the `HelloWorld` program again:

```
public class HelloWorld
{ public static void main(String[] args)
  { System.out.println("Hello, World!");
  }
}
```

The first line declares a class named `HelloWorld`. Every Java program begins this way. You can name your program whatever you want; any nonempty string of letters and digits can be used for the class name as long as it begins with a letter and contains no blanks.

The name of the class must be the same as the name of the file. For example, if you name your class `PlayTicTacToe`, like this:

```
public class PlayTicTacToe
{ public static void main(String[] args)
  { ...
  }
}
```

then it must be saved in a file name `PlayTicTacToe.java`.

The second line begins with the left brace character "{". This is required immediately after the class name. Some programmers put it at the end of the first line instead of at the beginning of the second line. The difference is only a matter of style; it doesn't matter to the compiler as long as it appears immediately after the main class name. Note that the last symbol in the program is the right brace "}" standing alone on the last line. These two braces form the program *block*, enclosing the program's body. Vertically aligning matching left and right braces, as we do consistently in this book, facilitates the reading of larger complex programs.

The second line contains the four words `public`, `static`, `void`, and `main`, followed by a parenthesized phrase. The word `public` here means the same as on the first line: that the contents of the following block are accessible from all other classes. The word `static` means that the method being defined applies to the class itself rather than to objects of the class. These concepts are explained in Chapter 4. The word `void` means that the method being defined has no return value. The word `main` is the name of the method being defined, just as `HelloWorld` is the name of the class being defined.

The parenthesized string that follows the word `main` on the second line is the *parameter list* for the `main` method. It declares the method's parameters, which are local variables used to transmit information to the method from the outside world. The parameter list for the `main` method always has this form:

```
(String[] args)
```

It states that this method has one parameter. Its name is `args`, and it is an array of `String` objects. These concepts are explained in Chapters 5 and 8.

The third line of the program contains the single executable statement in the program:

```
System.out.println("Hello, World!");
```

Note that this statement is contained within a block delimited by braces "{" and "}". The statement tells the system to print (*i.e.*, display in the DOS command line window) the message "`Hello, World!`". This message is a character string, so it must be enclosed in quotation marks. You can put anything you want within the quotation marks; whatever is there will be printed. The parentheses indicate that this character string is the object that the `main()` method is sending to the `println()` method.

The word `println` is the name of the method that tells the system how to do the "printing." The suffix "`ln`" stands for "line," which means that after the message is printed, the cursor on the screen should be positioned at the beginning of the next line, so that the next output (if any) will appear on the next line.

The prefix "`System.out.`" means that "`System.out`" is the name of an object that belongs to the class where this method is defined. This object is the *receiver* of the print request made by the program.

Note that the parentheses containing the "`Hello, World!`" and the semicolon at the end of the statement are required.

1.7 COMMENTS

Computer programs are read by two kinds of entities: compilers and humans. The compiler requires the source code text to conform exactly to its syntax rules. For example, the semicolon must follow the right parenthesis on the third line of the `HelloWorld` program. Humans are not so particular about how instructions are given, but they often do need more explanation about what the instructions mean. Programming languages allow such explanations to be included with source code. They are called *comments*, and are ignored by the compiler.

There are two ways to write comments in Java. A *C style comment* begins with the symbol pair `/*` and ends with the symbol pair `*/`. A *C++ style comment* begins with the symbol pair `//` and ends with the end of the text line. The C style comments can be used between compilable code on the same line, like this:

```
public /* access */ class /* declaration */ HelloWorld
```

but this is not recommended. More often, Java programmers use the C style for a multi-line comment, like this:

```
/*  This program prints the single line of output:
    Hello, World!
*/
```

C++ style comments are often used to annotate declarations and statements, like this:

```
public class TestFrame              // tests the Frame class
{ public static void main(String[] args)
  { Frame frame = new Frame("Example 9.1");
    frame.setSize(250,100);         // 250 pixels wide and 100 pixels high
    frame.setVisible(true);         // displays the frame on the screen
  }
}
```

The text shown here in boldface is ignored by the compiler. Multi-line comments can also be done in the C++ style:

```
//  This program prints the single line of output:
//  Hello, World!
```

Adding comments to your programs is called *documenting your code*. This should be done whenever the purpose or meaning of the code might not be clear to human readers. It is also good to include a *header comment* at the beginning of every program that identifies the programmer and the program.

EXAMPLE 1.1 The `HelloWorld` Program

Here is our `HelloWorld` program again with a three-line header comment for identification:

```
Command Prompt
A:\ch01\ex01>dir
 Volume in drive A has no label.
 Volume Serial Number is 0000-0000

 Directory of A:\ch01\ex01

06/26/98  01:33p       <DIR>          .
06/26/98  01:33p       <DIR>          ..
06/26/98  05:42p                   215 HelloWorld.java
               3 File(s)           215 bytes
                              645,632 bytes free

A:\ch01\ex01>type HelloWorld.java
//  Programming with Java by John R. Hubbard
//  Copyright McGraw-Hill, 1988
//  Example 1.1

public class HelloWorld
{ public static void main(String[] args)
  { System.out.println("Hello, World!");
  }
}

A:\ch01\ex01>javac HelloWorld.java

A:\ch01\ex01>dir
 Volume in drive A has no label.
 Volume Serial Number is 0000-0000

 Directory of A:\ch01\ex01

06/26/98  01:33p       <DIR>          .
06/26/98  01:33p       <DIR>          ..
06/26/98  05:42p                   473 HelloWorld.class
06/26/98  05:42p                   215 HelloWorld.java
               4 File(s)           688 bytes
                              645,120 bytes free

A:\ch01\ex01>java HelloWorld
Hello, World!

A:\ch01\ex01>
```

The DOS Command Prompt window shows the result of the following commands:

```
dir
type HelloWorld.java
javac HelloWorld.java
dir
java HelloWorld
```

The comments on the first three lines are ignored by the compiler.

1.8 PROGRAMS WITH INPUT

Input is more error-prone than output. If the wrong kind of input is received, the program can crash (*i.e.*, fail abruptly). Such a run-time error is called an *exception*. Java provides special mechanisms for handling exceptions. The simplest version of this for input/output exceptions is to append the clause "throws IOException" to the declaration of the main() method.

EXAMPLE 1.2 Interactive Input

```
Command Prompt

A:\ch01\ex02>dir
 Volume in drive A has no label.
 Volume Serial Number is 0000-0000

 Directory of A:\ch01\ex02

06/26/98   01:33p        <DIR>          .
06/26/98   01:33p        <DIR>          ..
06/26/98   06:00p                   460 HelloAl.java
              3 File(s)             460 bytes
                              644,608 bytes free

A:\ch01\ex02>type HelloAl.java
//   Programming with Java by John R. Hubbard
//   Copyright McGraw-Hill, 1988
//   Example 1.2

import java.io.*;
public class HelloAl
{ public static void main(String[] args) throws IOException
  { InputStreamReader reader = new InputStreamReader(System.in);
    BufferedReader input = new BufferedReader(reader);
    System.out.print("Enter your name: ");
    String name = input.readLine();
    System.out.println("Hello, " + name + "!");
  }
}

A:\ch01\ex02>javac HelloAl.java

A:\ch01\ex02>dir
 Volume in drive A has no label.
 Volume Serial Number is 0000-0000

 Directory of A:\ch01\ex02

06/26/98   01:33p        <DIR>          .
06/26/98   01:33p        <DIR>          ..
06/26/98   06:00p                   460 HelloAl.java
06/26/98   06:01p                   948 HelloAl.class
              4 File(s)           1,408 bytes
                              643,584 bytes free

A:\ch01\ex02>java HelloAl
Enter your name: Al Gore
Hello, Al Gore!
```

The DOS dialog here is similar to that in Example 1.1: it displays the contents of the current folder, displays the contents of the `HelloAl.java` file, compiles the program in that file, displays the contents of the current folder again to confirm that the bytecode file `HelloAl.class` was created, and then runs the program.

The program prints the prompt

  `Enter your name:`

and then waits for input. When the user types

  `Al Gore`

and presses the Enter key, the system respond immediately with

  `Hello, Al Gore!`

The picture here shows the flow of the data through the five objects in the program from its input from the keyboard to its output at the video display screen. The five objects are named `System.in`, `reader`, `input`, `name`, and `System.out`. The `System.in` and `System.out` objects are defined in the `System` class. The other three objects are defined in the program (on the third, fourth, and sixth lines). All but the `name` object are drawn as conduits, piping the individual bytes and characters through the system. These objects are called *stream* objects because, like a stream of water, they allow the data to flow in a sequence.

The first line in the source code file is

  `import java.io.*;`

This tells the `javac` compiler to look in the `java.io` library for the definitions of the three i/o classes that are used in the program: `IOException`, `InputStream-Reader`, and `BufferedReader`.

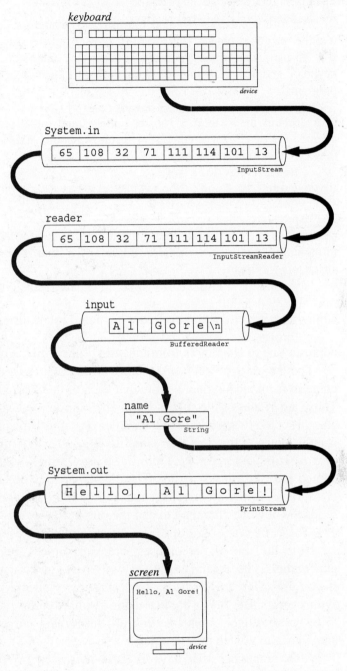

The fourth line defines the object `reader` to be an instance of the `InputStreamReader` class, binding it to the system input stream `System.in`. This means that the object `reader` will serve as a conduit, conveying data from the keyboard into the program.

The fifth line defines the object `input` to be an instance of the `BufferedReader` class, binding it to the `reader` object. This means that the object `input` can be used to extract input in a convenient way. In particular, it can use its `readLine()` method to read an entire line of characters from the keyboard and deliver them in the form of a `String` object. It does just that on the seventh line of the program:

```
String name = input.readLine();
```

This declares the `String` object `name` and initializes it with the string that is returned by the `input.readLine()` method. The result is that the `name` object contains whatever the user typed at the keyboard. That is then printed in the next statement:

```
Hello, Al Gore!
```

If you had entered `Tiger Woods` instead of `Al Gore`, this line would have printed

```
Hello, Tiger Woods!
```

The expression `"Hello, " + name + "!"` means to concatenate (*i.e.*, string together) the three strings `"Hello, "`, `name`, and `"!"` to form a single string to be sent to the screen. The first and third of these are literal string constants. But `name` is the `String` variable that holds whatever string of characters was input.

Note that the `readLine()` method is analogous to the `println()` method. The statement

```
name = input.readLine();
```

copies a line of characters from the keyboard to the string `name`, while the statement

```
System.out.println(name);
```

copies a line of characters from the string `name` to the computer display screen.

The `reader` object is an instance of the `InputStreamReader` class. It reads the bytes that come in from the keyboard. Note that each of the 8 bytes read is an integer in the range 0 to 127. These are values of the `byte` type. The `input` object is an instance of the `BufferedReader` class. It converts each byte in the reader object into a value of the `char` type. The `name` object is an instance of the `String` class. Its `readLine()` method copies all the characters up to the next *newline character* (\n) into its `name` string. Note that the newline character itself is not copied into the `name` string. The `System.out` object is an instance of the `PrintStream` class. Its `println()` method sends all the characters that are passed to it to the screen and then sends the newline character to end the output line.

The "`throws IOException`" clause allows the use of the `readLine()` method.

Note the use of parentheses, brackets, braces, and semicolons in these examples. This punctuation is necessary, exactly as written. If you omit any of it, your program will not compile. If you are using an IDE (*e.g.*, CodeWarrior or JBuilder), the editor will help you locate such syntax errors. But if you are just using a simple editor like the Microsoft Notepad, you will have to be more diligent about getting all this syntax correct. This is a common but unavoidable annoyance to novice programmers.

Also remember that Java is *case-sensitive*: "`system.out.println`" is different from "`System.out.println`".

1.9 NUMERIC INPUT

The input in Example 1.2 was a *string*: a sequence of characters read as text. Computers distinguish between strings and numbers. They are stored and processed differently. For example, the `+` operator works on both types but with very different results: the expression `"Al" + "Gore"` is equal to the string `"Al Gore"`, while the expression `22 + 44` is equal to the number `66`. This section shows how to input numeric data.

Every object used in a Java program must be *declared* before it is used. This means, for example, that a line like

```
String myName;
```

must precede any use of the `myName` object. The declaration tells the compiler the type and the name of the object. The declaration may optionally include an initialization:

```
String myName = input.readLine();
```

Numeric variables are declared like this:

```
long m;       // m is a 64-bit integer
double x;     // x is a 64-bit floating-point (decimal) number
int n = 44;   // n is a 32-bit integer initialized to be 44
```

You could visualize these variables as shown here. Note that every variable always has some value. But if you don't initialize it, its value will be unpredictable.

m		x		n
4933056		801.67		44
long		double		int

EXAMPLE 1.3 Computing Your Year of Birth

This example inputs your current age (as of 1998) and then computes and prints your probable year of birth. Its purpose is simply to illustrate integer input.

```
Command Prompt

A:\ch01\ex03>type YearOfBirth.java
//    Programming with Java by John R. Hubbard
//    Copyright McGraw-Hill, 1988
//    Example 1.3

import java.io.*;

public class YearOfBirth
{ public static void main(String[] args) throws IOException
  { InputStreamReader reader = new InputStreamReader(System.in);
    BufferedReader input = new BufferedReader(reader);
    System.out.print("Enter your age: ");
    String text = input.readLine();
    int age = new Integer(text).intValue();
    System.out.println("You are " + age + " years old, now.");
    int year = 1998 - age;
    System.out.println("so you were probably born in " + year);
  }
}

A:\ch01\ex03>javac YearOfBirth.java

A:\ch01\ex03>java YearOfBirth
Enter your age: 32
You are 32 years old, now,
so you were probably born in 1966

A:\ch01\ex03>
```

Like the program in Example 1.2 on page 14, this also imports class files from the `java.io` library so it can use the `InputStreamReader` and `BufferedReader` classes. It also includes the "throws `IOException`" clause on the `main()` method so it can use the `readLine()` method. After it reads the input as a `String`, it converts the `text` data into an integer by the expression

```
new Integer(text).intValue()
```

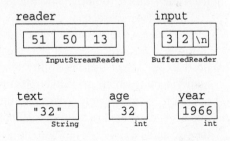

reader		input
51 | 50 | 13		3 | 2 |\n
InputStreamReader		BufferedReader

text	age	year
"32"	32	1966
String	int	int

This integer value is used to initialize the `int` variable `age`. The program prints that value, computes the user's `year` of birth from it, and then prints that year. Although not shown here, the flow of data through the stream objects is the same as in Example 1.2.

EXAMPLE 1.4 Computing the Area of a Circle

This program inputs the radius of a circle and then prints its area. It illustrates the processing of floating-point data.

```
Command Prompt

A:\ch01\ex04>type Area.java
//    Programming with Java by John R. Hubbard
//    Copyright McGraw-Hill, 1988
//    Example 1.4

import java.io.*;

public class Area
{ public static void main(String[] args) throws Exception
  { InputStreamReader reader = new InputStreamReader(System.in);
    BufferedReader input = new BufferedReader(reader);
    System.out.print("Enter the radius: ");
    String text = input.readLine();
    Double x = new Double(text);
    double r = x.doubleValue();
    System.out.println("The area of a circle of radius " + r);
    double area = Math.PI*r*r;
    System.out.println(" is " + area);
  }
}
                                          o

A:\ch01\ex04>javac Area.java

A:\ch01\ex04>java Area
Enter the radius: 100
The area of a circle of radius 100.0
 is 31415.926535897932

A:\ch01\ex04>
```

The structure of this program is nearly the same as that in the last two examples. The main difference here is the use of the object `x` and the variables `r` and `area`.

The object `x` is an instance of the `Double` class. The variable `r` is a variable of type `double`. They both represent the real number 100.0. The reason that we have these two separate objects representing the same thing is because of the different operations we have to perform on the value. As an instance of the `Double` class, the object `x` can obtain its value from the `text` object, which holds the value 100 in the four characters `'1'`, `'0'`, `'0'`, and

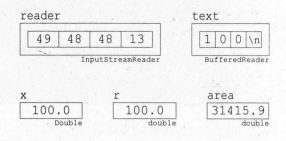

`'\n'` (the *newline* character). These flowed in from the `reader` object, which held the value 100 in the four bytes `49`, `48`, `48`, and `13` (the ASCII codes for the four characters `'1'`, `'0'`, `'0'`, and `'\n'`). So the `x` object has the ability to convert a numeric value from its character representation into its numeric representation. But implementing the formula $A = \pi r^2$ requires the use of the multiplication operator `*` which only works on numeric variables, not objects. (The difference between variables and objects is explained in Section 1.10 below.) So the object `x` had to be converted to the variable `r`, using the `doubleValue()` method on `x`.

Example 1.4 illustrates one of the fundamental principles of *object-oriented programming*: the choice of objects used in a program is based upon the operations that have to be performed. This program had to

1. input a floating-point number r;
2. apply the formula $A = \pi r^2$ to it;
3. output the result A.

Step 1 required the use of an `InputStreamReader` object and a `BufferedReader` object. Step 2 required the use of a `Double` object and the two variables `r` and `area`. Step 3 required the use of the `System.out` object.

1.10 VARIABLES AND OBJECTS

There are two kinds of entities that hold data in Java: variables and objects. A variable has a type and holds a single value. An object is an instance of a class and may contain many variables, the composite of whose values is called the *state* of the object. There are only nine possible types that variables can have. But programmers can define their own classes, so objects may *instantiate* an unlimited number of classes. Every variable has a unique name which is designated when the variable is declared. Objects have references instead of names, and they need not be unique. A variable is created when it is declared, and it remains alive until the method in which it is declared terminates. An object is created by using the `new` operator to invoke a *constructor*, and it dies when it has no references. If variables are the "nuts and bolts" of a program, then objects are its doors and windows.

EXAMPLE 1.5 The Circle Program Again

Here is the code from Example 1.4 on page 18:

```
import java.io.*;
public class Area
{ public static void main(String[] args) throws Exception
  { InputStreamReader reader = new InputStreamReader(System.in);
    BufferedReader input = new BufferedReader(reader);
    System.out.print("Enter the radius: ");
    String text = input.readLine();
    Double x = new Double(text);
    double r = x.doubleValue();
    System.out.println("The area of a circle of radius " + r);
    double area = Math.PI*r*r;
    System.out.println(" is " + area);
  }
}
```

This program uses two variables (`r` and `area`) and five objects (`reader`, `input`, `text`, `x`, and `System.out`). Both variables have type `double`. The objects are instances of the classes `InputStreamReader`, `BufferedReader`, `String`, `Double`, and `PrintStream`, respectively. Technically, `reader`, `input`, *etc.*, are the names of *references* to the three objects; objects themselves don't have names. But Java programmers usually refer to objects by the names of their references. It's simpler to say "the object `reader`" than "the object referred to by the reference `reader`."

A *reference* is a variable whose type is "reference to *Xxxx* class," where *Xxxx* is the name of some class. For example, text is a reference of type "reference to string class" in Example 1.5. So like other variables, every reference has a type.

Besides reference types, there are eight other types in Java. These are called *primitive* types, to distinguish them from reference types. Their names and values are:

boolean	either false or true
char	16-bit Unicode characters
byte	8-bit whole numbers: integers ranging from –128 to 127
short	16-bit whole numbers: integers ranging from –32,768 to 32,767
int	32-bit whole numbers: integers ranging from –2,147,483,648 to 2,147,483,647
long	64-bit whole numbers: integers ranging from ±9,223,372,036,854,775,807
float	32-bit decimal numbers: rationals ranging from $\pm 1.4 \times 10^{-45}$ to $\pm 3.4 \times 10^{38}$
double	64-bit decimal numbers: rationals ranging from $\pm 4.9 \times 10^{-324}$ to $\pm 1.8 \times 10^{308}$

The syntax for declaring a variable of any type is

```
type-name variable-name;
```

where *type-name* is the name of the type and *variable-name* is the name of the variable. For example, the declaration

```
int n;
```

declares the variable n with type int. All variables must be declared before they are used.

It is usually best to initialize a variable within its declaration. The syntax for that is

```
type-name variable-name = initial-value;
```

where *initial-value* is the value being given to the variable. For example, the declaration

```
char c = 'R';
```

declares the variable c with type char and initial value 'R'. We could then visualize the variable c as: This shows c as an object like a mailbox with contents 'R' and type char.

EXAMPLE 1.6 Primitive Data Types

This program simply declares and initializes eight variables, one for each of the eight primitive types, and then prints them.

```
public class PrintTypes
{ public static void main(String[] args)
  { boolean b = false;
    char c = 'R';
    byte j = 127;
    short k = 32767;
    int m = 2147483647;
    long n = 9223372036854775807L;    // 'L' is for "long"
    float x = 3.14159265F;            // 'F' is for "float"
    double y = 3.141592653589793238;
    System.out.println("b = " + b);
    System.out.println("c = " + c);
    System.out.println("j = " + j);
    System.out.println("k = " + k);
    System.out.println("m = " + m);
    System.out.println("n = " + n);
    System.out.println("x = " + x);
    System.out.println("y = " + y);
  }
}
```

Its output is

```
Command Prompt
A:\ch01\ex06>java PrintTypes
b = false
c = R
j = 127
k = 32767
m = 2147483647
n = 9223372036854775807
x = 3.1415927
y = 3.141592653589793

A:\ch01\ex06>
```

Note that the initial value for the `long` integer `n` ends with the letter `L`. This is necessary for literal values of `long` type. Similarly, literal values of `float` type must end with the letter `F`.

Also note that values of type char must be delimited with apostrophes:

```
char c = 'R';
```

Without the apostrophes, the declaration

```
char c = R;
```

would mean that the variable `c` is being initialized with the value of a symbolic constant named `R` whose actual value could be any character.

1.11 ARITHMETIC AND ASSIGNMENT OPERATORS

An *operator* is a function that has a special symbolic name and is invoked by using that symbol within an expression. Here are some examples of expressions that include Java operators:

n = 22	assignment operator
n += 22	assignment operator
++n	increment operator
n / 22	quotient operator
n % 22	remainder operator

These are illustrated in the following programming examples.

EXAMPLE 1.7 Increment and Decrement Operators

This example illustrates how the values of integer variables can be changed with the increment and the decrement operators: `++` and `--`. It also illustrates the use of the assignment operators `+=` and `-=`.

```
public class IncrementDecrement
{ public static void main(String[] args)
  { char c = 'R';
    byte j = 127;
    short k = 32767;
    System.out.println("c = " + c);
    ++c;
    System.out.println("c = " + c);
    ++c;
    System.out.println("c = " + c);
    System.out.println("j = " + j);
    --j;
    System.out.println("j = " + j);
```

```
      ++j;
      System.out.println("j = " + j);
      ++j;
      System.out.println("j = " + j);
      System.out.println("k = " + k);
      k -= 4;
      System.out.println("k = " + k);
      k += 5;
      System.out.println("k = " + k);
   }
}
```

This uses the same declarations for c, j, and k as in Example 1.6.

```
Command Prompt
A:\ch01>java IncrementDecrement
c = R
c = S
c = T
j = 127
j = 126
j = 127
j = -128
k = 32767
k = 32763
k = -32768

A:\ch01>
```

The expression ++c means to increment the variable c to its next value. Since its current value was 'R', this changes it to the next character 'S'. After printing that, it gets incremented to 'T'. Incrementing and decrementing ordinary integers works the same way.

This example also shows what happens when a variable gets incremented past its "last value": it wraps around to the lowest negative value. For example, the range of values for variables of type byte is –128 to 127, so when the variable j has the value 127 and gets incremented, its value becomes –128. Since this defies the rules of ordinary arithmetic, it is considered an error when it happens. It is called *integer overflow*. It is best avoided simply by using an integer type with a larger range.

The last part of this program uses the special assignment operators -= and +=. The statement
```
      k -= 4
```
simply means "subtract 4 from k." That changes its value from 32767 to 32763. Note that the last assignment causes integer overflow again.

EXAMPLE 1.8 Arithmetic

This example illustrates the use of the five integer arithmetic operators +, -, *, /, and %.
```
public class IntegerArithmetic
{ public static void main(String[] args)
   { int m = 25;
     int n = 7;
     System.out.println("m = " + m);
     System.out.println("n = " + n);
     int sum = m + n;
     System.out.println("m + n = " + sum);
     int difference = m - n;
     System.out.println("m - n = " + difference);
     int product = m * n;
     System.out.println("m * n = " + product);
```

```
        int quotient = m / n;
        System.out.println("m / n = " + quotient);
        int remainder = m % n;
        System.out.println("m % n = " + remainder);
    }
}
```

```
Command Prompt

A:\ch01>java IntegerArithmetic
m = 25
n = 7
m + n = 32
m - n = 18
m * n = 175
m / n = 3
m % n = 4

A:\ch01>
```

These operators work as you would expect. Note that the remainder operator gives the remainder from division: 25 % 7 = 4 because 4 is the remainder when 25 is divided by 7.

Review Questions

1.1   How old is the Java programming language?

1.2   What company developed the Java programming language?

1.3   What is source code?

1.4   Where does the source code come from?

1.5   What kind of files contain Java source code?

1.6   What is bytecode?

1.7   Where does bytecode come from?

1.8   What kind of files contain Java bytecode?

1.9   What does "portable" mean in the context of computer programming?

1.10 How is Java bytecode different from other low-level computer languages?

1.11 What is the difference between a compiler and an interpreter?

1.12 What is a Java virtual machine?

1.13 What is an "application."

1.14 What is a "developer."

1.15 What is the Java API?

1.16 What is an IDE?

1.17 What is the JDK?

1.18 What is the JIT?

1.19 What is the JVM?

1.20 What is the difference between a C style comment and a C++ style comment?

1.21 What is a "stream" object?

1.22 What is an exception?

1.23 What does "case-sensitive" mean?

1.24 What are the differences between a variable and an object?

1.25   What are the eight Java primitive types?

1.26   What is a reference type?

1.27   What is integer overflow?

Programming Problems

1.1   Modify Example 1.1 on page 13 so that it prints this message object:
```
String message = "Hello, World!";
```

1.2   Write and run a Java program that initializes a String object with your first name and then prints it on three separate lines.

1.3   Write and run a Java program that initializes a String object with your first name and then prints it three times on the same line, separated by spaces, like this:
```
John John John
```

1.4   Write and run a Java program that prompts the user for his/her last name and first name separately and then prints a greeting like this:
```
Enter your last name: O'Connor
Enter your first name: Sandra Day
Hello, Sandra Day O'Connor
```
(The boldface font here indicates the user input.)

1.5   Write and run a Java program that initializes an integer variable n with the value 5814 and then uses the quotient and remainder operators to extract and print each digit of n. The output should look like this:
```
n = 5814
The digits of n are 5, 8, 1, and 4
```
Hint: use n/1000 to extract the thousands digit from n, and use n %= 1000 to remove the thousands digit from n.

1.6   Write and run a Java program that inputs an integer that represents a temperature on the Fahrenheit scale and then computes and prints its equivalent Celsius value in decimal form. Use the conversion formula $C = 5(F - 32)/9$.

Supplemental Programming Problems

1.7   Write and run a Java program that inputs an integer that represents a temperature on the Celsius scale and then computes and prints its equivalent Fahrenheit value in decimal form. Use the conversion formula $F = 1.8C + 32$.

1.8   It has been observed that crickets tend to chirp in the summer at a rate that is related to the temperature by the formula $T = (c + 40)/10$, where c the number of chirps per minute and T is the temperature in Fahrenheit degrees. Write and run a Java program that inputs the number of chirps per minute and outputs the temperature in decimal form.

Answers to Review Questions

1.1   As of 1998, Java is 7 years old.

1.2   Java was developed at Sun Microsystems, Inc.

1.3   *Source code* is the plain text that makes up part or all of a computer program.

1.4   Source code is written by computer programmers, usually using an editor.

1.5   Java source code is saved in files with names that end with ".java".

1.6   *Bytecode* is the intermediate-level computer language translation of a Java source code program.

1.7   Bytecode is produced by the Java compiler when it compiles Java source code.

1.8   Java bytecode is saved in files with names that end with ".class".

1.9   A computer program is *portable* if it can be run on different kinds of computers.

1.10   Java bytecode programs are portable.

1.11   A compiler translates a source code program into machine language program that can then be run many times on the same kind of computer. An interpreter translates and executes each statement of the source code separately whenever it is needed.

1.12   A Java *virtual machine* is a software system that translates and executes Java bytecode.

1.13   In the context of computing, an *application* is a computer program that is intended to be used by non-programmers.

1.14   In the context of computing, a *developer* is a programmer who creates useful applications.

1.15   The acronym API stands for "Application Programming Interface." The *Java API* is the set of all the libraries that define the standard Java classes and interfaces.

1.16   The acronym IDE stands for "Integrated Development Environment." It describes a commercial software system designed to facilitate the development of computer programs. (See Appendixes B and C.)

1.17   The acronym JDK stands for "Java Development Kit." It describes the set of files that can be downloaded from Sun Microsystems for developing Java applications. It includes the Java compiler and the Java API.

1.18   The acronym JIT stands for "Just-In-Time," which is the name for the Java bytecode compiler that can be used to compile Java .class files into machine-specific executable programs.

1.19   The acronym JVM stands for "Java Virtual Machine." (See Question 1.12.)

1.20   A C style comment begins with /* and ends with */, like this:
```
    int size;  /* the size of the object */
```
A C++ style comment begins with // and extends to the end of the line, like this:
```
    int size;  // the size of the object
```

1.21   A *stream object* is an object through which data flows from or to other objects. For example, the System.in, reader, input, and System.out objects in Example 1.2 on page 14 are stream objects.

1.22   An *exception* is a run-time error.

1.23   A software environment (*e.g.*, a programming language or operating system) is *case-sensitive* if it distinguishes uppercase letters from their lowercase versions. Java is case-sensitive; DOS isn't.

1.24   A variable can have only one value at a time; an object can have many fields, each with its own value. A variable has a unique name; an object has one or more reference variables instead of a name. A variable has a type which is either one of the eight primitive types or a reference type; an object is an instance of a class which may be one of the Java library classes or one defined by the programmer. A variable is created by its declaration; an object has to be created by a constructor function that is invoked with the new operator.

1.25   The eight Java *primitive types* are boolean, char, byte, short, int, long, float, and double.

1.26   A *reference type* is a type that refers to a specific class, so that any variable declared to have that reference type can refer only to instances (objects) of that class.

1.27   When a program tries to increase the value of an integer variable above its maximum possible value, *integer overflow* occurs.

Solutions to Programming Problems

1.1
```
public class NamedConstant
{ public static void main(String[] args)
  { String message = "Hello, World!";
    System.out.println(message);
  }
}
```

1.2
```
public class PrintName
{ public static void main(String[] args)
  { String name = "John";
    System.out.println(name);
    System.out.println(name);
    System.out.println(name);
  }
}
```

1.3
```
public class PrintNameOnOneLine
{ public static void main(String[] args)
  { String name = "John";
    System.out.println(name + " " + name + " " + name);
  }
}
```

1.4
```
public class PrintNames
{ public static void main(String[] args)
  { final int LEN = 20 ;
    byte[] buffer1 = new byte[LEN];
    System.out.print("Enter your last name: ");
    try { System.in.read(buffer1, 0, LEN) ; }
    catch (Exception e) {}
    String lname = new String(buffer1) ;
    byte[] buffer2 = new byte[LEN];
    System.out.print("Enter your first name: ");
    try { System.in.read(buffer2, 0, LEN) ; }
    catch (Exception e) {}
    String fname = new String(buffer2) ;
    System.out.println("Hello, " + fname.trim() + " "
       + lname.trim());
  }
}
```

1.5
```
public class ExtractDigits
{ public static void main(String[] args)
  { int n = 5814;
    System.out.println("n = " + n);
    System.out.print("The digits of n are ");
    System.out.print(n/1000);
    n %= 1000;
    System.out.print(", " + n/100);
    n %= 100;
    System.out.print(", " + n/10);
    n %= 10;
    System.out.println(", and " + n);
  }
}
```

1.6
```
import java.io.*;
public class FahrenheitToCelsius
{ public static void main(String[] args) throws IOException
  { InputStreamReader reader = new InputStreamReader(System.in);
    BufferedReader input = new BufferedReader(reader);
    System.out.print("Enter Fahrenheit temperature: ");
    String text = input.readLine();
    int fahrenheit = new Integer(text).intValue();
    System.out.print(fahrenheit + " degrees Fahrenheit = ");
    double celsius = 5.0*(fahrenheit - 32.0)/9.0;
    System.out.println(celsius + " degrees Celsius.");
  }
}
```

Chapter 2

Strings

A *string* is a sequence of characters. Words, sentences, and names are strings. The message
"Hello, World!" is a string. This chapter describes the two fundamental string classes in Java:
String and StringBuffer.

2.1 THE string CLASS

The simplest type of string in Java is an object of the String class. These objects are
immutable; they cannot be changed.

EXAMPLE 2.1 A SIMPLE string OBJECT

This program prints some of the properties of a String object named alphabet.
```
public class Alphabet
{ public static void main(String[] args)
  { String alphabet = "ABCDEFGHIJKLMNOPQRSTUVWXYZ";
    System.out.println(alphabet);
    System.out.println("This string contains " + alphabet.length()
      + " characters.");
    System.out.println("The character at index 4 is "
      + alphabet.charAt(4));
    System.out.println("The index of the character Z is "
      + alphabet.indexOf('Z'));
    System.out.println("The hash code for this string is "
      + alphabet.hashCode());
  }
}
```
The object named alphabet is declared on the third line to be an instance of the String class
and is initialized with the string literal value "ABCDEFGHIJKLMNOPQRSTUVWXYZ". It looks like this:

The rest of the program consists of five output statements that generate the output:
```
ABCDEFGHIJKLMNOPQRSTUVWXYZ
This string contains 26 characters.
The character at index 4 is E
The index of the character Z is 25
The hash code for this string is -1127252723
```

The first output statement simply prints the string represented by object alphabet. The second
output statement invokes the length() method to print the number of characters in the string.

The third output statement invokes the charAt() method to print the character at index position 4
in the string. Note that this (the letter "E") is actually the fifth character in the string. The *index number* of
a character in a string is always the number of characters that precede it. The letter "E" has the index
number 4 in the string "ABCDEFGHIJKLMNOPQRSTUVWXYZ" because it is preceded by 4 characters.

The fourth output statement invokes the `indexOf()` method to print the index number of the letter "Z" in the `alphabet` string. That is the number 25 because the letter "Z" is preceded by 25 characters in the string.

The last output statement invokes the `hashCode()` method to print the hash value of the string. In Java, every `String` object has a unique integer value, called its *hash code*. This is computed from the Unicode values of the characters in the string. The hash value of the string "ABCDEFGHIJKLMNOPQRSTUVWXYZ" is –1,127,252,723. This number has no meaning other than serving as a numerical label for the object. Hash values are used as storage locators when the objects are stored in tables. Although each `String` object has one and only one hash code, the same number may be the hash code for more than one object.

2.2 SUBSTRINGS

A *substring* is a string whose characters form a contiguous part of another string. The `String` class includes a `substring()` method for extracting substrings. This method is illustrated in the next example.

EXAMPLE 2.2 Substrings

```
public class Substrings
{ public static void main(String[] args)
  { String alphabet = "ABCDEFGHIJKLMNOPQRSTUVWXYZ";
    System.out.println(alphabet);
    System.out.println("The substring from index 4 to index 8 is "
      + alphabet.substring(4, 8));
    System.out.println("The substring from index 4 to index 4 is "
      + alphabet.substring(4, 4));
    System.out.println("The substring from index 4 to index 5 is "
      + alphabet.substring(4, 5));
    System.out.println("The substring from index 0 to index 8 is "
      + alphabet.substring(0, 8));
    System.out.println("The substring from index 8 to the end is "
      + alphabet.substring(8));
  }
}
```
The output is
```
ABCDEFGHIJKLMNOPQRSTUVWXYZ
The substring from index 4 to index 8 is EFGH
The substring from index 4 to index 4 is
The substring from index 4 to index 5 is E
The substring from index 0 to index 8 is ABCDEFGH
The substring from index 8 to the end is IJKLMNOPQRSTUVWXYZ
```

This program uses the same object `alphabet` as in Example 2.1 on page 27. It has six output statements. The first prints the entire string. The second output statement invokes the `substring()` method to print the substring that begins with the character at index 4 (the letter "E") and ends with the character at index 7 (the letter "H"). Note that the length of the substring is the difference between the two index numbers: 8 – 4 = 4 characters.

The third output statement prints a substring of length zero (4 – 4 = 0). This is called the *empty string*. Note that since the empty string is unique, the call `alphabet.substring(14, 14)` would have the same effect as `alphabet.substring(4, 4)`. But the call `alphabet.substring(41, 41)` would fail because there is no character in the `alphabet` object with index number 44.

The fourth output statement prints the substring of the first 8 characters, and the last output statement prints the substring of all but the first 8 characters. Note that the last call uses only one parameter.

2.3 CHANGING CASE

Java distinguishes uppercase (capital letters) from lowercase. Its `String` class includes methods for changing all the letters of a string to uppercase or to lowercase. These methods are illustrated in the next example.

EXAMPLE 2.3 Uppercase and Lowercase

This program shows how to change all the characters in a string to lowercase or to uppercase:

```
public class ChangingCase
{ public static void main(String[] args)
  { String sbis = "StringBufferInputStream";
    System.out.println(sbis);
    String sbislc = sbis.toLowerCase();
    System.out.println(sbislc);
    String sbisuc = sbis.toUpperCase();
    System.out.println(sbisuc);
  }
}
```

The output is

```
StringBufferInputStream
stringbufferinputstream
STRINGBUFFERINPUTSTREAM
```

The `toLowerCase()` method returns a new string with the same characters in lowercase. The `toUpperCase()` method performs the obvious analogous task.

2.4 CONCATENATION

We have already used the concatenation operator "+" for strings. (See Example 1.2 on page 14.) The next example shows how it can be used to form larger strings from smaller string.

EXAMPLE 2.4 Concatenation

```
public class Concatenation
{ public static void main(String[] args)
  { String first = "James";
    String last = "Gosling";
    System.out.println(first + last);
    System.out.println(first + " " + last);
    System.out.println(last + ", " + first);
    String name = first + " " + last;
    System.out.println(name);
  }
}
```

The output is
```
JamesGosling
James Gosling
Gosling, James
James Gosling
```

Note that we can concatenate `String` objects such as first and last with *literal strings* such as " " (the string containing one blank) and ", " (the string containing a comma followed by a blank).

2.5 LOCATING A CHARACTER WITHIN A STRING

The `String` class's `indexOf()` and `lastIndexOf()` methods returns the index number of a character in a string.

EXAMPLE 2.5 Searching for Characters in a String

```
public class SearchingForChars
{ public static void main(String[] args)
  { String str = "This is the Mississippi River.";
    System.out.println(str);
    int i = str.indexOf('s');
    System.out.println("The first index of 's' is " + i);
    int j = str.indexOf('s', i+1);
    System.out.println("The next index of 's' is " + j);
    int k = str.indexOf('s', j+1);
    System.out.println("The next index of 's' is " + k);
    k = str.lastIndexOf('s');
    System.out.println("The last index of 's' is " + k);
    System.out.println(str.substring(k));
  }
}
```
The output is
```
This is the Mississippi River.
The first index of 's' is 3
The next index of 's' is 6
The next index of 's' is 14
The last index of 's' is 18
sippi River.
```

To see how this works, visualize the `str` object like this:

The call `str.indexOf('s')` returns 3, the index of the first `'s'` in the `str` object. After that, the value of `i` is 3, so the call `str.indexOf('s', i+1)` searches the `str` string beginning at index number `i+1` = 4. The first `'s'` from there forward is at index number 6, so that call assigns 6 to `j`. The third call begins searching at index number `j+1` = 7 and finds the next `'s'` at index number 14. The call `str.lastIndexOf('s')` returns the value 18, which is the index of the last `'s'` in the string.

Note that in Example 2.5, two different versions of the `indexOf()` method are being used here: one has a single parameter, and the other has two parameters. This is called *overloading*, using the same name for different methods. It is quite common in Java. The compiler can tell which method is being called by its distinctive parameter list: a single character parameter is different from a list of a character parameter followed by an integer parameter.

2.6 REPLACING CHARACTERS IN A STRING

The `String` class includes a method named `replace()` which replaces every occurrence of one character with another.

EXAMPLE 2.6 Replacing Characters in a String

```
public class Replacing
{ public static void main(String[] args)
  { String inventor = "Charles Babbage";
    System.out.println(inventor);
    System.out.println(inventor.replace('B', 'C'));
    System.out.println(inventor.replace('a', 'o'));
    System.out.println(inventor);
  }
}
```
The output is
```
Charles Babbage
Charles Cabbage
Chorles Bobboge
Charles Babbage
```

The call `inventor.replace('a', 'o')` replaces every occurrence of `'a'` in the string with the letter `'o'`, thereby transforming "Charles Babbage" into "Chorles Bobboge".

This example also illustrates *composition of methods*. The sixth line of the program
```
    System.out.println(inventor.replace('a', 'o'));
```
composes the `replace()` method with the `println()` method. That means that the object returned by the `replace()` method is immediately passed to the `println()` method. In this case, that is the `String` object that represents the string "Chorles Bobboge". This is an *anonymous object*: it has no name. It is not the same as the (immutable) `String` object named inventor which keeps its original string "Charles Babbage" as the last output shows.

Composition is an efficient way to avoid proliferation of object names. To obtain the same results as in the program in Example 2.6 without using composition would require the declaration of two extra `String` objects.

2.7 REPRESENTING A PRIMITIVE VALUE IN A STRING

Primitive values such as 47 are made up of ordinary characters. The float value 3.14 is read and printed as the string consisting of the four characters `'3'`, `'.'`, `'1'`, and `'4'`. So it is not surprising that we might need to create a `String` object that represents a primitive value, or to create a primitive variable whose value is taken from a `String` object.

EXAMPLE 2.7 Converting Primitive Types to Strings

This program uses the `String` class's `valueOf()` method to convert primitive values to strings.

```
public class TestValueOf
{ public static void main(String[] args)
  { boolean b = true;
    char c = '$';
    int n = 44;
    double x = 3.1415926535897932;
    System.out.println("b = " + b);
    System.out.println("c = " + c);
    System.out.println("n = " + n);
    System.out.println("x = " + x);
    String strb = String.valueOf(b);
    String strc = String.valueOf(c);
    String strn = String.valueOf(n);
    String strx = String.valueOf(x);
    System.out.println("strb = " + strb);
    System.out.println("strc = " + strc);
    System.out.println("strn = " + strn);
    System.out.println("strx = " + strx);
  }
}
```

The output is

```
b = true
c = $
n = 44
x = 3.141592653589793
strb = true
strc = $
strn = 44
strx = 3.141592653589793
```

EXAMPLE 2.8 Converting Strings into Primitive Types

This program shows how to do arithmetic on numerical values that are embedded within a string.

```
public class TestConversions
{ public static void main(String[] args)
  { String today = "May 18, 1998";
    String todaysDayString = today.substring(4, 6);
    int todaysDayInt = Integer.parseInt(todaysDayString);
    int nextWeeksDayInt = todaysDayInt + 7;
    String nextWeek = today.substring(0, 4) + nextWeeksDayInt
      + today.substring(6);
    System.out.println("Today's date is " + today);
    System.out.println("Today's day is " + todaysDayInt);
    System.out.println("Next week's day is " + nextWeeksDayInt);
    System.out.println("Next week's date is " + nextWeek);
  }
}
```

The output is

```
Today's date is May 18, 1998
Today's day is 18
```

```
Next week's day is 25
Next week's date is May 25, 1998
```

This program defines three `String` objects (today, todaysDayString, and nextWeek) and two `int` variables (todaysDayInt and nextWeeksDayInt). They can be visualized like this:

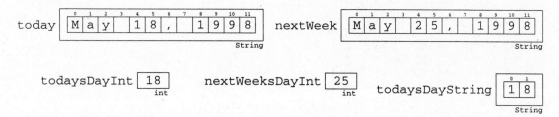

The execution of the statement

        `int todaysDayInt = Integer.parseInt(todaysDayString);`
carries out the following tasks:

1. It declares the variable `todaysDayInt` with type `int`.
2. It invokes the `parseInt()` method that is defined in the `Integer` class, passing the `String` object named `todaysDayString` to it.
3. The `parseInt()` method reads the two characters `'1'` and `'8'` from the `todaysDayString` string, converts them to their equivalent numerical values 1 and 8, combines them to form the integer 18, and then returns that `int` value.
4. The returned value 18 is used to initialize the `int` variable `todaysDayInt`.

As an integer, the value 18 is increased to 25 in the next statement simply by adding 7 to it. Then the `String` class's `substr()` method and concatenation operator can be used to build the `nextWeek` string, containing the substring "25".

Note that converting a `String` object to an `int` value requires the explicit invocation of the `parseInt()` method defined in the `Integer` class, but converting an integer value into a string can be done implicitly by concatenation.

The previous example used the `Integer` class. This is called a *wrapper class* in Java because it encapsulates or "wraps up" the primitive type `int`. Each of the eight primitive types has a corresponding wrapper class. Their names are `Boolean`, `Character`, `Byte`, `Short`, `Integer`, `Long`, `Float`, and `Double`. The purpose of a wrapper class is to provide methods for primitive types. For example, the `Integer` class provides the `parseInt()` method for `int` variables. Wrapper classes are covered in Chapter 6.

2.8 SUMMARY OF THE `string` CLASS METHODS

These are the methods that are defined in the `StringBuffer` class in Java v.1.1. They are described by examples which assume that `b` and `b1` are `boolean` variables; `c` is a `char` variable; `i`, `j`, and `k` are `int` variables; `n` is a `long` variable; `x` is a `float` variable; `y` is a `double` variable; `a` is a `char` array; `buf` is a `StringBuffer` object; `s`, `s1`, and `s2` are `String` objects; and `o` is any object:

```
String str = new String();
String str = new String(a);
String str = new String(buf);
String str = new String(s);
String str = new String(a, i, j);
String str = String.copyValue(a);
String str = String.copyValue(a, i, j);
String str = String.valueOf(b);
String str = String.valueOf(c);
String str = String.valueOf(i);
String str = String.valueOf(n);
String str = String.valueOf(x);
String str = String.valueOf(y);
String str = String.valueOf(a);
String str = String.valueOf(a, i, j);
String str = String.valueOf(o);
s = str.toString();
i = str.length();
c = str.charAt(i);
buf.getChars(i, j, a, k);
i = str.compareTo(s);
s = str.concat(s1);
b = str.endsWith(s1);
b = str.startsWith(s1);
b = str.startsWith(s1, i);
b = str.equals(s1);
b = str.equalsIgnoreCase(s1);
i = str.hashCode();
i = str.indexOf(c);
i = str.indexOf(c, i);
i = str.indexOf(s);
i = str.indexOf(s, i);
i = str.lastIndexOf(c);
i = str.lastIndexOf(c, i);
i = str.lastIndexOf(s);
i = str.lastIndexOf(s, i);
b = str.regionMatches(i, s, j, k);
b = str.regionMatches(b1, i, s, j, k);
s = str.substring(i);
s = str.substring(i, j);
a = str.toChar();
s = str.toLowerCase();
s = str.toLowerCase(i);
s = str.toUpperCase();
s = str.toUpperCase(i);
s = str.trim();
```

For more details and examples see the book **[Chan1]** listed in Appendix F.

2.9 THE `StringBuffer` CLASS

The `String` class is one of the most useful classes in Java. But its instances (objects) suffer the restriction of being *immutable*: they cannot be changed. In all the examples above, whenever a string was modified, it had to be done by constructing a new `String` object, either explicitly or implicitly. Java provides the separate `StringBuffer` class for string objects that need to be changed. The reason for this dichotomy is that providing the flexibility for changing a string requires substantial overhead (more space and complexity). In situations where you don't need to change the string, the simpler `String` class is preferred.

EXAMPLE 2.9 Using `StringBuffer` Objects

```
public class TestStringBuf
{ public static void main(String[] args)
  { StringBuffer buf = new StringBuffer(10);
    System.out.println("buf = " + buf);
    System.out.println("buf.length() = " + buf.length());
    System.out.println("buf.capacity() = " + buf.capacity());
  }
}
```
The output is
```
buf =
buf.length() = 0
buf.capacity() = 10
```

The first executable statement (on the third line) creates an empty `StringBuffer` object named `buf` with a capacity for 10 characters: This illustrates an essential feature of `StringBuffer` objects: they can have unused character cells; `String` objects cannot.

buf

StringBuffer

EXAMPLE 2.10 Modifying `StringBuffer` Objects

This program illustrates the flexibility of `StringBuffer` objects. It creates only one object, `buf`, which is then modified several times using the concatenation operator and the `append()` method.
```
public class TestAppending
{ public static void main(String[] args)
  { StringBuffer buf = new StringBuffer(10);
    buf.append("It was");
    System.out.println("buf = " + buf);
    System.out.println("buf.length() = " + buf.length());
    System.out.println("buf.capacity() = " + buf.capacity());
    buf.append(" the best");
    System.out.println("buf = " + buf);
    System.out.println("buf.length() = " + buf.length());
    System.out.println("buf.capacity() = " + buf.capacity());
    buf.append(" of times.");
    System.out.println("buf = " + buf);
    System.out.println("buf.length() = " + buf.length());
    System.out.println("buf.capacity() = " + buf.capacity());
  }
}
```
The output is
```
buf = It was
buf.length() = 6
buf.capacity() = 10
buf = It was the best
buf.length() = 15
```

```
buf.capacity() = 22
buf = It was the best of times.
buf.length() = 25
buf.capacity() = 46
```

The `StringBuffer` object `buf` is initialized to be empty with a capacity of 10 characters. After the statement

```
    buf.append("It was");
```
executes, 6 of its 10 characters are in use: After the next call to the `append()` method

```
    buf.append(" the best");
```
the object is expanded to a capacity of 22 characters, of which 15 are in use:

Note the difference between the *length* and the *capacity* of the `buf` object. The length increases by the number of characters appended to the string. The capacity is increased only when the current capacity is exceeded by the new length.

The capacity of a `StringBuffer` object is changed automatically by the operating system whenever necessary. The only control that the programmer has is initializing it when the object is created, as was done in Example 2.9 on page 35. When the capacity is changed, the entire object has to be restructured and moved in the computer's memory. To avoid this overhead it is best to initialize the object with a sufficient capacity.

The `StringBuffer` class is good for building a string by accumulating sequences of characters as is done with input. But it is not very good for editing a string, as the next example shows.

EXAMPLE 2.11 Replacing `StringBuffer` Objects

This program illustrates how to modify the contents of a buffer.

```
public class BufReplacing
{ public static void main(String[] args)
  { StringBuffer buf = new StringBuffer();
    buf.append("It was the best of times.");
    System.out.println("buf = " + buf);
    System.out.println("buf.length() = " + buf.length());
    System.out.println("buf.capacity() = " + buf.capacity());
    buf.setCharAt(11, 'w');
    System.out.println("buf = " + buf);
    buf.setCharAt(12, 'o');
    System.out.println("buf = " + buf);
    buf.insert(13, "r");
    System.out.println("buf = " + buf);
  }
}
```

The output is

```
buf = It was the best of times.
buf.length() = 25
buf.capacity() = 34
```

```
buf = It was the west of times.
buf = It was the wost of times.
buf = It was the worst of times.
```

To change the string from "It was the best of times." to "It was the worst of times.", we had to change two characters by invoking the setCharAt() method twice, and then we had to invoke the insert() method to insert a new character. This shows that the StringBuffer class is not very good at editing strings. It would have been easier to build the second string from scratch.

EXAMPLE 2.12 Converting StringBuffer Objects to String Objects

```java
public class TestToString
{ public static void main(String[] args)
  { StringBuffer buf = new StringBuffer("it was the age of wisdom,");
    System.out.println("buf = " + buf);
    System.out.println("buf.length() = " + buf.length());
    System.out.println("buf.capacity() = " + buf.capacity());
    String str = buf.toString();
    System.out.println("str = " + str);
    System.out.println("str.length() = " + str.length());
    buf.append(" " + str.substring(0, 18) + "foolishness,");
    System.out.println("buf = " + buf);
    System.out.println("buf.length() = " + buf.length());
    System.out.println("buf.capacity() = " + buf.capacity());
    System.out.println("str = " + str);
  }
}
```

The output is

```
buf = it was the age of wisdom,
buf.length() = 25
buf.capacity() = 41
str = it was the age of wisdom,
str.length() = 25
buf = it was the age of wisdom, it was the age of foolishness,
buf.length() = 56
buf.capacity() = 84
str = it was the age of wisdom,
```

The buf object is created with a length of 25 characters and a capacity of 41 characters by initializing it with the literal String object "it was the age of wisdom,". (Note that this literal has 25 characters.) This illustrates an alternative method for initializing StringBuffer objects: you can specify its numerical capacity explicitly (making its length 0), as was done in Example 2.9 on page 35, or you can specify its initial string contents explicitly, making its length equal to the number of characters in that string and letting the operating system set its initial capacity.

The statement
```
String str = buf.toString();
```
creates the String object str to hold the 25-character string that is in the StringBuffer object buf. The statement
```
buf.append(" " + str.substring(0, 18) + "foolishness,");
```
modifies the StringBuffer object buf by adding another clause to it. This has no effect on the independent str object, as the last line of output shows.

Unlike its capacity, the length of a StringBuffer object can be reset explicitly by the programmer. Decreasing it truncates the string. Increasing it pads the string with null characters.

(The *null character* is the unique character that cannot be detected when printed or displayed on the screen.) The next example shows the effect of decreasing a buffer's length.

EXAMPLE 2.13 Resetting the Length and Reversing `StringBuffer` Objects

This program illustrates the `setLength()` method and the `reverse()` method.

```
public class TestSetLength
{ public static void main(String[] args)
    { StringBuffer buf
        = new StringBuffer("It is a far, far better thing that I do");
      System.out.println("buf = " + buf);
      System.out.println("buf.length() = " + buf.length());
      System.out.println("buf.capacity() = " + buf.capacity());
      buf.setLength(60);
      System.out.println("buf = " + buf);
      System.out.println("buf.length() = " + buf.length());
      System.out.println("buf.capacity() = " + buf.capacity());
      buf.setLength(30);
      System.out.println("buf = " + buf);
      System.out.println("buf.length() = " + buf.length());
      System.out.println("buf.capacity() = " + buf.capacity());
      buf.reverse();
      System.out.println("buf = " + buf);
      System.out.println("buf.length() = " + buf.length());
      System.out.println("buf.capacity() = " + buf.capacity());
    }
}
```

The output is

```
buf = It is a far, far better thing that I do
buf.length() = 39
buf.capacity() = 55
buf = It is a far, far better thing that I do
buf.length() = 60
buf.capacity() = 112
buf = It is a far, far better thing
buf.length() = 30
buf.capacity() = 112
buf =  gniht retteb raf ,raf a si tI
buf.length() = 30
buf.capacity() = 112
```

The statement
```
buf.setLength(60);
```
increases the buffer's length from 39 to 60 characters by appending 21 null characters to it. But this change cannot be seen from the buffer's output. (Null characters are invisible.) The statement
```
buf.setLength(30);
```
decreases the buffer's length from 60 to 30 characters by removing its last 30 characters: the 9 characters in the substring "`that I do`" and the 21 null characters that had been appended previously. Note that the capacity is not decreased.

The statement
```
buf.reverse();
```
reverses the string in the `buf` object. This is not a very useful method, but it does illustrate the ability of `StringBuffer` objects to modify themselves.

2.10 SUMMARY OF THE `StringBuffer` CLASS METHODS

These are the methods that are defined in the `StringBuffer` class in Java v.1.1. They are described by examples which assume that `b` is a `boolean` variable; `c` is a `char` variable; `i`, `j`, and `k` are `int` variables; `n` is a `long` variable; `x` is a `float` variable; `y` is a `double` variable; `a` is a `char` array; `s` is a `String` object; and `o` is any object:

```
StringBuffer buf = new StringBuffer();
StringBuffer buf1 = new StringBuffer(100);
StringBuffer buf2 = new StringBuffer(s);
s = buf.toString();
i = buf.length();
i = buf.capacity();
c = buf.charAt(i);
buf.setCharAt(i, c);
buf.getChars(i, j, a, k);
buf.setLength(i);
buf.ensureCapacity(i);
buf.append(b);
buf.append(c);
buf.append(i);
buf.append(n);
buf.append(x);
buf.append(y);
buf.append(a);
buf.append(o);
buf.append(s);
buf.append(a, i, j);
buf.insert(i, b);
buf.insert(i, c);
buf.insert(i, i);
buf.insert(i, n);
buf.insert(i, x);
buf.insert(i, y);
buf.insert(i, a);
buf.insert(i, o);
buf.insert(i, s);
buf.reverse();
```

For more details and examples see the books **[Chan1]** and **[Chan2]** listed in Appendix F.

Review Questions

2.1 What substring is returned by the call `alphabet.substring(6, 10)`?

2.2 How long is the substring returned by the call `alphabet.substring(9, 16)`?

2.3 Why would the call `alphabet.substring(14, 14)` have the same effect as the call `alphabet.substring(4, 4)`?

2.4 Why would the call `alphabet.substring(41, 41)` fail?

2.5 What is "overloading?"

2.6 What is "composition of methods?"

2.7 What is the main difference between the `String` class and the `StringBuffer` class?

2.8 What is the difference between the length of a `StringBuffer` object and its capacity?

Programming Problems

2.1   Modify Example 2.1 on page 27 so that it prints your name and its attributes.

2.2   Modify Example 2.2 on page 28 so that it prints your father's name and its attributes.

2.3   Write and run a Java program that does the following:

1. Declare a `String` object named `s` containing the string "`Call me Ishmael.`"
2. Print the entire string.
3. Use the `length()` method to print the length of the string.
4. Use the `charAt()` method to print the first character in the string.
5. Use the `charAt()` and the `length()` methods to print the last character in the string.
6. Use the `indexOf()` and the `substring()` methods to print the first word in the string.

2.4   Rewrite the program in Example 2.6 on page 31 so that it does not use composition.

2.5   Write and run a Java program that enters a 10-digit string as a typical U.S. telephone number, extracts the 3-digit area code, the 3-digit "exchange," and the remaining 4-digit number as separate strings, prints them, and then prints the complete telephone number in the usual formatting. A sample run might look like this:

```
Enter 10-digit telephone number: 1234567890
You entered 1234567890
The area code is 123
The exchange is 456
The number is 7890
The complete telephone number is (123)456-7890
```

2.6   The *Y2K Problem* is that many thousands of old software systems around the world use only two digits for the year in stored dates. On January 1, 2000, those dates are likely to be misinterpreted by the software as January 1, 1900, causing unpredictable errors and system crashes. ("Y2K" stands for "Year 2 Thousand"). Some experts predict that the total cost of repairing the software and recovering from the problem will exceed $200,000,000,000! Write a Java program that inputs a date in the form *mm/dd/yy* and outputs in the expanded form *mm/dd/19yy*. For example, the input `06/30/98` would be printed as `06/30/1998`.

Supplementary Programming Problems

2.7   Write and run a Java program that inputs a persons name in the form *First Middle Last* and then prints it in the form *Last, First M.*, where "M." is the person's middle initial. For example, the input

```
William Jefferson Clinton
```

would produce the output

```
Clinton, William J.
```

2.8   Write and run a Java program that capitalizes a two-word name. For example, the input

```
noRtH    CARolIna
```

would produce the output

```
North Carolina
```

Answers to Review Questions

2.1   The call `alphabet.substring(6, 10)` returns the substring "GHIJ".

2.2   The substring returned by the call `alphabet.substring(9, 16)` has length $16 - 9 = 7$.

2.3   The calls `alphabet.substring(14, 14)` and `alphabet.substring(4, 4)` would have the same effect because both return the unique empty string.

2.4   The call `alphabet.substring(41, 41)` fails because there is no character in the string `alphabet` with index number 41. The last character ('Z') has index number 25.

2.5   The term *overloading* refers to the ability to declare different methods with the same name.

2.6   We say that two or more methods are *composed* when the return value of one is used directly as the input to another, as in Example 2.6 on page 31.

2.7   Instances (objects) of the `String` class are immutable: they cannot be changed. Instances of the `StringBuffer` class do not have that constraint.

2.8   The *length* of a `StringBuffer` object is the number of characters it contains. Its *capacity* is the number of characters it can contain without being expanded.

Solutions to Programming Problems

2.1   Your solution will be slightly different unless you have the same name as the author of this book:

```java
public class MyName
{ public static void main(String[] args)
  { String name = "John R. Hubbard";
    System.out.println(name);
    System.out.println("This string contains " + name.length()
      + " characters.");
    System.out.println("The character at index 4 is "
      + name.charAt(4));
    System.out.println("The index of the character Z is "
      + name.indexOf('Z'));
    System.out.println("The hash code for this string is "
      + name.hashCode());
  }
}
```

Note that the character at index 4 is the blank character. Also note that since the character 'Z' is not in this string, the `indexOf()` method returns the value –1.

2.2   Your solution will be slightly different unless you are one of the author's siblings:

```java
public class MyFather
{ public static void main(String[] args)
  { String name = "Willard W. Hubbard III";
    System.out.println(name);
    System.out.println("The substring from index 4 to index 8 is "
      + name.substring(4, 8));
    System.out.println("The substring from index 4 to index 4 is "
      + name.substring(4, 4));
    System.out.println("The substring from index 4 to index 5 is "
      + name.substring(4, 5));
    System.out.println("The substring from index 0 to index 8 is "
      + name.substring(0, 8));
    System.out.println("The substring from index 8 to the end is "
      + name.substring(8));
  }
}
```

2.3   ```
public class Ishmael
{ public static void main(String[] args)
   { String s = "Call me Ishmael.";
     System.out.println(s);
     System.out.println("The length of the string is "
        + s.length());
     System.out.println("The first character is " + s.charAt(0));
     System.out.println("The last character is "
        + s.charAt(s.length()-1));
     System.out.println("The first word is "
        + s.substring(0, s.indexOf(' ')));
   }
}
```

**2.4**   ```
public class Replacing
{ public static void main(String[] args)
   { String inventor = "Charles Babbage";
     System.out.println(inventor);
     String temp = inventor.replace('B', 'C');
     System.out.println(temp);
     temp = inventor.replace('a', 'o');
     System.out.println(temp);
     System.out.println(inventor);
   }
}
```

2.5   ```
import java.io.*;
public class TelephoneNumbers
{ public static void main(String[] args) throws IOException
   { InputStreamReader reader = new InputStreamReader(System.in);
     BufferedReader input = new BufferedReader(reader);
     System.out.print("Enter 10-digit telephone number: ");
     String telephone = input.readLine();
     System.out.println("You entered " + telephone);
     String areaCode = telephone.substring(0,3);
     System.out.println("The area code is " + areaCode);
     String exchange = telephone.substring(3,6);
     System.out.println("The exchange is " + exchange);
     String number = telephone.substring(6);
     System.out.println("The number is " + number);
     System.out.println("The complete telephone number is "
        + "(" + areaCode + ")" + exchange + "-" + number);
   }
}
```

**2.6**   ```
import java.io.*;
public class FixY2K
{ public static void main(String[] args) throws IOException
   { InputStreamReader reader = new InputStreamReader(System.in);
     BufferedReader input = new BufferedReader(reader);
     System.out.print("Enter 10-digit telephone number: ");
     String date = input.readLine();
     System.out.println("You entered " + date);
     String firstPart = date.substring(0,6);
     String secondPart = date.substring(6);
     date = firstPart + "19" + secondPart;
     System.out.println("The expanded form is " + date);
   }
}
```

Chapter 3

Selection

3.1 THE `if` STATEMENT

The `if` statement allows for *conditional* execution. The statement that is included within it will be executed only if its condition is true. The syntax for the `if` statement is

```
if (condition) statement;
```

where `condition` is a boolean expression. A *boolean expression* is an expression whose value has type `boolean`.

EXAMPLE 3.1 Testing a Random Integer for Negativity

This program uses a *random number generator* to generate a random integer. It then reports whether the integer is negative:

```
import java.util.Random;
public class Example0301
{ public static void main(String[] args)
  { Random random = new Random();
    int n = random.nextInt();
    System.out.println("n = " + n);
    if (n < 0) System.out.println("****  n < 0");
    System.out.println("Goodbye.");
  }
}
```

The first line "imports" the `Random` class which is used on the fourth line to instantiate a random number generator named `random`. It generates a random integer named `n` on the fifth line. The `if` statement on the seventh line evaluates the condition `(n < 0)`. If it is true, the string `"****  n < 0"` is printed. If the condition is false (*i.e.*, `n` is not negative) then that string is not printed and execution proceeds immediately to the next line. The last executable statement is independent of the `if` statement, so it executes regardless of the condition.

Here are the results of three consecutive runs of this program:

```
n = 720138778
Goodbye.
```

```
n = -101963997
****  n < 0
Goodbye.
```

```
n = 492857803
Goodbye.
```

You can see that the values of `n` generated by the `random` are unpredictable. When they are negative the extra `println()` statement executes.

The examples in this chapter use the `Random` class which is defined in the `java.util` package. This is part of the standard Java class library which is in the JDK. It is located in the

43

jdk folder src/java/util (C:\jdk1.1.6\src\java\util\Random.class on the author's Windows PC). The import statement simply tells the Java compiler that it will need the definitions in that file to compile this program. Without it, the compiler would not know what Random is. You can generate random numbers in your programs by instantiating a Random object (as done on the fourth line of the program in Example 3.1) and then invoking one of its next... methods. The nextInt() method generates a random integer (as done on the fifth line of the program in Example 3.1). The nextDouble() method generates a random real number (see Example 3.3).

A *random number* is a variable whose value is produced by some method that makes it unpredictable, or at least difficult to predict. Java's nextInt() method generates integers in the range –2,147,483,648 to 2,147,483,647 in such a way that any large set of them will be uniformly distributed in this range. Similarly, the nextFloat() and nextDouble() methods generate rational numbers that are uniformly distributed in the range 0 to 1.

By defining Random to be a class, Java encapsulates the idea of a random number generator. The object random in Example 3.1 is an *instance* of that class. We think of it as a "black box;' *i.e.*, a thing that contains some unknown mechanism for generating random numbers. Whenever we "ask" it for a random integer by invoking its method random.nextInt(), it provides us with one. We don't need to know how it does that. Indeed, we're better off not having to think about how it is done, just as we're better off not having to think about how the computer delivers our email for us.

3.2 THE if...else STATEMENT

The if...else statement is the if statement with an added else clause. It works the same way as the if statement except that, when the condition is false the statement within the else clause executes. The syntax for the if...else statement is

```
if (condition) statement1;
else statement2;
```

Either *statement1* or *statement2* executes, depending upon whether the *condition* is true or false.

EXAMPLE 3.2 Testing Two Random Integers for Their Minimum

This program uses the random number object random to generate the two integers m and n. Then it determines which is smaller and reports the results.

```
import java.util.Random;
public class Example0302
{ public static void main(String[] args)
  { Random random = new Random();
    int m = random.nextInt();
    System.out.println("m = " + m);
    int n = random.nextInt();
    System.out.println("n = " + n);
    if (m < n) System.out.println("The minimum is " + m);
    else System.out.println("The minimum is " + n);
  }
}
```

This is similar to the program in Example 3.1. Here is the output from three consecutive runs:

```
m = 1589634066
n = -716919032
The minimum is -716919032
```

```
m = -1439894098
n = -59632402
The minimum is -1439894098
```

```
m = -411845037
n = 567066459
The minimum is -411845037
```

3.3 THE `if...else if...` STATEMENT COMBINATION

The `if...else` statement allows for conditional execution based upon two alternatives. If you have more than two possible alternatives, you can link together a sequence of `if...else` statements.

EXAMPLE 3.3 Choosing among Four Alternatives

This program generates a random real number in the range 0 to 1 and then reports into which of four disjoint intervals it falls:

```
import java.util.Random;
public class Example0303
{ public static void main(String[] args)
  { Random random = new Random();
    double t = random.nextDouble();
    System.out.println("t = " + t);
    if (t < 0.25) System.out.println("0 <= t < 1/4");
    else if (t < 0.5) System.out.println("1/4 <= t < 1/2");
    else if (t < 0.75) System.out.println("1/2 <= t < 3/4");
    else System.out.println("3/4 <= t < 1");
  }
}
```

Here are the results of three consecutive runs of this program:

```
t = 0.5979526952214973
1/2 <= t < 3/4
```

```
t = 0.8205623262672468
3/4 <= t < 1
```

```
t = 0.058669499596328056
0 <= t < 1/4
```

3.4 NESTED CONDITIONALS

The syntax of the `if` and `if...else` statements allows any statement to be used in either its `if` clause or its `else` clause. That means that we can put other `if` or `if...else` statements inside an `if` or and `if...else` statement. This is called *nesting* statements inside other statements. Generally, such combinations should be used sparingly because they are error-prone and their logic can be misunderstood.

The `if...else if` combination illustrated in Section 3.3 is actually a form of nested conditionals. That can be seen by reformatting the code in Example 3.3 like this:

```
if (t < 0.25) System.out.println("0 <= t < 1/4");
else
  if (t < 0.5) System.out.println("1/4 <= t < 1/2");
  else
    if (t < 0.75) System.out.println("1/2 <= t < 3/4");
    else System.out.println("3/4 <= t < 1");
```

Although this formatting is structurally more consistent with the general indentation conventions used for nested statements, most programmers prefer the unindented form for the `if...else if` combination because its alternative statements are conceptually parallel.

EXAMPLE 3.4 Determining the Order of Three Numbers

This program uses pairwise comparisons to determine the increasing order of three randomly generated real numbers:

```
import java.util.Random;
public class Example0304
{ public static void main(String[] args)
  { Random random = new Random();
    float a = random.nextFloat();
    System.out.println("a = " + a);
    float b = random.nextFloat();
    System.out.println("b = " + b);
    float c = random.nextFloat();
    System.out.println("c = " + c);
    if (a < b)
      if (b < c) System.out.println("a < b < c");
      else
        if (a < c) System.out.println("a < c < b");
        else  System.out.println("c < a < b");
    else
      if (a < c) System.out.println("b < a < c");
      else
        if (b < c) System.out.println("b < c < a");
        else  System.out.println("c < b < a");
  }
}
```

Either `a` is less than `b` or it isn't. If it is, then three possibilities are left: a < b < c, a < c < b, or c < a < b. The two conditionals inside the first sort out those possibilities. Similarly, the three possibilities in the case that `a` is greater than `b` are sorted out in the `else` clause of the first `if` statement.

A diagram of the logic in this example is shown at the top of the next page.

Note the way that the interior `if..else` statements are indented in Example 3.4. Careful formatting like this will help you (and others who read your Java code) to understand the logic in conditionals structures like this. Such structures can produce the worst kind of bugs: logical run-time errors that the system cannot help you find. For example, suppose you omit the second `else` in Example 3.4, leaving this code instead:

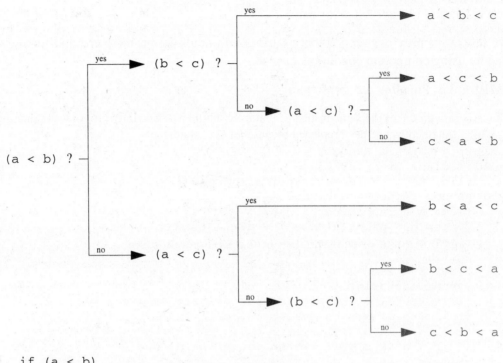

```
if (a < b)
    if (b < c) System.out.println("a < b < c");
    else
        if (a < c) System.out.println("a < c < b");
    else
        if (a < c) System.out.println("b < a < c");
    else
        if (b < c) System.out.println("b < c < a");
        else  System.out.println("c < b < a");
```

The program compiles and runs without complaint. However, it gives perplexingly erroneous results!

Here is a general rule that will help you debug such logical errors:

Rule: In nested `if` statements, each `else` is paired with the last previously unpaired `if`.

Using this rule, you can see how the compiler groups the `ifs` and `elses` in the erroneous code shown above:

```
if (a < b)
    if (b < c) System.out.println("a < b < c");
    else
        if (a < c) System.out.println("a < c < b");
        else
            if (a < c) System.out.println("b < a < c");
            else
                if (b < c) System.out.println("b < c < a");
                else System.out.println("c < b < a");
```

This is very different from what was intended. If `b < a`, nothing gets printed. And if `c < a < b`, it prints `c < b < a`.

Note that these examples seem to exclude the possibility that any two randomly generated numbers could be equal. Although not impossible, the chances are less than one in a four billion.

3.5 COMPOUND STATEMENTS

We saw in the previous section that nested conditionals are prone to error. Often they can be avoided by using compound conditions instead.

EXAMPLE 3.5 Parallel `if` Statements

This program produces the same results as that in Example 3.4. The only difference is that the nested `if...else` statements have been replaced by parallel `if` statements.

```
import java.util.Random;
public class Example0305
{ public static void main(String[] args)
  { Random random = new Random();
    float a = random.nextFloat();
    System.out.println("a = " + a);
    float b = random.nextFloat();
    System.out.println("b = " + b);
    float c = random.nextFloat();
    System.out.println("c = " + c);
    if (a < b && b < c) System.out.println("a < b < c");
    if (a < c && c < b) System.out.println("a < c < b");
    if (b < a && a < c) System.out.println("b < a < c");
    if (b < c && c < a) System.out.println("b < c < a");
    if (c < a && a < b) System.out.println("c < a < b");
    if (c < b && b < a) System.out.println("c < b < a");
  }
}
```

The expression `(a < b && b < c)` is read "a is less than b and b is less than c." It is false unless both conditions `(a < b)` and `(b < c)` are true. Since we know what the six possible orderings are, we can test them all with these six independent statements.

Note that those six `if` statements are logically equivalent to the combination statement

```
if (a < b && b < c) System.out.println("a < b < c");
else if (a < c && c < b) System.out.println("a < c < b");
else if (b < a && a < c) System.out.println("b < a < c");
else if (b < c && c < a) System.out.println("b < c < a");
else if (c < a && a < b) System.out.println("c < a < b");
else System.out.println("c < b < a");
```

This is more efficient, but a little less intuitive. Generally, it is better to sacrifice speed for simplicity, especially when complex logic can lead to errors.

Warning: The expression `(a < b < c)` is <u>not</u> a valid boolean expression. You have to split it up, either into the two separate conditions `(a < b)` and `(b < c)` as in Example 3.4, or use the compound condition `(a < b && b < c)` as in Example 3.5.

3.6 OPERATORS

The symbol `&&` is one of the *logical operators* used in Java programs. Two others are `||` for "or" and `!` for "not." Logical operators combine boolean expressions to form compound boolean expressions, just as the *arithmetic operators* `+`, `-`, `*`, `/`, and `%` combine arithmetic expressions to form compound arithmetic expressions. In contrast, the *relational operators* `<`, `>`, `==`, `!=`, `<=` and `<=` combine arithmetic expressions to form boolean expressions.

If `ex1` and `ex2` are boolean expressions, then

`ex1 && ex2`	is `false` unless both `ex1` and `ex2` are `true`
`ex1 || ex2`	is `true` unless both `ex1` and `ex2` are `false`
`!ex1`	is `true` if and only if `ex1` is `false`

The rules for the arithmetic and relational operators are more obvious. For example, if `ex1` and `ex2` are arithmetic expressions, then `ex1 <= ex2` is true unless the value of `ex1` is greater than the value of `ex2`: "`2 <= 6`" is true, but "`2 <= -6`" is false.

EXAMPLE 3.6 Using the `||` Operator

```
import java.util.Random;
public class Example0306
{ public static void main(String[] args)
  { Random random = new Random();
    float t = random.nextFloat();
    System.out.println("t = " + t);
    if (t < 0.25 || t >= 0.75)
      System.out.println("Either t < 0.25 or t >= 0.75");
    else
      System.out.println("0.25 <= t < 0.75");
  }
}
```

The condition `(t < 0.25 || t >= 0.75)` is true if and only if `t` is not in the interval from 0.25 to 0.75.

EXAMPLE 3.7 Combining Several Boolean Expressions

Like the arithmetic operators, the logical operators may be chained, combining more than two expressions. The `if` condition in this program combines five boolean expressions.

```
public class Example0307
{ public static void main(String[] args)
  { final int LEN = 255;
    byte buffer[] = new byte[LEN];
    System.out.print("Enter your first name: ");
    try { System.in.read(buffer, 0, LEN); }
    catch (Exception e) {}
    String name = new String(buffer);
    System.out.println("Hello, " + name.trim());
    char c = name.charAt(0);
    System.out.println("The first letter of your name is " + c);
    if (c == 'A' || c == 'E' || c == 'I' || c == 'O' || c == 'U')
      System.out.println("That is a vowel.");
  }
}
```

Here are two sample runs:

```
Enter your first name: Albert
Hello, Albert
The first letter of your name is A
That is a vowel.
```

```
Enter your first name: John
Hello, John
The first letter of your name is J
```

3.7 ORDER OF EVALUATION

When you use several different operators in a combined expression, it is important to know in what order the compiler will evaluate the operators. The order for arithmetic operators is familiar. For example, in the expression

    9 - 4 * 2

the multiplication operator is evaluated before the subtraction operator, producing $9 - (4*2) = 1$, not $(9 - 4)*2 = 10$.

Here are the rules that Java uses for evaluating operators

- In unary expressions `op exp` (*prefix*) and `exp op` (*postfix*), the expression `exp` is evaluated first, and then the operation `op` is performed on that value.

- In the binary expression `exp1 && exp2`, the expression `exp1` is evaluated first. If it is false, the value of the entire expression is immediately determined to be false without evaluating `exp2`.

- In the binary expression `exp1 || exp2`, the expression `exp1` is evaluated first. If it is true, the value of the entire expression is immediately determined to be true without evaluating `exp2`.

- In any other binary expressions `exp1 op exp2`, the expression `exp1` is evaluated first, the expression `exp2` is evaluated second, and then the operation `op` is performed on those values.

- In a compound expression `exp1 op1 exp2 op2 exp3` where operator `op1` has higher precedence or the same precedence as operator `op2`, the order is: evaluate `exp1`, evaluate `exp2`, apply `op1` to those two values, evaluate `exp3`, apply `op2` to those two values.

- In a compound expression `exp1 op1 exp2 op2 exp3` where operators `op1` has lower precedence than operator `op2`, the order is: evaluate `exp2`, evaluate `exp3`, apply `op2` to those two values, evaluate `exp1`, apply `op1` to those two values.

- The precedence priorities for the logical, arithmetic, and relational operators are:
1. ++ (postfix increment), -- (postfix decrement)
2. ++ (prefix increment), -- (prefix decrement), !
3. *, /, %
4. +, -
5. <, >, <=, >=
6. ==, !=
7. &&
8. ||

EXAMPLE 3.8 Evaluating a Complex Expression

Evaluate the expression

    a * b - c != a / b + c && -- a > b ++ || b % -- c > 0

where the given values of a, b, and c are 5, 3, and 1, respectively.

The precedence levels for the are

```
     ③   ④   ⑥   ③   ④   ⑦ ②   ⑤   ① ⑧   ③ ②   ⑤
     a * b - c != a / b + c && -- a > b ++ || b % -- c > 0
```

These levels affect the order of evaluation which can be indicated by the following parenthesization:

```
(((a*b - c) != (a/b + c)) && (--a > b++)) || (b%(--c) > 0)
```

The last operation to be evaluated is the `||` operator. According to the third rule given above, this requires the evaluation of its left side

```
((a*b - c) != (a/b + c)) && (--a > b++)
```

first. In this expression, the last operation to be evaluated is the `&&` operator. According to the second rule given above, this requires the evaluation of its left side

```
(a*b - c) != (a/b + c)
```

which is

```
(5*3 - 1) != (5/3 + 1)
```

which is to true because 14 != 2. Then the right side

```
--a > b++
```

is evaluated. The expression `b++` applies the *postfix increment operator*, evaluating to the same value as b itself, but then adding 1 to b <u>after</u> that expression has been applied. So the value of `b++` is 3. Next, the expression `--a` applies the *prefix decrement operator* which subtracts 1 from a and then evaluates to that reduced value. So the value of `--a` is 4. Then since 4 > 3, the expression

```
--a > b++
```

evaluates to true. That produces the value true for the compound condition

```
((a*b - c) != (a/b + c)) && (--a > b++)
```

Now, according to the third rule given above, the complete expression evaluates to true, without evaluating the right-hand expression

```
b%(--c) > 0
```

Note that if the right-hand expression had to be evaluated, it could crash the program, because the expression `b%(--c)` would attempt division by zero.

The second and third rules for evaluating expressions allow the complete expression to be evaluated without evaluating the right-hand side in the cases where the value of the right-hand side is irrelevant. This is called *short circuiting*. It allows statements like

```
if (d != 0 && c/d > 2) System.out.println("o.k.");
```

to execute without hazard.

3.8 boolean VARIABLES

The primitive type `boolean` is the simplest of all. The only two values that a `boolean` variable can have are `false` and `true`. Although simple, `boolean` variables can help simplify a program with complex logic.

EXAMPLE 3.9 Implementing the Quadratic Formula

The *quadratic formula* gives the solution(s) to a quadratic equation of the form $ax^2 + bx + c = 0$. For given values of the parameters a, b, and c, the formula solves the equation for x.

This is the general quadratic formula:

$$x = \frac{-b \pm \sqrt{b^2 - 4ac}}{2a}$$

Its implementation requires the consideration of special cases. For example, if $a = 0$, the division cannot be performed.

An analysis of the different possibilities is shown in a diagram at the top of the next page.

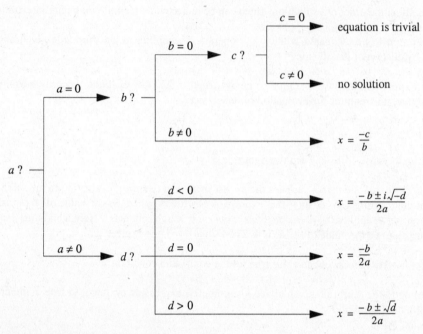

Here, d is the *discriminant*: $d = b^2 - 4ac$.

In this implementation, we define 9 boolean variables, one for each of the branches in our analysis. This allows a clean separation of the various cases:

```
import java.util.Random;
import java.lang.Math;
public class Example0309
{ public static void main(String[] args)
  { Random random = new Random();
    float a = random.nextFloat();
    float b = random.nextFloat();
    float c = random.nextFloat();
    double d = b*b - 4*a*c;
    boolean linear = (a == 0);
    boolean constant = (linear && b == 0);
    boolean trivial = (constant && c == 0);
    boolean noSolution = (constant && c != 0);
    boolean unique = (linear && b != 0);
    boolean quadratic = (!linear);
    boolean complex = (quadratic && d < 0);
    boolean equal = (quadratic && d == 0);
    boolean distinct = (quadratic && d > 0);
    System.out.println("The coefficients of "
      + "the function f(x) = a*x^2 + b*x + c are:");
    System.out.println("\ta = " + a);
    System.out.println("\tb = " + b);
    System.out.println("\tc = " + c);
    System.out.print("The equation f(x) = 0 is ");
    if (linear) System.out.print("linear ");
    if (trivial) System.out.print("and trivial.");
    if (noSolution) System.out.println("with no solution.");
```

```
      if (unique)
      { double x = -c/b;
        double y = a*x*x + b*x + c;
        System.out.println("with unique solution x = " + -c/b);
        System.out.println("Check: f(x) = " + y);
      }
      if (quadratic) System.out.print("quadratic with ");
      if (complex)
      { double re = -b/(2*a);
        double im = Math.sqrt(-d)/(2*a);
        System.out.println("complex solutions:\n\tx1 = " + re
          + " + " + im + "i\n\tx2 = " + re + " - " + im + "i");
      }
      if (equal)
      { double x = -b/(2*a);
        double y = a*x*x + b*x + c;
        System.out.println("real solution x = " + x);
        System.out.println("Check: f(x) = " + y);
      }
      if (distinct)
      { double s = Math.sqrt(d);
        double x1 = (-b + s)/(2*a);
        double x2 = (-b - s)/(2*a);
        double y1 = a*x1*x1 + b*x1 + c;
        double y2 = a*x2*x2 + b*x2 + c;
        System.out.println("real solutions:\n\tx1 = " + x1
          + "\n\tx2 = " + x2);
        System.out.println("Check:\tf(x1) = " + y1 + "\n\tf(x2) = "
          + y2);
      }
    }
  }
}
```

The program generates its own random coefficients for the quadratic equation, applies the analysis, and prints the results. In the case (distinct) where the equation has two distinct real roots, their values are checked by evaluating the original quadratic function $f(x) = ax^2 + bx + c$. The value should be 0.

Here are two sample runs:

```
The coefficients of the function f(x) = a*x^2 + b*x + c are:
    a = 0.21762687
    b = 0.14400232
    c = 0.36107045
The equation f(x) = 0 is quadratic with complex solutions:
    x1 = -0.3308468163013458 + 1.2448561059400642i
    x2 = -0.3308468163013458 - 1.2448561059400642i
```

```
The coefficients of the function f(x) = a*x^2 + b*x + c are:
    a = 0.17408675
    b = 0.6870155
    c = 0.1355514
The equation f(x) = 0 is quadratic with real solutions:
    x1 = -0.20829920536441746
    x2 = -3.738098068431407
Check:f(x1) = -1.1046030534700435E-8
    f(x2) = -1.104603031265583E-8
```

Note the values f(x1) and f(x2) in the second run. Albegraically, they should be exactly 0. The letter "E" in the value -1.1046030534700435E-8 stands for "exponent." It means that the value is the number in front of the "E" multiplied by 10 to the power after the "E". So the value -1.1046030534700435E-8 means about $-1.1046 \times 10{-8} = -0.000000011046$. That's pretty close to 0.

The exponential form -1.1046030534700435E-8 is called *floating-point notation* because it comes from letting the decimal point "float" to the left or right to normalize the number so that its decimal form can be expressed with one digit to the left of the decimal. The *exponent* (the integer that follows the "E") is the number of places that the decimal point should be shifted to convert the normalized form back to the correct value. A negative exponent means move the point to the right; positive means move it to the left. In this example, it was moved 8 digits to the right. The normalized decimal form is called the *mantissa*. The mantissa in this example is -1.1046030534700435.

Why isn't $f(x_1)$ exactly equal to 0 in Example 3.9? The answer lies at the very heart of computing and is tied to one of the fundamental principles of mathematics. The fact is that there are two kinds of numbers in the real world: those that are used for counting and those that are used for measuring. The counting numbers are called *integers* and are always exact. (You can't have approximately three books.) The measuring numbers are called *rational numbers* and are never exact. (The circumference of a tree cannot be exactly 22/7 feet.) Computers store integers as int types (short, int, and long) and are able to perform arithmetic on them exactly. They store rational numbers as float types (float and double) and make errors each time they perform arithmetic on them. These are called *round-off errors*. The more arithmetic performs, the more the error accumulates. Using type double (so-called because it doubles the number bytes used, yielding 16 significant digits instead of 7) helps alleviate the problem. But there is no escaping it: computer arithmetic with float types is erroneous.

3.9 THE CONDITIONAL OPERATOR

Java includes a special *ternary* operator, called the *conditional operator*, which is handy for abbreviating simple if..else statements. Its syntax is

```
( condition ? expr1 : expr2 )
```

The value of this operation is either the value of expr1 or the value of expr2, according to whether the condition is true or false.

EXAMPLE 3.10 Using the Conditional Operator

This program gets two random floats and then uses the condition operator to determine which is the smaller and which is the larger of the two.

```
import java.util.Random;
public class Example0310
{ public static void main(String[] args)
  { Random random = new Random();
    float x = random.nextFloat();
    System.out.println("x = " + x);
    float y = random.nextFloat();
    System.out.println("y = " + y);
    float min = ( x < y ? x : y );
    float max = ( x > y ? x : y );
    System.out.println("min = " + min);
```

```
        System.out.println("max = " + max);
    }
}
```

3.10 ASSIGNMENT OPERATORS

The standard assignment operator is represented by the equals sign "=". Its syntax is

```
    var = expr;
```

This operation evaluates the expression `expr` and then assigns that value to the variable `var`. For example,

```
    int m;
    m = 44;
```

declares `m` to be an `int` and then assigns the value 44 to it. Note that an assignment is not the same as an initialization, such as

```
    int n = 44;
```

If `op` is a binary operator, `expr` an expression, and `var` a variable, then

```
    var op= expr;
```

has the same effect as the assignment

```
    var = var op expr;
```

provided that that assignment makes sense. For example,

```
    n += 7;
```

has the same effect as

```
    n = n + 7;
```

they both increase the value of `n` by 7. Combination assignment operators such as `+=` and `%=` are handy abbreviations. They are more intuitive (algebraically, the "equation" $n = n + 7$ makes no sense) and sometimes even run a little faster.

3.11 THE switch STATEMENT

The `switch` statement is similar to the `if...else if` combination for processing one of a set of alternatives. It is more specialized because it requires that the conditions that determine the alternatives have the form `(var == const)`, where `var` is an integer variable. The syntax is

```
    switch (var)
    { case const1:
        stmt-seq1
      case const2:
        stmt-seq2
      case const3:
        stmt-seq3
      etc.
      default:
        stmt-seqN
    }
```

where `stmt-seq1;` is any sequence of zero or more statements, and `etc.` indicates that any number of case sections is possible. This is equivalent to

```
if (var == const1) { stmt-seq1 stmt-seq2 stmt-seq3 ... }
else if (var == const2) { stmt-seq2 stmt-seq3 ... }
else if (var == const3) { stmt-seq3 ... }
   etc.
else { stmt-seqN }
```

The order of the case sections is critical because of the "fall-through"

The default section is optional.

EXAMPLE 3.11 Using the `switch` Statement with Fallthrough

This program generates a random integer, uses the %= and += operators to restrict its range, and then uses a switch statement to print one or more lines to indicate which case(s) execute.

```
import java.util.Random;
public class Example0311
{ public static void main(String[] args)
   { Random random = new Random();
     int n = random.nextInt();
     System.out.println("n = " + n);
     n %= 3;
     n += 2;
     System.out.println("n = " + n);
     switch (n)
     { case 0: System.out.println("This is case 0.");
       case 1: System.out.println("This is case 1.");
       case 2: System.out.println("This is case 2.");
       case 3: System.out.println("This is case 3.");
       default: System.out.println("This is the default case.");
     }
   }
}
```

Originally, n could be any integer in the range –2147483648 to 2147483647. The statement
```
n %= 3;
```
changes its value to one in the range –2 to 2. Then the statement
```
n += 2;
```
changes its value to one in the range 0 to 4. Then the switch statement then causes execution to jump to the case that matches the value of n. The program continues, executing each statement from that line to the end.

Here are two sample runs:
```
n = -751325274
n = 2
This is case 2.
This is case 3.
This is the default case.
```

```
n = -804020549
n = 0
This is case 0.
This is case 1.
This is case 2.
This is case 3.
This is the default case.
```

Note that each case section is executed, one after the other, after the selected case section is reached. This is called a *fall through*.

Usually the case statement is intended to implement a logical set of alternatives that are mutually exclusive, the way that the `if...else if` combination is used. This requires the use of the `break` statement to avoid the fall through from one case to the next, as illustrated in the next example.

EXAMPLE 3.12 Using the `break` Statement to Prevent Fall Through

This program generates a random test score in the range 50 to 100 and then uses a case statement to print exactly one grade report.

```
import java.util.Random;
public class Example0312
{ public static void main(String[] args)
  { Random random = new Random();
    float x = random.nextFloat();
    System.out.println("x = " + x);
    int score = Math.round(50*x + 50);
    System.out.println("Your test score was = " + score);
    switch (score/10)
    { case 10:
      case 9:
        System.out.println("That is an A. Outstanding!");
        break;
      case 8:
        System.out.println("That is a B. Nice work!");
        break;
      case 7:
        System.out.println("That is a C. You can do better!");
        break;
      case 6:
        System.out.println("That is a D. See me after class.");
        break;
      default:
        System.out.println("That is an F. Get a job.");
    }
  }
}
```
Here is a sample run:
```
x = 0.75739926
Your test score was = 88
That is a B. Nice work!
```

The method `nextFloat()` delivers a `float` in the range 0 to 1. In this run, `x` gets the value 0.75739926. The `round()` method defined in the `Math` class rounds a float to the nearest `int`. In this case, it rounds the number 87.869963 (50*0.75739926 + 50) to 88. That yields 8 for the expression `score/10`, so the `switch` statement causes execution to branch to the `println()` statement inside the `case 8` section. That prints the line about the grade B. Then the `break` statement right after it causes execution to branch again, this time to the end of the entire `switch` block, which is at the end of the program. Without the `break` statement, execution would "fall through," printing the following lines about the C, D, and F grades.

Note that the `switch` statement uses four Java keywords: `break`, `case`, `default`, and `switch`. The `break` statement is used in other contexts, but the other three keywords are used only in `switch` statement.

Review Questions

3.1   Determine which of the following pairs of boolean expressions are equivalent. For those that are not, give an example where one is true and the other is false. Assume that a, b, and c are boolean variables.

   a. !(a || b) and !a || b;
   b. !(a && b) and !a || !b;
   c. !(a || !b) and !a && b;
   d. !!!a and !a;
   e. a && (b || c) and a && b || c;
   f. a && (b || c) and (c || b) && a;
   g. a && (b || c) and a && b || a && c;
   h. a || (b && c) and a || b && a || c;

3.2   What is "short circuiting?"

3.3   How is the `if...else if` combination more general than a `switch` statement?

3.4   What is a "fall through?"

3.5   What's wrong with this code:

```
switch (n)
{ case 1:
    a = 11;
    b = 22;
    break;
  case 2:
    c = 33;
    break;
    d = 44;
}
```

Programming Problems

3.1   Write and run a Java program that generates a random integer, tests whether it is positive, and reports that it is if it is.

3.2   Write and run a Java program that generates two random integers, determines their minimum, and prints it.

3.3   Write and run a Java program that generates four random integers, determines their maximum, and prints it.

3.4   Write and run a Java program that generates a random double, determines which quintile of the unit interval it is in, and reports it. A *quintile* is one of the five equal sized pieces of the whole. The quintiles of the unit interval are 0 to 1/5, 1/5 to 2/5, 2/5 to 3/5, 3/5 to 4/5, and 4/5 to 1.

3.5   Write and run a Java program that generates three random floats and then prints them in their increasing order.

3.6   Write and run a Java program that generates a random integer and reports whether it is divisible by 2, by 3, or by 5. Hint: *n* is divisible by *d* if the remainder from dividing *n* by *d* is 0.

3.7   Write and run a Java program that inputs three names and then prints them in their increasing alphabetical order. Use the `String` class method `compareTo()`. For example, if s1 is the string ABACADABRA and s2 is the string ABLE, then s1.compareTo(s2) will be a negative integer, s2.compareTo(s2) will be a 0, and s2.compareTo(s1) will be a positive integer. So the condition `(s1.compareTo(s2) <= 0)` can be used to determine whether `s1` precedes `s2` *lexicographically* (*i.e.*, according to the dictionary ordering).

3.8 Write and run a Java program that generates a random year between 1800 and 2000 and then reports whether it is a leap year. A *leap year* is is an integer greater than 1584 that is either divisible by 400 or is divisible by 4 but not 100. To generate an integer in the range 1800 to 2000, use

```
int year = Math.round(200*x + 1800);
```

where `x` is a random float. The `round()` method of the `Math` class returns the integer nearest the float passed to it. The transformation $y = 200x + 1800$ converts a number in the range $0 \le x < 1$ into a number in the range $1800 \le y < 2000$.

3.9 Write and run a Java program that generates a random integer and then uses nested `if...else` statements to determine whether it is divisible by 2, 3, 5, 6, 10, 15, or 30.

3.10 Modify the program in Example 3.12 on page 57 so that it prints appropriate "+" or "–" modifiers to the letter grades. Scores that end in 0 or 1 get a "–", and those that end in 8 or 9 get a "+". For example, 78 gets a "C+" and 90 gets an "A–".

3.11 Write and run a Java program that inputs a month name and then processes it by:

a. extract the first three letters;

b. capitalize them;

c. print that abbreviation;

d. extract each of the three letters as separate char variables;

e. use nested `if...else` statements to identify the number of the month from the char variables;

f. print the number of the month.

Here is a sample run:

```
Enter the month: February
You entered: February
Its abbreviation is: FEB
This is month number 2
```

3.12 Modify the program for Problem 3.11, replacing the nested `if...else` statements with 12 parallel `if` statements. Use the `startsWith()` method in the `String` class. For example,

```
if (month.startsWith("FEB")) n = 2;
```

Supplementary Programming Problems

3.13 Write and run a Java program that generates a random integer, tests whether it is even, and reports that it is if it is.

3.14 Write and run a Java program that generates two random integers, determines their maximum, and prints it.

3.15 Write and run a Java program that generates four random integers, determines their minimum and their maximum, and prints them both.

3.16 Write and run a Java program that generates a random double, determines which decile of the unit interval it is in, and reports it. A *decile* is one of the ten equal sized pieces of the whole. The first decile of the unit interval is the subinterval from 0.0 to 0.1, the second decile is the subinterval from 0.1 to 0.2, the third decile is the subinterval from 0.2 to 0.3, *etc*.

3.17 Extend the program for Problem 3.12 so that it also prints the number of days in the month. Here is a sample run:

```
Enter the month: February
FEBRUARY is month number 2
It has 28 days.
```

Answers to Review Questions

3.1   *a.* These are not equivalent: if b is true, then !(a || b) is false, but !a || b is true.
    b. !(a && b) and !a || !b are equivalent.
    c. !(a || !b) and !a && b are equivalent.
    d. !!!a and !a are equivalent.
    e. These are not equivalent: if a is false and c is true, then a && (b || c) false, but a && b || c is true.
    f. a && (b || c) and (c || b) && a are equivalent.
    g. a && (b || c) and a && b || a && c are equivalent.
    h. These are not equivalent: if a and b are false and c is true, then a || (b && c) is false, but a || b && a || c is true.

3.2 The term "short circuiting" refers to the feature of the && and || operators that prevents the second operand from being evaluated unless necessary. If the value of the first operand in an && expression is false, then the complete expression is immediately given the value false without evaluating the second operand. Similarly, if the value of the first operand in an || expression is true, then the complete expression is immediately given the value true without evaluating the second operand.

3.3 The switch statement must be controlled by a single integer control variable, and each case section must correspond to a single constant value for the variable. The if...else if combination allows any kind of condition after each if. For example, Example 3.3 uses inequalities in its conditions.

3.4 The term "fall through" refers to the way the switch statement executes its various case sections. Every statement that follows the selected case section will be executed unless a break statement is encountered.

3.5 The statement d = 44; is unreachable.

Solutions to Programming Problems

3.1
```
import java.util.Random;
public class TestPositive
{ public static void main(String[] args)
  { Random random = new Random();
    int n = random.nextInt();
    System.out.println("n = " + n);
    if (n > 0) System.out.println("n > 0");
  }
}
```

3.2
```
import java.util.Random;
public class PrintMinimum
{ public static void main(String[] args)
  { Random random = new Random();
    int m = random.nextInt();
    System.out.println("m = " + m);
    int n = random.nextInt();
    System.out.println("n = " + n);
    if (m < n) System.out.println("Their minimum is " + m);
    else System.out.println("Their minimum is " + n);
  }
}
```

3.3

```
import java.util.Random;
public class MaxOfFour
{ public static void main(String[] args)
  { Random random = new Random();
    int n1 = random.nextInt();
    System.out.println("n1 = " + n1);
    int n2 = random.nextInt();
    System.out.println("n2 = " + n2);
    int n3 = random.nextInt();
    System.out.println("n3 = " + n3);
    int n4 = random.nextInt();
    System.out.println("n4 = " + n4);
    int max = n1;
    if (n2 > max) max = n2;
    if (n3 > max) max = n3;
    if (n4 > max) max = n4;
    System.out.println("Their maximum is " + max);
  }
}
```

3.4

```
import java.util.Random;
public class Quintiles
{ public static void main(String[] args)
  { Random random = new Random();
    double x = random.nextDouble();
    System.out.print("x = " + x + ", which is in the ");
    if (x < 0.2) System.out.println("first quintile.");
    else if (x < 0.4) System.out.println("second quintile.");
    else if (x < 0.6) System.out.println("third quintile.");
    else if (x < 0.8) System.out.println("fourth quintile.");
    else System.out.println("fifth quintile.");
  }
}
```

3.5

```
import java.util.Random;
public class SortThreeFloats
{ public static void main(String[] args)
  { Random random = new Random();
    float a = random.nextFloat();
    System.out.println("a = " + a);
    float b = random.nextFloat();
    System.out.println("b = " + b);
    float c = random.nextFloat();
    System.out.println("c = " + c);
    if (a < b)
      if (b < c) System.out.println(a + " < " + b + " < " + c);
      else
        if (a < c) System.out.println(a + " < " + c + " < " + b);
        else  System.out.println(c + " < " + a + " < " + b);
    else
      if (a < c) System.out.println(b + " < " + a + " < " + c);
      else
        if (b < c) System.out.println(b + " < " + c + " < " + a);
        else  System.out.println(c + " < " + b + " < " + a);
  }
}
```

3.6

```
import java.util.Random;
public class TestDivisibility
{ public static void main(String[] args)
  { Random random = new Random();
    int n = random.nextInt();
    System.out.println("n = " + n);
```

```
                  if (n%2 == 0) System.out.println("n is divisible by 2");
                  if (n%3 == 0) System.out.println("n is divisible by 3");
                  if (n%5 == 0) System.out.println("n is divisible by 5");
                }
             }
```

3.7
```
        import java.io.*;
        public class SortThreeStrings
        { public static void main(String[] args) throws IOException
          { final int LEN = 255;
            byte buffer[] = new byte[LEN];
            System.out.println("Enter three names, one per line:");
            int n = 0;
            try { n = System.in.read(buffer, 0, LEN); }
            catch (Exception e) {}
            String s1 = new String(buffer);
            s1 = s1.substring(0, n-2);
            try { n = System.in.read(buffer, 0, LEN); }
            catch (Exception e) {}
            String s2 = new String(buffer);
            s2 = s2.substring(0, n-2);
            n = System.in.read(buffer, 0, LEN);
            String s3 = new String(buffer);
            s3 = s3.substring(0, n-2);
            System.out.println(s1 + ", " + s2 + ", " + s3);
            if (s1.compareTo(s2) <= 0 && s2.compareTo(s3) <= 0)
              System.out.println(s1 + " <= " + s2 + " <= " + s3);
            if (s1.compareTo(s3) <= 0 && s3.compareTo(s2) <= 0)
              System.out.println(s1 + " <= " + s3 + " <= " + s2);
            if (s2.compareTo(s1) <= 0 && s1.compareTo(s3) <= 0)
              System.out.println(s2 + " <= " + s1 + " <= " + s3);
            if (s2.compareTo(s3) <= 0 && s3.compareTo(s1) <= 0)
              System.out.println(s2 + " <= " + s3 + " <= " + s1);
            if (s3.compareTo(s2) <= 0 && s2.compareTo(s1) <= 0)
              System.out.println(s3 + " <= " + s2 + " <= " + s1);
            if (s3.compareTo(s1) <= 0 && s1.compareTo(s2) <= 0)
              System.out.println(s3 + " <= " + s1 + " <= " + s2);
          }
        }
```

3.8
```
        import java.util.Random;
        public class TestLeapYear
        { public static void main(String[] args)
          { Random random = new Random();
            float x = random.nextFloat();
            System.out.println("x = " + x);
            int year = Math.round(200*x + 1800);
            System.out.println("The year is " + year);
            if (year%400 == 0 || year%100 != 0 && year%4 == 0)
              System.out.print("That is a leap year.");
            else
              System.out.print("That is not a leap year.");
          }
        }
```

3.9
```
        import java.util.Random;
        public class Problem0309
        { public static void main(String[] args)
          { Random random = new Random();
            int n = random.nextInt();
            System.out.println("n = " + n);
```

```
        if (n%2 == 0)
          if (n%3 == 0)
            if (n%5 == 0) System.out.println("n is divisible by 30");
            else System.out.println("n is divisible by 6 but not 5");
          else
            if (n%5 == 0)
              System.out.println("n is divisible by 10 but not 3");
            else
              System.out.println("n is divisible by 2 but not 3 or 5");
        else
          if (n%3 == 0)
            if (n%5 == 0)
              System.out.println("n is divisible by 15 but not 2");
            else
              System.out.println("n is divisible by 3 but not 2 or 5");
          else
            if (n%5 == 0)
              System.out.println("n is divisible by 5 but not 6");
            else
              System.out.println("n is not divisible by 2, 3, or 5");
      }
    }
```

3.10
```
    import java.util.Random;
    public class LetterGrades
    { public static void main(String[] args)
      { Random random = new Random();
        float x = random.nextFloat();
        System.out.println("x = " + x);
        int score = Math.round(50*x + 50);
        System.out.println("Your test score was = " + score);
        switch (score/10)
        { case 10:
            System.out.print("That is is an A+");
            break;
          case 9:
            System.out.print("That is is an A");
            break;
          case 8:
            System.out.print("That is a B");
            break;
          case 7:
            System.out.print("That is a C");
            break;
          case 6:
            System.out.print("That is a D");
            break;
          default:
            System.out.print("That is an F");
        }
        if (score >= 60 && score < 100)
          if (score%10 > 7) System.out.print("+");
          else if (score%10 < 2) System.out.print("-");
      }
    }
```

3.11
```
import java.util.Random;
public class MonthNumbers
{ public static void main(String[] args) throws IOException
  { InputStreamReader reader = new InputStreamReader(System.in);
    BufferedReader input = new BufferedReader(reader);
    System.out.print("Enter the month: ");
    String month = input.readLine();
    month = month.trim().toUpperCase();
    System.out.println("You entered: " + month);
    String abbr = month.substring(0,3);
    abbr = abbr.toUpperCase();
    System.out.println("Its abbreviation is: " + abbr);
    int n = 0;
    char c0 = abbr.charAt(0);
    char c1 = abbr.charAt(1);
    char c2 = abbr.charAt(2);
    if (c0 == 'A')
      if (c1 == 'P') n = 4;
      else if (c1 == 'U') n = 8;
    if (c0 == 'D') n = 12;
    if (c0 == 'F') n = 2;
    if (c0 == 'J')
      if (c1 == 'A') n = 1;
      else if (c1 == 'U')
        if (c2 == 'L') n = 7;
        else if (c2 == 'N') n = 6;
    if (c0 == 'M')
      if (c1 == 'A')
        if (c2 == 'R') n = 3;
        else if (c2 == 'Y') n = 5;
    if (c0 == 'N') n = 11;
    if (c0 == 'O') n = 10;
    if (c0 == 'S') n = 9;
    if (n > 0) System.out.println("This is month number " + n);
    else System.out.println("That word is not valid");
  }
}
```

3.12
```
import java.io.*;
public class MonthNumbers
{ public static void main(String[] args) throws IOException
  { InputStreamReader reader = new InputStreamReader(System.in);
    BufferedReader input = new BufferedReader(reader);
    System.out.print("Enter the month: ");
    String month = input.readLine();
    month = month.trim().toUpperCase();
    int n = 0;
    if (month.startsWith("JAN")) n = 1;
    if (month.startsWith("FEB")) n = 2;
    if (month.startsWith("MAR")) n = 3;
    if (month.startsWith("APR")) n = 4;
    if (month.startsWith("MAY")) n = 5;
    if (month.startsWith("JUN")) n = 6;
    if (month.startsWith("JUL")) n = 7;
    if (month.startsWith("AUG")) n = 8;
    if (month.startsWith("SEP")) n = 9;
    if (month.startsWith("OCT")) n = 10;
    if (month.startsWith("NOV")) n = 11;
    if (month.startsWith("DEC")) n = 12;
    if (n > 0) System.out.println(month + " is month number " + n);
    else System.out.println(month + " is not a valid month name.");
  }
}
```

Chapter 4

Iteration

The first computer was designed by the English mathematician Charles Babbage (1792-1871) designed in the 1830s. Its purpose was "to do these calculations by steam." He was referring to the tabulation of trigonometric tables upon which safe navigation was dependent. At the time all the tables had been computed by hand and were full of errors. Babbage recognized that *iteration*, the repetition of elementary computations, was a natural task for automatic computers. Because his colleague Ada Byron Lovelace (1815-1852) described in 1843 how a computer would do iteration, she has been dubbed the world's first computer programmer.

Modern computers perform far more important tasks than tabulating functions. But most of those tasks usually depend upon iteration at some level. This is because most useful programs use data objects that contain sequences of numbered elements, as described in Chapter 8. These sequences are easily processed by iteration statement blocks. Such programming statements are called *loops*, because the flow of execution "loops back" to the beginning of the block. Like most modern programming languages, Java has three loop statements: the `for` statement, the `while` statement, and the `do...while` statement.

4.1 THE `for` STATEMENT

The syntax of the `for` statement is

```
for ( expr1; expr2; expr3 )
    stmt;
```

where `expr1` and `expr3` are any expressions, `expr2` is a boolean expression, and `stmt` is any statement or block of statements. The three expressions are used to control the iteration of the statement or block in this order:

1. evaluate `expr1`;
2. evaluate the condition `expr2`; if false, exit from the loop;
3. execute the complete block of statements;
4. evaluate `expr3`;
5. evaluate the condition `expr2`; if true, go back to step 3.

Steps 3–5 constitute one iteration of the loop. Step 1 is the *initialization*; step 4 is the *update* and `expr2` is the *continuation condition*. Note that the continuation condition is checked only <u>after</u> all the statements in the block are executed, not during or between them.

In most cases, the three control expressions are coordinated by means of a control variable, called an *index* or *counter*, which counts each iteration of the loop. That common structure is

```
for (int i = begin; i < end; i++)
{ stmnt1;
  stmnt2;
  etc.
}
```

where `i` is the index variable, `begin` is its first value, and `end-1` is its last value. The loop executes in this order:

1. declare i of type int and initialize it with the value *begin*;
2. if (i >= *end*), exit from the loop;
3. executes the complete block of statements;
4. increment i;
5. if (i < *end*), go back to step 3.

Note that, in this form, the number of iterations is equal to the difference *end* - *begin*. The most common control structure is

```
for (int i = 0; i < n; i++) ...
```

In this case, the loop executes exactly *n* times.

EXAMPLE 4.1 The Babbage Function

In 1820, Charles Babbage requested financial support from the British government to build his computer. (This was the first government grant proposal in history.) In describing how his computer would tabulate functions, he gave the explicit example of the function $f(x) = x^2 + x + 41$. This is a curious polynomial because it seems to generate only prime numbers. This is the program that Babbage's Difference Engine would have executed:

```
public class Example0401
{ public static void main(String[] args)
  { for (int x = 0; x < 10; x++)
    { int y = x*x + x + 41;
      System.out.println("\t" + x + "\t" + y);
    }
  }
}
```

The output is

```
    0    41
    1    43
    2    47
    3    53
    4    61
    5    71
    6    83
    7    97
    8    113
    9    131
```

Note that the index is named x in this loop.

EXAMPLE 4.2 Accumulating a Sum

This program generates 5 random numbers in the range 0.0 to 1.0 and accumulates their sum:

```
import java.util.Random;
public class Example0402
{ public static void main(String[] args)
  { Random random = new Random();
    float sum = 0;
    for (int i = 0; i < 5; i++)
    { float x = random.nextFloat();
      sum += x;
      System.out.println("\tx = " + x + "\t\tsum = " + sum);
    }
  }
}
```

Here is a sample run:
```
x = 0.19246513    sum = 0.19246513
x = 0.20723224    sum = 0.39969736
x = 0.33193415    sum = 0.7316315
x = 0.42326802    sum = 1.1548996
x = 0.14011943    sum = 1.295019
```

EXAMPLE 4.3 Testing Primality

This program generates a random integer in the range 2 to 100 and then tests it for primality. (Recall that a *prime number* is an integer greater than 2 whose only divisors are 1 and itself.)
```
import java.util.Random;
public class Example0403
{ public static void main(String[] args)
  { Random random = new Random();
    float x = random.nextFloat();
    System.out.println("x = " + x);
    int n = (int)Math.floor(99*x+2);
    for (int d = 2; d < n; d++)
      if (n%d == 0)
      { System.out.println(n + " is not prime.");
        return;
      }
    System.out.println(n + " is prime.");
  }
}
```
Here are two sample runs:
```
x = 0.28460586
28 is not prime.
```
```
x = 0.7978597
79 is prime.
```

The float x is a random number in the range $0.0 \le x < 1.0$, so $0.0 \le 99*x < 99.0$, and consequently $2.0 \le 99*x+2 < 101.0$. The floor() method of the Math class returns a double whose value is the largest integer less than or equal to the number passed to it. So $2.0 \le$ Math.floor(99*x+2) ≤ 100.0. The (int) prefix converts that double value to an int value so that it can be used to initialize the int variable n. So n is initialized with one of the 99 integers from 2, 3, ..., 100. For example, in the second run shown above, x is given the float value 0.7978597. From that, the floor() method receives the value 79.78597 and returns the double value 79.0. (Note that this truncates the fractional part, even if it is greater than 0.5.) That value is then converted to the int value 79 before it is used to initialize n. Changing the type of a numerical value this way is called *type casting*.

Inside the for loop, n is tested by d. The condition (n%d == 0) is true if and only if n is divisible by d. If it is, then n cannot be prime, so at that point the println() method reports that n is not prime and the program terminates. The return statement terminates the main() method, which ends the program abruptly, preventing the loop from finishing. On the other hand, if the condition (n%d == 0) is false for every potential divisor d in the range from 2 to n-1, then n has no divisors and is therefore a prime number. In that case the loop terminates normally and the println() that follows the loop executes.

There are several ways to stop iteration. The normal way in a for loop is for its continuation condition to become false. That happens when x increments to 10 in Example 4.1 and when i

increments to 5 in Example 4.2. It also happens when d increments to n in Example 4.3 if it
gets that far. But the loop in Example 4.3 can also stop if the return statement inside the loop
gets to execute. That not only stops the loop, but it also stops the entire program. That is a rather
radical way to stop a loop. A better way is to use a break statement, as illustrated in the next
example.

EXAMPLE 4.4 Using a `break` Statement to Stop a Loop

This is a modification of the program in Example 4.3. It uses a boolean variable named
isNotPrime and a break statement to break out of the loop when a divisor is found.

```
import java.util.Random;
public class Example0404
{ public static void main(String[] args)
  { Random random = new Random();
    float x = random.nextFloat();
    System.out.println("x = " + x);
    int n = (int)Math.floor(101*x);
    boolean isNotPrime = (n < 2);
    for (int d = 2; d < n; d++)
    { isNotPrime = (n%d == 0);
      if (isNotPrime) break;
    }
    if (isNotPrime) System.out.println(n + " is not prime.");
    else System.out.println(n + " is prime.");
  }
}
```

Here is a sample run:

```
x = 0.07461572
7 is prime.
```

In this version, n is initialized with an integer in the range 0 to 100. Then the boolean variable
isNotPrime is declared and initialized to either true or false according to whether n < 2 or not. (0
and 1 are, by definition, not primes.)

The for loop here is controlled the same way as the for loop in Example 4.3: the index d begins
with the value 2 and increments up through n-1 before stopping at n, unless some other event
interrupts the loop. In this case, that event would be the break statement. The isNotPrime variable
is reset to be true or false according to whether d divides n. If and when it does, the break statement
executes, transferring execution control to the first statement that follows the loop. That is the last if
statement, which prints that n either is not or is prime according to whether the isNotPrime variable
is true or false.

The break statement works the same way in loops as in switch statements: it causes
execution to jump to the first statement that follows the block within which it occurs.

4.2 THE `while` STATEMENT

The for loop is the best way to perform iteration when the repetitions are naturally tied to
an index such as x, i, and d in the previous examples. But if there is no natural counting
variable to control the iteration, then a more general while statement is usually the best choice.

The syntax for the `while` loop is

```
while ( expr )
   stmt;
```

where `expr` is a boolean expression, and `stmt` is any statement or block of statements.

EXAMPLE 4.5 The Fibonacci Sequence

The *Fibonacci sequence* is defined recursively by the equations

$$\begin{cases} F_0 = 0 \\ F_1 = 1 \\ F_n = F_{n-1} + F_{n-2} \end{cases}$$

If we let $n = 2$ and then substitute the first two equations into the third, we get

$$F_2 = F_1 + F_0 = 1 + 0 = 1$$

Repeating this process with $n = 3$ yields

$$F_3 = F_2 + F_1 = 1 + 1 = 2$$

and $n = 4$ yields

$$F_4 = F_3 + F_2 = 2 + 1 = 3$$

The process is the same on each iteration: add the last two numbers. It is called a *recursive* process because each computed number "recurs" again on the right side of the next two equations. It is very efficient because it allows us to define an infinite sequence using only three equations. The down side is that we cannot compute the nth number until after we have computed the n numbers that precede it.

This program uses a `while` loop to implement the definition of the Fibonacci sequence. It prints all the Fibonacci numbers less than 1000:

```
public class Example0405
{ public static void main(String[] args)
   { System.out.print("0, 1");
      int fib0 = 0;
      int fib1 = 1;
      int fib2 = fib1 + fib0;
      while (fib2 < 1000)
      { fib0 = fib1;
         fib1 = fib2;
         fib2 = fib1 + fib0;
         System.out.print(", " + fib1);
      }
   }
}
```

The output is

```
0, 1, 1, 2, 3, 5, 8, 13, 21, 34, 55, 89, 144, 233, 377, 610, 987
```

Note that this sequence is *exponential*: the number of 3-digit numbers is the same as the number of 2-digit numbers.

EXAMPLE 4.6 Using a `while` Loop to Test Primality

This is a modification of the program in Example 4.4. Its `boolean` variable, named `isPrime`, is the opposite of that in Example 4.4. It partially controls the `while` loop that is used in place of the `for` loop.

```
import java.util.Random;
public class Example0406
{ public static void main(String[] args)
  { Random random = new Random();
    float x = random.nextFloat();
    System.out.println("x = " + x);
    int n = (int)Math.floor(101*x);
    boolean isPrime = (n > 1);
    int d = 2;
    while (isPrime && d < n)
      isPrime = (n % d++ != 0);
    if (isPrime) System.out.println(n + " is prime.");
    else System.out.println(n + " is not prime.");
  }
}
```

The other control variable `d` must be initialized explicitly to 2 before the `while` loop begins. Then we used the postfix increment operator in the expression `(n%d++ == 0)` to increment `d` from 2 to `n`. This boolean expression has the value either true or false. That value is assigned to the variable `isPrime` which will stop the loop if and when it is assigned the value false.

These two previous examples illustrate two different reasons for using a `while` loop in place of a `for` loop. We had to use a `while` loop in Example 4.5 because we did not know in advance how many iterations would be needed to compute all the Fibonacci numbers less than 1000. The primary reason for using a `while` loop in Example 4.6 was to simplify the `for` loop from Example 4.4 by removing the `break` statement. In most cases a `for` loop can be translated easily into a `while` loop, and *vice versa*. For example, the `while` loop in Example 4.5 could have been replaced by

```
for (int fib2 = 1; fib2 < 1000; fib2 = fib1 + fib0)
{ fib0 = fib1;
  fib1 = fib2;
  System.out.print(", " + fib1);
}
```

But many programmers consider this an abuse of the `for` statement, like pounding a nail with a wrench; the `for` statement was designed to be controlled by an index variable that counts the iterations. Others prefer to use the `for` loop whenever it works because it is more structured. In general, the best strategy is to choose the statement that seems most natural and yields code that is easy to understand. If your code is not clear, it should be reformulated.

4.3 SOME NUMBER CRUNCHING

Although Java is not the best programming language for scientific computation, it is adequate. This section illustrates its use on some common algorithms.

EXAMPLE 4.7 The Discrete Binary Logarithm

The *logarithm* of a positive number x with *base b* is the power of b that equals x:

$$y = \log_b x \iff b^y = x$$

The *binary logarithm* of a positive number x is the power of 2 that equals x. The *discrete binary logarithm* of a positive number x is the greatest integer power of 2 that is less than or equal to x. This is the same as the number of times 1 can be doubled before it exceeds x.

This program computes the discrete binary logarithm of a random number between 2 and 1,000,000:

```
import java.util.Random;
public class Example0407
{ public static void main(String[] args)
  { Random random = new Random();
    float x = random.nextFloat();
    x = 999999*x+2;
    int y = 0;
    int n = 1;
    while (n <= x)
    { n *= 2;
      ++y;
      System.out.println("n = " + n + "     \ty = " + y);
    }
    --y;
    System.out.println("                                     x: " + x);
    System.out.println("  Discrete binary logarithm of x: " + y);
    float lgx = (float)(Math.log(x)/Math.log(2.0));
    System.out.println("Continuous binary logarithm of x: " + lgx);
  }
}
```

The `while` loop doubles `n` until it exceeds `x`. The variable `y` counts the number of iterations, so it is the discrete binary logarithm of `x`.

Here is a sample run:

```
n = 2          y = 1
n = 4          y = 2
n = 8          y = 3
n = 16         y = 4
n = 32         y = 5
n = 64         y = 6
n = 128        y = 7
n = 256        y = 8
n = 512        y = 9
n = 1024       y = 10
n = 2048       y = 11
n = 4096       y = 12
n = 8192       y = 13
n = 16384      y = 14
n = 32768      y = 15
n = 65536      y = 16
n = 131072     y = 17
n = 262144     y = 18
n = 524288     y = 19
                              x: 954202.9
   Discrete binary logarithm of x: 19
Continuous binary logarithm of x: 19.863937
```

In this run, the number n had to be doubled 19 times before it exceeded 954,202.9.

The last line of output checks the result by comparing it to the continuous binary logarithm of x. The method Math.log() returns the natural logarithm (base e), so we had to use the standard formula for converting bases:

$$\log_2 x \ = \ \frac{\log_e x}{\log_e 2}$$

This confirms that the discrete binary logarithm is the floor of the (continuous) binary logarithm.

The next uses an if statement inside a while loop.

EXAMPLE 4.8 The Euclidean Algorithm

The *Euclidean Algorithm* computes the greatest common divisor (g.c.d.) of two given positive integers. Its name comes from the fact that it is given in Euclid's *Elements*, the great mathematical encyclopedia written about 2300 years ago.

The g.c.d. of two integers is the largest integer that divides both of them. For example, the g.c.d. of 66 and 84 is 6 because it is the largest in the set of their common divisors {1, 2, 3, 6}.

A common use of the g.c.d. is to reduce fractions. For example, the fraction 66/84 is reduced to 11/14 simply by dividing both 66 and 84 by their g.c.d. 6.

This program generates two random integers in the range 2 to 1000 and then uses a while loop to reduce them until one of them reaches 0; at that point, Euclid proved, the other must equal the greatest common divisor of the two original numbers.

```
import java.util.Random;
public class Example0408
{ public static void main(String[] args)
  { Random random = new Random();
    float x = random.nextFloat();
    int m = Math.round(999*x + 2);
    x = random.nextFloat();
    int n = Math.round(999*x + 2);
    System.out.println("m = " + m + "\t\tn = " + n);
    while (m > 0)
    { if (m < n)
      { int temp = m;
        m = n;
        n = temp;
        System.out.println("m = " + m + "\t\tn = " + n);
      }
      m -= n;
    }
    System.out.println("The g.c.d. of m and n is " + n);
  }
}
```

Here are two sample runs:

```
m = 832         n = 752
m = 752         n = 80
m = 80          n = 32
m = 32          n = 16
The g.c.d. of m and n is 16
```

```
m  =  141          n  =  488
m  =  488          n  =  141
m  =  141          n  =  65
m  =  65           n  =  11
m  =  11           n  =  10
m  =  10           n  =  1
The g.c.d. of m and n is 1
```

In the first run, the randomly generated numbers are $m = 832$ and $n = 752$. Inside the `while` loop, the condition $(m < n)$ is false, so the next four statements are skipped and `m -= n` executes, subtracting 752 from m reducing its value to 80. Now the continuation condition $(m > 0)$ is still true so the loop iterates again. This time, the condition $(m < n)$ is true, so the next four statements execute. The first three of these perform a *swap*; their effect is to interchange the values of m and n, giving m the value 752 and n the value 80. This way, m will always be the larger number when the decrement m `-=` n executes. On this iteration, that decrement reduces m to $752 - 80 = 672$. The next eight iterations continue reducing m to 592, 512, 432, 352, 272, 192, 112, and finally 32. After that, another swap occurs, making $m = 80$ and $n = 32$. Then m gets reduced twice more, to 48 and 16. Another swap occurs, making $m = 32$ and $n = 16$. Then m gets reduced to 16 and finally 0. That stops the loop, leaving n with the value 16, which must be the g.c.d.

We saw in the analysis of the execution of the program in Example 4.8 that m will always be the larger of the two numbers before the statement m `-=` n in the while loop. That fact is essential to the success of the algorithm. It is an example of what software engineers call a *loop invariant*: a condition at a particular point within a loop that must always be true. Loop invariants are used to prove (mathematically) that a program is correct.

The proof that the Euclidean Algorithm is correct hinges on the fact that subtracting n from m does not change their g.c.d. That is: $gcd(m, n) = gcd(m-n, n)$. This is a fact from number theory that is not difficult to verify. In the program, it is a loop invariant. And it proves that the program is correct because it means that the g.c.d. of the original two numbers must be the same as the g.c.d. of the last two numbers before m becomes zero, and those last two numbers are both equal to the final value of n.

4.4 THE `do...while` STATEMENT

The `do...while` statement is essentially the same as the `while` statement with its continuation condition put at the end of the loop instead of the beginning. The only difference is that the `do...while` loop executes once before the condition is evaluated.

The syntax for the `do...while` loop is

```
do
   stmt
while ( expr );
```

where `expr` is a boolean expression, and `stmt` is any statement or block of statements.

EXAMPLE 4.9 The Factorial Function

The *factorial function* of a positive integer n is the product of all the integers from 1 to n. For example, the factorial of 5 is $1 \cdot 2 \cdot 3 \cdot 4 \cdot 5 = 120$. This is usually expressed as $5! = 120$. The value of $0!$ is 1, by definition.

This program generates a random integer in the range 0 to 20 and then computes and prints its factorial:

```
import java.util.Random;
public class Example0409
{ public static void main(String[] args)
   { Random random = new Random();
     float x = random.nextFloat();
     int n = Math.round(21*x);
     long f = 1;
     int k = 1;
     do
        f *= k++;
     while (k <= n);
     System.out.println(n + "! = " + f);
   }
}
```

After initializing n, f, and k, the do...while loop multiplies f by all the numbers from 1 to n. This is done by means of the assignment statement

```
        f *= k++;
```

which multiplies f by k and then increments k.

Here are three sample runs:

```
5! = 120
```

```
17! = 355687428096000
```

```
0! = 1
```

In the first run, n is initialized to 5, f to 1, and k to 1. The first iteration changes f to $1 \cdot 1 = 1$ and k to 2. The second iteration changes f to $1 \cdot 2 = 2$ and k to 3. The third iteration changes f to 2 $\cdot 3 = 6$ and k to 4. The fourth iteration changes f to $6 \cdot 4 = 24$ and k to 5. The fifth iteration changes f to $24 \cdot 5 = 120$ and k to 6. That stops the loop and prints 120.

The second run reveals how large the factorial numbers are. This integer 355,687,428,096,000 is much larger than the maximum int value (2,147,483,647). That's why we used type long for f.

The third run produces 0! = 1, which is true by definition. In this case, the loop executes once, multiplying $1 \cdot 1$ for f and incrementing k to 1.

The above analysis of the first run of the program in Example 4.9 illustrates an important debugging strategy that all successful programmers do. It is called *tracing* the execution by hand. Its main purpose is to check the logic of a program to see if it will do what was intended. Although somewhat tedious, tracing is often the best way to uncover logical errors in a program.

The table shown at right summarizes the trace made above: This *tracing table* shows at a glance that the program logic is correct.

Tracing also helps the programmer find ways to improve his/her code. There is almost always more than one way to solve a problem (*i.e.*, write a program). The first solution is usually not the best. Modifications can often be found to make the program run faster, use less memory, or even be simpler to understand. In our competitive world, efforts toward such improvements are usually rewarded.

f	k
1	1
1	2
2	3
3	6
24	4
120	6

EXAMPLE 4.10 Testing Primality Again

This program modifies that in Example 4.6 on page 70 by replacing its `while` loop with a `do...while` loop:

```
import java.util.Random;
public class Example0410
{ public static void main(String[] args)
  { Random random = new Random();
    float x = random.nextFloat();
    System.out.println("x = " + x);
    int n = Math.round(97*x + 2);
    boolean isPrime;
    int d = 2;
    do
      isPrime = (n % d++ != 0);
    while (isPrime && d < n);
    if (isPrime) System.out.println(n + " is prime.");
    else System.out.println(n + " is not prime.");
  }
}
```

The `do...while` loop executes the statement

```
      isPrime = (n%d++ != 0);
```

once before it evaluates the continuation condition `(isPrime && d < n)`. Consequently, if n has the value 1, that statement will set the `isPrime` variable to `true` on that automatic first iteration, and that would produce an incorrect result (1 is not prime, by definition). This version of the program avoids that difficulty by restricting random numbers that n can be given to the range 2 to 99. It's an artificial fix, but necessary to avoid erroneous results.

Example 4.10 shows that `do...while` loops are a little more prone to error than `while` loops because they limit the control you have on the first iteration. So in general, it is better to use a while loop unless there is a good reason to have the loop iterate once unconditionally. An example of such a situation is given in Example 4.12 on page 76.

4.5 MORE NUMBER CRUNCHING

The next two examples implement classic numerical algorithms where the `do...while` statement is typically used.

EXAMPLE 4.11 The Babylonian Algorithm for Computing Square Roots

Over 5000 years ago the ancient Babylonians discovered a method for computing the square root of 2. They probably used that number (about 1.4) to construct right angles for the foundations of their buildings. This iterative algorithm is still the simplest way to compute square roots.

If x is any number close to $\sqrt{2}$, then x^2 will be close to 2, which makes x close to $2/x$. But $2/x$ will be on the other side of $\sqrt{2}$ from x. That is, if x less than $\sqrt{2}$, then $2/x$ will be greater than $\sqrt{2}$, and *vice versa*. For example, suppose that $x = 1.6$. Then $2/x = 1.25$, which is on the other side of $\sqrt{2}$. That "crossing over the limit" is the key to the algorithm because it means that the average of x and $2/x$ must be between them and therefore closer to the objective $\sqrt{2}$. So the Babylonian Algorithm consists of choosing some number x that is close to $\sqrt{2}$, and then repeatedly replacing x by its average with $2/x$. That's what the statement

```
      x = (x + 2.0/x)/2;
```

does in the following program:

```
import java.util.Random;
public class Example0411
{ public static void main(String[] args)
  { final double TOL = 0.5E-15;
    Random random = new Random();
    double x = random.nextDouble();
    System.out.println("\tx = " + x);
    do
    { x = (x + 2.0/x)/2;
      System.out.println("\tx = " + x);
    }
    while (Math.abs(x*x - 2.0) > TOL*2*x);
    System.out.println("sqrt(2.0) = " + Math.sqrt(2.0));
  }
}
```

Here is a sample run:

```
        x = 0.8211882540816451
        x = 1.6283416959199273
        x = 1.4282925660893104
        x = 1.4142829523392502
        x = 1.4142135640753595
        x = 1.414213562373095
sqrt(2.0) = 1.4142135623730951
```

The program uses a constant named TOL (for "tolerance") to control its do...while loop. The value of this constant is 0.5×10^{-15}. The continuation condition

```
(Math.abs(x*x - 2.0) > TOL*2*x)
```

means that the absolute value of $x^2 - 2$ is greater than $0.5 \times 10^{-15}(2x)$, which is algebraically equivalent to the condition that the distance between x and $(x + 2/x)/2$ is greater than 0.5×10^{-15}. By continuing the loop until that condition is false, we guarantee that our answer will be accurate to 15 decimal places. That's the best we can expect with type double.

The variable x is initialized with a random value between 0 and 1. In the sample run, that value is about 0.82. On each iteration, the current value of x is replaced by the average of x and 2/x. This causes x to jump back and forth on either side of its limit, 1.4142135623730951...

Notice how fast the sequence converges to its limit. The first iterate (1.628...) is accurate to 1 digit, the second to 2, the third to 5, the fourth to 9, and the fifth to 16. Each iteration doubles the number of accurate digits! This is called *quadratic convergence*.

It is also interesting to observe here that it doesn't much matter what number you begin with. No matter where it starts, the sequence seeks the same limit $\sqrt{2}$ and it takes only 5 iterations to get there with 16 digit accuracy.

EXAMPLE 4.12 The Bisection Algorithm for Solving Equations

Algebra is a good way to exercise your brain. But it really isn't very good for solving equations. Most equations cannot be solved complete by any algebraic techniques. Instead, their solutions must be approximated by numerical methods. The Bisection Method is a simple example.

This algorithm uses the classic *divide and conquer* strategy. Begin with an interval that contains the unknown solution. Divide it in half, discard the half that does not contain the solution, and repeat.

This program implements the Bisection Algorithm to solve the equation

$$\sqrt{x} = \cos x$$

It has the same solutions as the equation

$$\sqrt{x}-\cos x = 0$$

Its solutions are the x-intercepts of the graph of the equation

$$y = \sqrt{x}-\cos x$$

We know that there must be a solution within the interval from 0 to $\pi/2$ because at $x = 0$, $y = \sqrt{0}-\cos 0 = 0$ $- 1 = -1 < 0$, and at $x = \pi/2$, $y = \sqrt{\pi/2}-\cos\pi/2 = \sqrt{\pi/2}-0 > 0$. A continuous curve cannot be below the x-axis at one point and above it at another without crossing it in between.

```
public class Example0412
{ public static void main(String[] args)
  { final double TOL = 0.5E-7;
    double a = 0;
    double b = Math.PI/2;
    double x, y;
    do
    { x = (a + b)/2;
      y = Math.sqrt(x) - Math.cos(x);
      System.out.println("a = " + (float)a + "\tx = " + (float)x
        + "\tb = " + (float)b + "\ty = " + (float)y);
      if (y < 0) a = x;
      else b = x;
    } while (b - a > TOL);
    System.out.println("sqrt(x) = " + (float)Math.sqrt(x));
    System.out.println(" cos(x) = " + (float)Math.cos(x));
  }
}
```

The do...while loop uses the same kind of continuation condition as in Example 4.11. The loop continues iterating until the length of the interval is less than 0.5×10^{-7}. This guarantees that our answer will be correct to 7 decimal place. This use of a *tolerance constant* is the standard way to control *convergence loops*.

Here is a sample run:

```
a = 0.0          x = 0.7853982    b = 1.5707964    y = 0.17912014
a = 0.0          x = 0.3926991    b = 0.7853982    y = -0.29722247
a = 0.3926991    x = 0.5890486    b = 0.7853982    y = -0.06397458
a = 0.5890486    x = 0.6872234    b = 0.7853982    y = 0.055978928
a = 0.5890486    x = 0.638136     b = 0.6872234    y = -0.0043733763
a = 0.638136     x = 0.6626797    b = 0.6872234    y = 0.025704984
a = 0.638136     x = 0.65040785   b = 0.6626797    y = 0.010641771
a = 0.638136     x = 0.6442719    b = 0.65040785   y = 0.003128247
a = 0.638136     x = 0.64120394   b = 0.6442719    y = -6.2404445E-4
a = 0.64120394   x = 0.6427379    b = 0.6442719    y = 0.0012517304
a = 0.64120394   x = 0.64197093   b = 0.6427379    y = 3.1375035E-4
a = 0.64120394   x = 0.64158744   b = 0.64197093   y = -1.5517019E-4
a = 0.64158744   x = 0.6417792    b = 0.64197093   y = 7.928429E-5
a = 0.64158744   x = 0.64168334   b = 0.6417792    y = -3.79444E-5
a = 0.64168334   x = 0.64173126   b = 0.6417792    y = 2.0669584E-5
a = 0.64168334   x = 0.6417073    b = 0.64173126   y = -8.637498E-6
a = 0.6417073    x = 0.6417193    b = 0.64173126   y = 6.0160205E-6
a = 0.6417073    x = 0.6417133    b = 0.6417193    y = -1.3107443E-6
a = 0.6417133    x = 0.6417163    b = 0.6417193    y = 2.3526366E-6
a = 0.6417133    x = 0.6417148    b = 0.6417163    y = 5.2094583E-7
a = 0.6417133    x = 0.64171404   b = 0.6417148    y = -3.948993E-7
a = 0.64171404   x = 0.6417144    b = 0.6417148    y = 6.302324E-8
```

```
a = 0.64171404   x = 0.6417142    b = 0.6417144    y = -1.6593803E-7
a = 0.6417142    x = 0.64171433   b = 0.6417144    y = -5.14574E-8
a = 0.64171433   x = 0.6417144    b = 0.6417144    y = 5.782921E-9
sqrt(x) = 0.80107075
 cos(x) = 0.80107075
```

Each iteration replaces either a or b with their average which is the number midway between them. The choice of which endpoint to change depends upon whether the value of the function $\sqrt{x}-\cos x$ is negative or positive. If it is negative, then the target solution (which is the point where the function's graph crosses the x-axis) must be between the midpoint $(a+b)/2$ and b, so we reset a to that value to make the new interval the right half of the previous interval. If the function is positive, then we reset b to be the midpoint, which makes the left half the new interval. On the first iteration, the midpoint $x = 0.7853982$ and $y = 0.17912014$, which is positive, so b is reset to x.

At the end of the program, the answer $x = 0.6417144$ is checked by evaluating both $\sqrt{x}$ and $\cos x$ to see that they agree there.

Note that this algorithm converges much more slowly than the Babylonian Algorithm. But it is much more general. It can be used to solve almost any equation that uses known continuous functions.

4.6 NESTED LOOPS

The statement within a loop can be any kind of statement. Usually it is a block of statements, and often some of those statements themselves are loops. In that case, they are called *nested loops*.

EXAMPLE 4.13 Printing a Multiplication Table

This program uses two nested `for` loops to print a multiplication table:

```java
public class Example0413
{ public static void main(String[] args)
  { final int SIZE = 15;
    for (int x = 1; x <= SIZE; x++)
    { for (int y = 1; y <= SIZE; y++)
      { int z = x*y;
        if (z < 10) System.out.print(" ");
        if (z < 100) System.out.print(" ");
        System.out.print(" " + z);
      }
      System.out.println();
    }
  }
}
```

The output is shown at the top of the next page.

The outer loop iterates 15 times. On each iteration of the outer loop, the inner loop iterates 15 times. On each iteration of the inner loop, the product z is computed and printed with a prefix of blanks. The number of blanks in the prefix depends upon the number of digits in z so that the number in each column of the resulting table are right-justified. For example, when x is 13 and y is 10, z is 130, which has 3 digits, so its prefix has only 1 blank. But when x is 3 and y is 2, z is 6, which has only 1 digit, so its prefix has 3 blanks. This way, every product is printed in a *field* of 4 characters.

1	2	3	4	5	6	7	8	9	10	11	12	13	14	15
2	4	6	8	10	12	14	16	18	20	22	24	26	28	30
3	6	9	12	15	18	21	24	27	30	33	36	39	42	45
4	8	12	16	20	24	28	32	36	40	44	48	52	56	60
5	10	15	20	25	30	35	40	45	50	55	60	65	70	75
6	12	18	24	30	36	42	48	54	60	66	72	78	84	90
7	14	21	28	35	42	49	56	63	70	77	84	91	98	105
8	16	24	32	40	48	56	64	72	80	88	96	104	112	120
9	18	27	36	45	54	63	72	81	90	99	108	117	126	135
10	20	30	40	50	60	70	80	90	100	110	120	130	140	150
11	22	33	44	55	66	77	88	99	110	121	132	143	154	165
12	24	36	48	60	72	84	96	108	120	132	144	156	168	180
13	26	39	52	65	78	91	104	117	130	143	156	169	182	195
14	28	42	56	70	84	98	112	126	140	154	168	182	196	210
15	30	45	60	75	90	105	120	135	150	165	180	195	210	225

EXAMPLE 4.14 Validating Identification Numbers

Validation checking is a common method in software that uses identification numbers. Such numbers usually include one character that is used to check the internal consistency of the string to minimize errors. For example, nearly every book published is given a 10-character ISBN (International Standard Book Number) that identifies it and its publisher. The last character of each ISBN is a "check digit," computed from the other 9 digits by an algorithm that will give a different value if any of the other 9 digits are transposed. Consequently, transposition errors or single digit errors are easily detected because their check digit will be incorrect.

This program uses a `for` loop nested inside a `do` loop to check the digits of an 8-digit identification number for its validity. It uses the same kind of algorithm that ISBNs use: the sum

$$d_1 + 2d_2 + 3d_3 + 4d_4 + 5d_5 + 6d_6 + 7d_7 + 8d_8$$

should be a multiple of 9, where d_1 is the first digit, d_2 is the first digit, *etc*. (With the ISBNs, the corresponding 10 digit sum must be a multiple of 11.) This uniquely determines the last digit.

```java
public class Example0414
{ public static void main(String[] args)
   { final int LEN = 8;
     byte buf[] = new byte[LEN+2];
     boolean isValid;
     String id;
     do
     { System.out.print("Enter your " + LEN + "-digit ID number: ");
       try { System.in.read(buf, 0, LEN+2); }
       catch (Exception e) {}
       id = new String(buf);
       id = id.trim();
       int check = 0;
       for (int i = 0; i < LEN; i++)
         check += (i+1)*buf[i];
       isValid = (check%(LEN+1) == 0);
       if (isValid) System.out.println("Thank you.");
       else System.out.println(id + " is not a valid ID number.");
     } while (!isValid);
     System.out.println("Your ID number is " + id);
   }
}
```

Here is a sample run:

```
Please enter your 8-digit ID number: 97542300
97542300 is not a valid ID number.
Please enter your 8-digit ID number: 97543300
97543300 is not a valid ID number.
Please enter your 8-digit ID number: 97543200
Thank you.
Your ID number is 97543200
```

In this run, the user's correct ID number is 97543200. Its check sum, $d_1 + 2d_2 + 3d_3 + 4d_4 + 5d_5 + 6d_6 + 7d_7 + 8d_8$, is divisible by 9: $9 + 2·7 + 3·5 + 4·4 + 5·3 + 6·2 + 7·0 + 8·0 = 81$. The first attempt entered 97542300, which transposed the 5th and 6th digits. That error was detected by the check-sum algorithm: $9 + 2·7 + 3·5 + 4·4 + 5·2 + 6·3 + 7·0 + 8·0 = 82$, which is not divisible by 9. The second attempt entered 97543300, which simply mistyped the 6th digit. That error was also detected by the check-sum algorithm: $9 + 2·7 + 3·5 + 4·4 + 5·3 + 6·3 + 7·0 + 8·0 = 87$, which is not divisible by 9. The third attempt got it right.

The `do` loop iterates once each time the user enters an ID number. It repeats until the entered ID number is correct. The `for` loop computes the check sum which is valid only if it is divisible by 9.

EXAMPLE 4.15 Finding Substrings

This program uses a `for` loop nested inside another `for` loop to search a string for a substring. The `indexOf()` method does the same thing, so it is used at the end of the program to confirm the results. This program also illustrates the use of a labeled `break` statement.

```java
public class Example0415
{ public static void main(String[] args)
  { final int LEN = 100;
    System.out.print("Enter a string: ");
    byte buf1[] = new byte[LEN];
    try { System.in.read(buf1, 0, LEN); }
    catch (Exception e) {}
    String s1 = new String(buf1);
    s1 = s1.trim();
    int n1 = s1.length();
    System.out.print("Enter a substring: ");
    byte buf2[] = new byte[LEN];
    try { System.in.read(buf2, 0, LEN); }
    catch (Exception e) {}
    String s2 = new String(buf2);
    s2 = s2.trim();
    int n2 = s2.length();
    System.out.println("n1 = " + n1 + "\tn2 = " + n2);
    boolean found = false;
    int k = 0;
  stop:
    for (int i = 0; n2 + i <= n1; i++)
      for (int j = 0; j < n2; j++)
      { System.out.println(i + " " + j);
        if (s1.charAt(i+j) != s2.charAt(j)) break;
        if (j+1 == n2)
        { found = true;
          k = i;
          break stop;
        }
      }
```

```
        System.out.print("Using this algorithm, the substring \"" + s2);
        if (found) System.out.println("\" was found at index " + k);
        else System.out.println("\" was not found.");
        k = s1.indexOf(s2);
        System.out.print("Using the indexOf() method, this substring ");
        if (found) System.out.println(" was found at index " + k);
        else System.out.println(" was not found.");
    }
}
```

The program reads two strings from standard input: the string `s1` to be searched, and the substring `s2`. It prints their lengths and then runs the nested `for` loops to do the search. If `s1` is found to be a substring of `s2`, it sets the value of the `boolean` variable `found` to `true`, saves the index `k`, and then executes a labeled `break` statement to break out of both loops simultaneously. Then it reports the results and uses the `indexOf()` method to check them. The value of `k` is the index in `s1` of the first character of the substring `s2`.

The inner `for` loop uses the `charAt()` method to compare consecutive characters in `s1` with those in `s2`, beginning at index `i` in `s1` and index 0 in `s2`. If it finds a mismatch, it breaks out of the inner loop and resumes with the next iteration of the outer loop. If that doesn't happen, then when ($j ==$ $n2-1$), all `n2` characters of `s2` have been matched and the substring has been found. The `println()` inside the inner loop is included so we can trace the search as it executes.

Here is a sample run:

```
Enter a string: ABACADABRA
Enter a substring: ABR
n1 = 10n2 = 3
0  0
0  1
0  2
1  0
2  0
2  1
3  0
4  0
4  1
5  0
6  0
6  1
6  2
Using this algorithm, the substring "ABR" was found at index 6
Using the indexOf() method, this substring  was found at index 6
```

The string ABACADABRA has 10 characters and the substring ABR has 3. The inner loop iterates 3 times when $i = 0$, once when $i = 1$, twice when $i = 2$, once when $i = 3$, twice when $i = 4$, once when $i = 2$, and three times when $i = 6$. That is where the substring is found.

A labeled `break` statement is a break statement that jumps to the next statement that follows the labeled statement. Typically, the labeled statement is a loop containing another loop that contains the break statement, thereby allowing execution to break out of both loops simultaneously. The compiler recognizes the line

```
        stop:
```

as a label because it ends with a colon (:). The label itself can be any valid identifier. Note that this line itself is not a Java statement; it serves only as a prefix to label the statement that follows.

EXAMPLE 4.16 Three Nested Loops

This program uses three nested `for` loops to illustrate that the labeled `break` statement need not break out of the nest completely. Here, it terminates the current iterations of the middle and inner loops, proceeding on to the next iteration of the outer loop.

```
public class Example0416
{ public static void main(String[] args)
    { for (int i = 0; i < 3; i++)
        { resume:
            for (int j = 0; j < 3; j++)
            { for (int k = 0; k < 3; k++)
                { System.out.print("\n" + i + " " + j + " " + k);
                  if (i == 1 && j == 2 && k == 0) break resume;
                }
                System.out.print("\tEnd of k loop; j = " + j);
            }
            System.out.print("\tEnd of j loop; i = " + i);
        }
        System.out.println("\tEnd of i loop.");
    }
}
```

The break occurs when i = 1, j = 2, and k = 0. Since the label `resume` labels the j loop, the `print()` statement that follows it is executed next. Since that is the last statement within the i loop, that outer loop continues, starting its next iteration with i = 2.

Here is the output:

```
0 0 0
0 0 1
0 0 2    End of k loop; j = 0
0 1 0
0 1 1
0 1 2    End of k loop; j = 1
0 2 0
0 2 1
0 2 2    End of k loop; j = 2    End of j loop; i = 0
1 0 0
1 0 1
1 0 2    End of k loop; j = 0
1 1 0
1 1 1
1 1 2    End of k loop; j = 1
1 2 0    End of j loop; i = 1
2 0 0
2 0 1
2 0 2    End of k loop; j = 0
2 1 0
2 1 1
2 1 2    End of k loop; j = 1
2 2 0
2 2 1
2 2 2    End of k loop; j = 2    End of j loop; i = 2    End of i loop.
```

Review Questions

4.1   What is a continuation condition?

4.2   What does a `break` statement do?

4.3   What does a labeled `break` statement do?

4.4   When would you use a labeled `break` statement instead of an unlabeled one?

4.5   What is a loop invariant?

4.6   What's wrong with the following program?

```
public class Example0405
{ public static void main(String[] args)
  { System.out.print(0);
    int fib0 = 0;
    int fib1 = 1;
    int fib2 = 1;
    while (fib2 < 1000);
    { fib0 = fib1;
      fib1 = fib2;
      fib2 = fib0 + fib1;
      System.out.print(", " + fib1);
    }
    try { System.in.read(); }
    catch (Exception e) {}
  }
}
```

4.7   What is tracing, and why is it a worthwhile activity for programmers?

4.8   Predict the output from the following program. Then run it to confirm your prediction:

```
public class Question0408
{ public static void main(String[] args)
  { int count = 0;
    for (int i = 0; i < 3; i++)
      resume:
        for (int j = 0; j < 4; j++)
          for (int k = 0; k < 5; k++)
          { ++count;
            if (i == 1 && j == 2 && k == 3) break resume;
          }
    System.out.println("\tcount = " + count);
  }
}
```

4.9   Predict the output from the following modification of the program from Question 4.8. Then run it to confirm your prediction:

```
public class Question0409
{ public static void main(String[] args)
  { int count = 0;
    for (int i = 0; i < 3; i++)
    { resume:
        for (int j = 0; j < 4; j++)
          for (int k = 0; k < 5; k++)
          { ++count;
            if (i == 1 && j == 2 && k == 3) break resume;
          }
      System.out.println("\tcount = " + count);
    }
  }
}
```

4.10 What does the definition
```
final double TOL = 0.5E-15;
```
do in the program in Example 4.11 on page 75?

Programming Problems

4.1 Write and run a program that tabulates the sine function for 17 equally spaced values of x in the range 0 to π. Use the constant `Math.PI` and the `Math.sin()` method. Your output should look like this:
```
0.0                        0.0
0.19634954084936207        0.19509032201612825
0.39269908169872414        0.3826834323650898
0.5890486225480862         0.5555702330196022
0.7853981633974483         0.7071067811865475
0.9817477042468103         0.8314696123025452
1.1780972450961724         0.9238795325112867
1.3744467859455345         0.9807852804032304
1.5707963267948966         1.0
1.7671458676442586         0.9807852804032304
1.9634954084936207         0.9238795325112867
2.1598449493429825         0.8314696123025455
2.356194490192345          0.7071067811865476
2.552544031041707          0.5555702330196022
2.748893571891069          0.3826834323650899
2.945243112740431          0.1950903220161286
3.141592653589793          1.2246063538223773E-16
```

4.2 Write and run a program that prints the average of 5 random integers. Your output should look like this:
```
average = 9.448290208E8
```

4.3 Write and run a program that tests the summation formula

$$\sum_{i=1}^{n} i = \frac{n(n+1)}{2}$$

Generate a random integer n in the range 0 to 100, sum the integers from 1 to n, compute the value of the expression on the right, and then print both values to see that they agree. Your output should look like this:
```
x = 0.12363869
n = 14
sum =        105
n*(n+1)/2 = 105
```

4.4 Modify the program in Example 4.3 on page 67 so that: even numbers are processed before the for loop begins and only odd values of `d` less than or equal to the square root of n are used in the loop.

4.5 The Babbage function (Example 4.1 on page 66) generates more than 20 prime numbers. Modify the program to find out how large x can be before the value of $x^2 + x + 41$ is not prime. You can use the code from Example 4.10 on page 75 to tell which numbers are prime.

4.6 Modify the Fibonacci program in Example 4.5 on page 69 by replacing the `while` loop with the `for` loop shown on page 70, and then run it to see that it is correct.

4.7   Write and run a program that tests the summation formula

$$\sum_{i=1}^{n} i^2 = \frac{n(n+1)(2n+1)}{6}$$

Generate a random integer n in the range 0 to 100, sum the integers from 1 to n, compute the value of the expression on the right, and then print both values to see that they agree.

4.8   Write and run a program that tests the summation formula

$$\sum_{i=1}^{n} i^2 = \frac{n^2(n+1)^2}{4}$$

Generate a random integer n in the range 0 to 100, sum the integers from 1 to n, compute the value of the expression on the right, and then print both values to see that they agree.

Supplementary Programming Problems

4.9   Write and run a program that tests the summation formula

$$\sum_{i=0}^{\infty} \frac{1}{i!} = e$$

Generate a random integer n in the range 0 to 20, sum the numbers $1/i!$ from 1 to n, and then print the sum, the constant e, and their difference to see how closely they agree. (Recall that e is the constant 2.718281828..., the base of the natural logarithm.) Use the constant `Math.E`. Your output should look like this:

```
x = 0.04224533
n = 6
sum =                  91
n*(n+1)*(2*n+1)/6 = 91
```

4.10   Write and run a program that generates a random integer n in the range 0 to 10 and then tabulates the sine function for n equally spaced values of x in the range 0 to π. Use the constant `Math.PI` and the `Math.sin()` method.

4.11   Write and run a program that generates a random integer n in the range 0 to 10 and then tabulates the tangent function for n equally spaced values of x in the range 0 to $\pi/2$. Use the constant `Math.PI` and the `Math.tan()` method.

4.12   Write and run a program that generates a random integer n in the range 0 to 10 and then tabulates the natural logarithm function for n equally spaced values of x in the range 1 to e. Use the constant `Math.E` and the `Math.log()` method.

4.13   Write and run a program that tests the summation formula

$$\sum_{i=1}^{\infty} \frac{1}{i^2} = \frac{\pi^2}{6}$$

Generate a random integer n in the range 0 to 100, sum the numbers $1/i^2$ from 1 to n, compute value of the expression on the right, and then print both values and their difference to see how closely they agree.

Answers to Review Questions

4.1   A *continuation condition* is a boolean expression that is used to control a loop. The loop repeats as long as the value of the expression is true. For example, in the loop

```
for (int x = 0; x < 10; x++)
{ int y = x*x + x + 41;
  System.out.println("\t" + x + "\t" + y);
}
```

in Example 4.1 on page 66, the express ion x < 10 is the continuation condition for that loop. It continues iterating as long as it is true.

4.2   A break statement terminates the current loop and proceeds to the first statement that follows that loop. For example in Example 4.4 on page 68, the break statement in the loop

```
for (int d = 2; d < n; d++)
{ isNotPrime = (n%d == 0);
  if (isNotPrime) break;
}
```

stops the loop and executes the next statement that follows it.

4.3   A labeled break statement terminates the current loop and proceeds to the first statement that follows the loop that is labeled by the identifier that follows the keyword break. For example, in Example 4.16 on page 82, the statement

```
if (i == 1 && j == 2 && k == 0) break resume;
```

contains a labeled break statement that terminates both the inner loop and the middle loop containing it.

4.4   The semicolon at the end of the line containing the keyword while is wrong. It marks the end of the loop, indicating to the compiler that the only statement within the loop is the *empty statement*, meaning "do nothing." That means nothing happens within the loop, so the control variable fib2 never changes and the loop never stops. That's called an *infinite loop*. It looks strange when it runs because the cursor is missing and the system does not respond to keystrokes or mouse actions. When that happens, press Ctrl + C to abort the process.

4.5   You would use a labeled break statement instead of an unlabeled one when you want to break out of two or more loops in a nested loop structure. For example, the labeled break statement in Example 4.16 on page 82 breaks out of two of the three nested loops.

4.6   A *loop invariant* is an assertion about the state of the variables (*i.e.*, their current values) at some point in a loop that is intended to be true on every iteration of the loop. For example, in Problem 4.2 on page 87, the loop

```
for (int i = 0; i < 50; i++)
  sum += random.nextDouble();
```

the assertion "sum equals the sum of all the random numbers generated so far" is a loop invariant; it should be true on every iteration of the loop.

4.7   Tracing a program means pretending you are the computer and you carry out all the steps of your program, keeping track of the values of each variable as it changes. For example, the table on page 74 shows a trace of the program in Example 4.9 on page 73. Tracing is one of the best ways to understand the details of the logic of your program which is essential for correcting logical errors ("bugs").

4.8   count = 20

4.9   count = 20
         count = 34
         count = 54

4.10 The definition

```
final double TOL = 0.5E-15;
```

in the program in Example 4.11 on page 75 defines the constant TOL to be 0.5×10^{-15}. This tiny number is used to determine when the value of x approximates $\sqrt{2}$ to 15 decimal places.

Solutions to Programming Problems

4.1
```java
public class Problem0401
{ public static void main(String[] args)
  { final int N = 16;
    double x, y;
    for (int n = 0; n <= N; n++)
    { x = n*Math.PI/N;
      y = Math.sin(x);
      System.out.println("\t" + x + "\t" + y);
    }
  }
}
```

4.2
```java
import java.util.Random;
public class Problem0402
{ public static void main(String[] args)
  { Random random = new Random();
    double sum = 0.0;
    for (int i = 0; i < 5; i++)
      sum += random.nextInt();
    System.out.println("average = " + sum/5);
  }
}
```

4.3
```java
import java.util.Random;
public class Problem0403
{ public static void main(String[] args)
  { Random random = new Random();
    float x = random.nextFloat();
    System.out.println("x = " + x);
    int n = (int)Math.floor(99*x+2);
    System.out.println("n = " + n);
    int sum = 0;
    for (int i = 1; i <= n; i++)
      sum += i;
    int form = n*(n+1)/2;
    System.out.println("sum =          " + sum);
    System.out.println("n*(n+1)/2 = " + form);
  }
}
```

4.4
```java
import java.util.Random;
import java.lang.Math;
public class Problem0404
{ public static void main(String[] args)
  { Random random = new Random();
    float x = random.nextFloat();
    System.out.println("x = " + x);
    int n = Math.round(99997*x + 2);
    boolean isPrime = (n==2 || n%2>0);
    int d = 3;
    double sqrtn = Math.sqrt(n);
    while (isPrime && d <= sqrtn)
    { if (n%d++ == 0) isPrime = false;
      d += 2;
    }
    if (isPrime) System.out.println(n + " is prime.");
    else System.out.println(n + " is not prime.");
  }
}
```

4.5   As the following program shows, the Babbage function actually generates 40 prime numbers before
hitting the first composite (non-prime) number:

```
public class Problem0405
{ public static void main(String[] args)
  { boolean isPrime;
    for (int x = 0; x < 50; x++)
    { int y = x*x + x + 41;
      System.out.print("\t" + x + "\t" + y);
      int d = 2;
      do isPrime = (y%d++ != 0);
      while (isPrime && d < y);
      if (isPrime) System.out.println("\tis prime.");
      else System.out.println("\tis not prime.");
    }
  }
}
```

4.6
```
public class Problem0406
{ public static void main(String[] args)
  { System.out.print("0, 1");
    int fib0 = 0;
    int fib1 = 1;
    for (int fib2 = 1 ; fib2 < 1000; fib2 = fib1 + fib0)
    { fib0 = fib1;
      fib1 = fib2;
      System.out.print(", " + fib1);
    }
  }
}
```

4.7
```
import java.util.Random;
public class Problem0407
{ public static void main(String[] args)
  { Random random = new Random();
    float x = random.nextFloat();
    System.out.println("x = " + x);
    int n = (int)Math.floor(99*x+2);
    System.out.println("n = " + n);
    int sum = 0;
    for (int i = 1; i <= n; i++)
      sum += i*i;
    int form = n*(n+1)*(2*n+1)/6;
    System.out.println("sum =                    " + sum);
    System.out.println("n*(n+1)*(2*n+1)/6 = " + form);
  }
}
```

4.8
```
import java.util.Random;
public class Problem0408
{ public static void main(String[] args)
  { Random random = new Random();
    float x = random.nextFloat();
    System.out.println("x = " + x);
    int n = (int)Math.floor(99*x+2);
    System.out.println("n = " + n);
    int sum = 0;
    for (int i = 1; i <= n; i++)
      sum += i*i*i;
    int form = n*n*(n+1)*(n+1)/4;
    System.out.println("sum =                  " + sum);
    System.out.println("n*n*(n+1)*(n+1)/4 = " + form);
  }
}
```

Chapter 5

Methods

A *method* is a sequence of declarations and executable statements encapsulated together like an independent mini-program. In other programming languages, methods are called *functions*, *procedures*, *subroutines*, and *subprograms*.

In Java, every executable statement must be within some method. Consequently, the methods are where the action is. Programmers design object-oriented programs by deciding first what specific actions have to be performed and what kinds of objects should perform them.

5.1 SIMPLE EXAMPLES

EXAMPLE 5.1 The `cube()` Method

This program tests a method named `cube()` that returns the cube of the integer passed to it:

```
public class TestCube
{ public static void main(String[] args)
  { for (int i = 0; i < 6; i++)
      System.out.println(i + "\t" + cube(i));
  }

  static int cube(int n)
  { return n*n*n;
  }
}
```

Here is its output:

```
0    0
1    1
2    8
3    27
4    64
5    125
```

The `main()` method contains a `for` loop which invokes the `println()` method 6 times. That method invokes the `cube()` method, passing the value of its argument `i` to its parameter `n`. So, for example, on the third iteration, `i = 2`, so the variable `n` is initialized to 2 inside the `cube()` method. It then computes the value 8 from the expression `n*n*n` and returns it to the `println()` method which prints it.

EXAMPLE 5.2 The `min()` Method

This program tests a method named `min()` that returns the minimum of its two integer arguments:

```
import java.util.Random;

public class TestMin
{ public static void main(String[] args)
  { Random random = new Random();
```

89

```
        for (int i = 0; i < 5; i++)
        { float x = random.nextFloat();
          int m = Math.round(100*x);
          x = random.nextFloat();
          int n = Math.round(100*x);
          int y = min(m, n);
          System.out.println("min(" + m + ", " + n + ") = " + y);
        }
    }
    static int min(int x, int y)
    { if (x < y) return x;
      else return y;
    }
}
```

Here is a sample run:

```
min(16, 18) = 16
min(83, 30) = 30
min(68, 96) = 68
min(17, 73) = 17
min(72, 26) = 26
```

The `random.nextFloat()` method returns a `float` value in the range 0.0 to 1.0. The expression `Math.round(100*x)` expands that value to the range 0.0 to 100.0 and then invokes the `Math.round()` method to produce an integer in the range 0 to 100. So the variables `m` and `n` are initialized with random integers in that range. They are then passed to the `min()` method which returns the smaller value, as the test run verifies.

5.2 LOCAL VARIABLES

A *local variable* is a variable that is declared in a method. They can be used only within that method, and they cease to exist when the method finishes its execution.

In Example 5.1, the variable `i` is local to `main()` and the parameter `n` is local to `cube()`. In Example 5.2, the variables `random, i, x, m, n,` and `y` are local to `main()`, and the parameters `x` and `y` are local to `min()`. Note that the localization of variables allows you to use the same name for different variables in the same program. The variable `y` that is local to `main()` is different and completely independent of the variable `y` that is local to `min()`.

EXAMPLE 5.3 Implementing the Factorial Function

This program tests a method named `f()` that implements the factorial function (see Example 4.9 on page 73). The method has one local variable: the variable `f` of type `long`.

```
public class TestFactorial
{ public static void main(String[] args)
    { for (int i = 0; i < 9; i++)
        System.out.println("f(" + i + ") = " + f(i));
    }
    static long f(int n)
    { long f = 1;
      while (n > 1)
        f *= n--;
      return f;
    }
}
```

Here is the output:

```
f(0) = 1
f(1) = 1
f(2) = 2
f(3) = 6
f(4) = 24
f(5) = 120
f(6) = 720
f(7) = 5040
f(8) = 40320
```

The for loop invokes the `f()` method 9 times. For example, when `i = 5`, the expression `f(i)` invokes `f()` passing 5 to its parameter `n`. Inside the method, the local variable `f` is initialized to 1 and then successively multiplied by 5, 4, 3, and 2, changing its value to 5, 20, 60, and 120 before the `while` loop stops. Then its current value (120) is returned to the `println()` method which prints it.

EXAMPLE 5.4 Implementing the Permutation Function

This program tests a method `p(n, k)` that returns the number of permutations of size `k` from a set of size `n`. That number is defined to be

$$p(n, k) = \prod_{i = n-k+1}^{n} i = (n-k+1)(n-k+2)\cdots(n-2)(n-1)(n)$$

For example, $p(8,6)$ would be $p(n,k)$ with $n = 8$ and $k = 6$, which is

$$p(8, 6) = \prod_{i = 3}^{8} i = (3)(4)(5)(6)(7)(8) = 20160$$

That means that if you have 8 different things (*e.g.*, the letters A, B, C, D, E, F, G, and H), then there are 20,160 different sequences of 6 of those things (*e.g.*, the sequences BGEADH).

```
public class TestPermutation
{ public static void main(String[] args)
  { for (int i = 0; i < 9; i++)
    { for (int j = 0; j <= i; j++)
        System.out.print(p(i,j) + "\t");
      System.out.println();
    }
  }
  static long p(int n, int k)
  { long p = 1;
    for (int i = 0; i < k; i++)
      p *= n--;
    return p;
  }
}
```

The output is shown at the top of the next page.

The `main()` method uses a pair of nested for loops to print the triangle of numbers. For example, when `i = 5`, the inner `j` loop iterates 6 times, with `j = 0, 1, 2, 3, 4,` and 5. For those arguments, the `p()` method returns 1, 5, 20, 60, 120, and 120, which are printed on the sixth line of the triangle.

The `p()` method computes permutations the same way that the `f()` method computes factorials. For example, when `i = 5` and `j = 3`, the invocation `p(i,j)` initializes the local variables `n = 5`, `k = 3`, and `p = 1`. Then its `for` loop iterates `k = 3` times, multiplying `p` by 5, 4, and 3, changing its value to 5, 20, and 60 which is returned to the `println()` method.

1								
1	1							
1	2	2						
1	3	6	6					
1	4	12	24	24				
1	5	20	60	120	120			
1	6	30	120	360	720	720		
1	7	42	210	840	2520	5040	5040	
1	8	56	336	1680	6720	20160	40320	40320

5.3 METHODS OFTEN INVOKE OTHER METHODS

We have already seen examples of methods that invoke other methods. In Example 5.1 on page 89, the `main()` method invokes the `println()`, which then invokes the `cube()` method.

EXAMPLE 5.5 Using the Factorial Method to Implement the Permutation Method

This example is nearly identical to Example 5.4. The only difference is that here the `p()` method invokes the factorial method `f()` to compute permutations. This implementation is based upon the identity

$$p(n, k) = (n-k+1)(n-k+2)\cdots(n-2)(n-1)(n) = \frac{1\cdot 2\cdot 3\cdots(n-1)(n)}{1\cdot 2\cdot 3\cdots(n-k-1)(n-k)} = \frac{n!}{(n-k)!}$$

For example, $p(7,3) = 5\cdot 6\cdot 7 = (1\cdot 2\cdot 3\cdot 4\cdot 5\cdot 6\cdot 7)/(1\cdot 2\cdot 3\cdot 4) = 7!/4!$. This is not a very efficient algorithm for computing permutations, but it is correct.

```
public class Example0505
{ public static void main(String[] args)
   { for (int i = 0; i < 9; i++)
      { for (int j = 0; j <= i; j++)
         System.out.print(p(i, j) + "\t");
        System.out.println();
     }
   }
   static long p(int n, int k)
   { return f(n)/f(n-k);
   }
   static long f(int n)
   { long f = 1;
     while (n > 1)
       f *= n--;
     return f;
   }
}
```

The output is identical to that in Example 5.4.

EXAMPLE 5.6 Computing Combinations

The number of combinations of size k from a set of size n (often pronounced "n choose k") is the number is defined to be

$$c(n, k) = \prod_{i=1}^{k} \frac{n-i+1}{i} = \left(\frac{n}{1}\right)\left(\frac{n-1}{2}\right)\cdots\left(\frac{n-k+2}{k-1}\right)\left(\frac{n-k+1}{k}\right)$$

For example, $c(8,3)$ would be $c(n,k)$ with $n = 8$ and $k = 3$, which is

$$c(8,3) = \prod_{i=1}^{3} \frac{n-i+1}{i} = \binom{8}{1}\binom{7}{2}\binom{6}{3} = 56$$

Note that, like the permutation function $p(n,k)$, the combination function $c(n,k)$ is a product of k factors.

This implementation of the combination function is based upon the identity

$$c(n,k) = \frac{(n-k+1)(n-k+2)\cdots(n-2)(n-1)(n)}{1 \cdot 2 \cdot 3 \cdots (k-2)(k-1)(k)} = \frac{p(n,k)}{k!}$$

For example, $c(8,3) = p(8,3)/3! = 336/6 = 56$.

```
public class TestCombination
{ public static void main(String[] args)
  { for (int i = 0; i < 9; i++)
    { for (int j = 0; j <= i; j++)
        System.out.print(c(i, j) + "\t");
      System.out.println();
    }
  }
  static long c(int n, int k)
  { return p(n, k)/f(k);
  }
  static long f(int n)
  { long f = 1;
    while (n > 1)
      f *= n--;
    return f;
  }
  static long p(int n, int k)
  { long p = 1;
    for (int i = 0; i < k; i++)
      p *= n--;
    return p;
  }
}
```

The output is

1								
1	1							
1	2	1						
1	3	3	1					
1	4	6	4	1				
1	5	10	10	5	1			
1	6	15	20	15	6	1		
1	7	21	35	35	21	7	1	
1	8	28	56	70	56	28	8	1

This triangle of numbers is known as *Pascal's Triangle*.

5.4 METHODS THAT INVOKE THEMSELVES

A method that invokes itself is called *recursive* and the resulting process is called *recursion*. Some fundamental processes are naturally recursive.

EXAMPLE 5.7 A Recursive Implementation of the Factorial Function

The factorial function can be defined recursively as

$$n! = \begin{cases} 1 & \text{if } n = 0 \\ n \cdot (n-1)! & \text{if } n > 0 \end{cases}$$

For example, $5! = 120 = 5 \cdot 24 = 5 \cdot 4!$. This leads to the following implementation:

```
public class Example0507
{ public static void main(String[] args)
  { for (int i = 0; i < 9; i++)
    System.out.println("f(" + i + ") = " + f(i));
  }

  static long f(int n)
  { if (n < 2) return 1;
    return n*f(n-1);
  }
}
```

The output is the same as in Example 5.3.

A recursive definition has two essential parts: its *basis*, which defines the function for the first one or few values, and its *recurrence relation*, which defines the nth value in terms of previous values. In Example 5.7, the basis is $0! = 1$, and the recurrence relation is $n! = n \cdot (n-1)!$.

Recursive methods generally should be used only when they are natural implementations of recursive functions and are significantly simpler than the corresponding iterative implementation.

The French mathematician Blaise Pascal (1623-62) discovered that when the coefficients in the polynomial expansions of the binomials $(1+x)^n$ are tabulated, the resulting triangle of numbers enjoys some surprising properties. The first 9 rows of that triangle are

```
1
1  1
1  2  1
1  3  3  1
1  4  6  4  1
1  5  10 10 5  1
1  6  15 20 15 6  1
1  7  21 35 35 21 7  1
1  8  28 56 70 56 28 8  1
```

You can see from Example 5.6 on page 92 that these numbers are the values of the combination function $c(n,k)$.

One of the more obvious properties of Pascal's Triangle is that each interior number is the sum of two in the previous row. For example, $56 = 21 + 35$. This is a recurrence relation that can be used to define all the binomial coefficients:

$$c(n, k) = \begin{cases} 1 & \text{if } k = 0 \text{ or } k = n \\ c(n-1, k) + c(n-1, k-1) & \text{if } 0 < k < n \end{cases}$$

We implement this in the next example.

EXAMPLE 5.8 Pascal's Triangle

This program tests a method that implements the recurrence relation from Pascal's Triangle.

```
public class PrintPascalsTriangle
{ public static void main(String[] args)
  { for (int i = 0; i < 9; i++)
    { for (int j = 0; j <= i; j++)
        System.out.print(c(i, j) + "\t");
      System.out.println();
    }
  }

  static long c(int n, int k)
  { if (k <=0 || k >= n) return 1;
    return c(n-1,k) + c(n-1,k-1);
  }
}
```

The output is the triangle shown above.

5.5 boolean METHODS

A *boolean method* is simply a method that returns type boolean. These methods are usually invoked as boolean expressions used to control loops and conditionals.

EXAMPLE 5.9 The isPrime() Method

This program tests a boolean method named isPrime() that tests its arguments for primality. The main() method prints those integers for which the isPrime() returns true:

```
public class TestPrimes
{ public static void main(String[] args)
  { for (int i = 0; i < 80; i++)
      if (isPrime(i)) System.out.print(i + " ");
  }

  static boolean isPrime(int n)
  { if (n < 2) return false;
    if (n == 2) return true;
    if (n%2 == 0) return false;
    for (int d = 3; d < Math.sqrt(n); d += 2)
      if (n%d == 0) return false;
    return true;
  }
}
```

The output is

2 3 5 7 9 11 13 17 19 23 25 29 31 37 41 43 47 49 53 59 61 67 71 73 79

These are the first 25 prime numbers.

5.6 void METHODS

A *void method* is a method whose return type is void. That means that the method does not return a value.

EXAMPLE 5.10 The `isLeapYear()` Method

This program tests two methods: the `boolean` method `isLeapYear()` and the `void` method `test()`:

```
public class TestLeapYear
{ public static void main(String[] args)
  { test(1492);
    test(1592);
    test(1600);
    test(1700);
    test(1776);
    test(1992);
    test(1999);
    test(2000);
  }

  static boolean isLeapYear(int n)
  { if (n < 1582) return false;
    if (n%400 == 0) return true;
    if (n%100 == 0) return false;
    if (n%4 == 0) return true;
    return false;
  }

  static void test(int n)
  { if (isLeapYear(n)) System.out.println(n + " is a leap near.");
    else System.out.println(n + " is not a leap near.");
  }
}
```
The output is
```
1492 is not a leap near.
1592 is a leap near.
1600 is a leap near.
1700 is not a leap near.
1776 is a leap near.
1992 is a leap near.
1999 is not a leap near.
2000 is a leap near.
```

Note that the `main()` method itself is a `void` method.

To make your code more readable, you should use verb phrases for name of `void` methods, predicate phrases for name of `boolean` methods, and noun phrases for name of all other methods.

5.7 OVERLOADING

You can use the same name for different methods as long as they have different parameter type lists. This practice is called *overloading*.

EXAMPLE 5.11 Using One `max()` Method to Implement Another

This program tests two methods, both named `max()`. They have the distinct parameter type lists `(int,int)` and `(int,int,int)`:

```
import java.util.Random;
public class TestMax
{ public static void main(String[] args)
    { Random random = new Random();
      for (int i = 0; i < 5; i++)
      { float x = random.nextFloat();
        int a = Math.round(100*x);
        x = random.nextFloat();
        int b = Math.round(100*x);
        x = random.nextFloat();
        int c = Math.round(100*x);
        System.out.println("max(" + a + "," + b + "," + c
          + ") = " + max(a, b, c));
      }
    }

    static int max(int m, int n)
    { if (m > n) return m;
      return n;
    }

    static int max(int n1, int n2, int n3)
    { return max( max(n1, n2), n3);
    }
}
```

Here is the output from a sample run:

```
max(34,43,19) = 43
max(11,36,65) = 65
max(8,40,46) = 46
max(67,44,4) = 67
max(58,48,19) = 58
```

A method's name and parameter type list is called its *signature*. For example, the signatures of the two methods in Example 5.11 are `max(int,int)` and `max(int,int,int)`. It is the method's signature that the compiler uses to locate its definition when it encounters its invocation. That is why overloaded methods must have different signatures.

Review Questions

5.1   What is a local variable?

5.2   What is a recursive method?

5.3   What are the two parts required of every recursive method?

5.4   What is a `void` method?

5.5   What is overloading?

Programming Problems

5.1   Write and test a method that implement the Babbage function $f(x) = x^2 + x + 41$ (see Example 4.1 on page 66):

```
static int f(int x)
```

5.2   Write and test a method that returns the maximum of two given integers:

```
static int max(int x, int y)
```

5.3   Write and test a method that returns the maximum of three given integers:

```
static int max(int x, int y, int z)
```

5.4   Write and test in the same program a method that returns the minimum and another method that returns the maximum of four given integers:

```
static int min(int x1, int x2, int x3, int x4)
static int max(int x1, int x2, int x3, int x4)
```

5.5   Modify the test program in Example 5.3 on page 90 so that it attempts to print the values of the factorial function from 0 to 25. Use the resulting output to see how big n can before integer overflow occurs.

5.6   Write and test a method that implements the permutation function p(n,k) (see Example 5.4 on page 91) using a while loop (like the one used to implement the factorial function in Example 5.3 on page 90) in place of the for loop.

5.7   Write and test a method that implements the combination function c(n,k) (see Example 5.6 on page 92) using the following equivalent definition

$$c(n, k) = \frac{n!}{k!(n-k)!}$$

Here $n!$ means the value of the factorial function $f(n)$ (see Example 5.3 on page 90). Have your program print *Pascal's Triangle*, like this:

```
1
1   1
1   2   1
1   3   3   1
1   4   6   4   1
1   5   10  10  5   1
1   6   15  20  15  6   1
1   7   21  35  35  21  7   1
1   8   28  56  70  56  28  8   1
```

5.8   Write and test a method that implements the combination function c(n,k) (see Example 5.6 on page 92) using alternate multiplication and division. For example, $c(8,3)$ would be computed by dividing 8 by 1 and then multiplying by 7 and then dividing by 2 and then multiplying by 6 and then dividing by 3.

5.9   The largest value of $c(n,k)$ for any n is where $k = n/2$. For example, $c(8,4) = 70$ while all the other $c(8,k) \le 56$. So by evaluating c(n,k/2), you can tell whether your implementation of the combination function would compute the entire nth row of Pascal's triangle correctly without suffering from integer overflow. Do that for both implementations (Example 5.7 and Example 5.8) to see which gives better results.

5.10   Write and test the following method that implements the power function:

```
static double pow(double x, int n)
```

This method returns the value of x raised to the power n. For example pow(2.0, -3) would return

$$2^{-3} = \frac{1}{2^3} = \frac{1}{8} = 0.125$$

For each value of pow(x,n) that you print, also print the value of Math.pow(x,n) to check your results.

5.11 Write and test the following method that implements the gcd function:
```
static long gcd(long m, long n)
```
This returns the greatest common divisor of m and n. (See Example 4.8 on page 72.)

5.12 Write and test the following method that implements the lcm function:
```
static long lcm(long m, long n)
```
This returns the least common multiple of m and n. For example lcm(24,40) should return 120 because it is the smallest number common to the set {24, 48, 72, 96, 120, 144, ...} of multiples of 24 and the set {40, 80, 120, 160, ...} of multiples of 40. Use your gcd() method from Problem 5.11 with the formula

$$\mathrm{lcm}(m, n) = \frac{m \cdot n}{\gcd(m, n)}$$

5.13 Write and test the following method that uses a loop to find the largest short integer that is less than or equal to the float passed to it:
```
static short floor(float x)
```
For example, floor(2.71828) would return 2, and floor(-3.3) would return –4. Use the Math.floor() method to check your test results.

5.14 Write and test the following method that returns digit number k of the positive integer n:
```
static int digit(long n, int k)
```
For example, digit(86421,3) would return 6, and digit(86421,7) would return 0.

5.15 Write and test the following method that implements the Fibonacci function recursively:
```
static long fib(int n)
```
(See Example 4.5 on page 69.)

5.16 Implement the gcd function (see Problem 5.11) recursively. Have your test program invoke both the iterative and the recursive implementations so you can check your results.

5.17 Implement the power function (see Problem 5.10) recursively. Have your test program also invoke the Math.pow() method to check your results.

5.18 Write and test the following recursive method that returns the nth triangular number:
```
static long t(int n)
```
The *triangular numbers* are 0, 1, 3, 6, 10, 15, 21, 28, ... Note that $t(n) = t(n–1) + n$ for $n > 1$.

5.19 Write and test the following recursive method that returns the nth square number:
```
static long s(int n)
```
The *square numbers* are 0, 1, 4, 9, 16, 25, 36, ... Note that $s(n) = s(n–1) + 2n – 1$ for $n > 1$.

5.20 Write and test the following recursive method that returns the nth Catalan number:
```
static long c(int n)
```
The *Catalan numbers* are 1, 1, 2, 5, 14, 42, 132, 429, ... Their recurrence relation is

$$c(n) = \sum_{i=0}^{n-1} c(i) \cdot c(n-1-i) = c(0) \cdot c(n-1) + c(1) \cdot c(n-2) + \cdots + c(n-2) \cdot c(1) + c(n-1) \cdot c(0)$$

You can check your results by using the explicit formula

$$c(n) = \frac{(2n)!}{n! \cdot (n+1)!}$$

For example, $c(3) = 6!/(3! \cdot 4!) = 720/144 = 5$. The Catalan numbers provide the solution to several diverse counting problems. One of those problems is to determine the number of different valid nestings of a set of n pairs of parentheses. For example, a set of 3 pairs of parentheses can be nested in $c(3) = 5$ ways: ()()(), ()(()), (())(), (()()), and ((())).

5.21 Implement the Babbage function (see Problem 5.1) recursively. Have your test program invoke both the explicit and the recursive implementations to check your results.

5.22 Write and test the following boolean method that determines whether the given number is a triangular number (see Problem 5.18):

```
static boolean isTriangular(long n)
```

Test this method by using it to identify all the triangular numbers less than 100.

5.23 Write and test the following boolean method that determines whether the given number is a square number (see Problem 5.19):

```
static boolean isSquare(long n)
```

Test this method by using it to identify all the square numbers less than 200.

Answers to Review Questions

5.1 A *local variable* is a variable that is declared within a method, as opposed to a field which is declared in a class. For example, the variable `i` is local to `main()` in Example 5.1 on page 89, and the reference `random` is a local variable to `main()` in Example 5.2.

5.2 A *recursive method* is a method that invokes itself. For example, the method `c()` in Example 5.8 on page 95 is recursive. The statement

```
return c(n-1,k) + c(n-1,k-1);
```

is within the method `c()` and it invokes `c()` twice.

5.3 Every recursive method must have a basis and a recurrence relation. The *basis* specifies the method's actions for one or more specific arguments. The *recurrence* specifies the method's actions by invoking the same method on smaller arguments.

5.4 A `void` method is one that does not return a value. The keyword `void` is used in place of a type for its return type.

5.5 Overloading refers to the occurrence of more than one method with the same name. This is legal provided that no two methods have the same name and the same parameter type lists.

Solutions to Programming Problems

5.1
```
public class Problem0501
{ public static void main(String[] args)
  { for (int i = 0; i < 10; i++)
      System.out.println(i + "\t" + f(i));
  }

  static int f(int x)
  { return x*x + x + 41;
  }
}
```

5.2
```
import java.util.Random;
public class Problem0502
{ public static void main(String[] args)
  { Random random = new Random();
    for (int i = 0; i < 5; i++)
    { float x = random.nextFloat();
      int m = Math.round(100*x);
      x = random.nextFloat();
      int n = Math.round(100*x);
      int y = max(m, n);
      System.out.println("max(" + m + ", " + n + ") = " + y);
    }
  }

  static int max(int x, int y)
  { if (x < y) return x;
    else return y;
  }
}
```

5.3
```
import java.util.Random;
public class Problem0503
{ public static void main(String[] args)
  { Random random = new Random();
    for (int i = 0; i < 5; i++)
    { float x = random.nextFloat();
      int n1 = Math.round(100*x);
      x = random.nextFloat();
      int n2 = Math.round(100*x);
      x = random.nextFloat();
      int n3 = Math.round(100*x);
      int y = max(n1, n2, n3);
      System.out.println("max(" + n1 + ", " + n2 + ", " + n3
        + ") = " + y);
    }
  }

  static int max(int x, int y, int z)
  { int m = x;
    if (y > m) m = y;
    if (z > m) m = z;
    return m;
  }
}
```

5.4
```
import java.util.Random;
public class Problem0504
{ public static void main(String[] args)
  { Random random = new Random();
    for (int i = 0; i < 5; i++)
    { float x = random.nextFloat();
      int n1 = Math.round(100*x);
      x = random.nextFloat();
      int n2 = Math.round(100*x);
      x = random.nextFloat();
      int n3 = Math.round(100*x);
      x = random.nextFloat();
      int n4 = Math.round(100*x);
      System.out.println("min(" + n1 + ", " + n2 + ", " + n3
        + ", " + n4 + ") = " + min(n1, n2, n3, n4));
      System.out.println("max(" + n1 + ", " + n2 + ", " + n3
        + ", " + n4 + ") = " + max(n1, n2, n3, n4));
    }
  }
```

```
static int min(int x1, int x2, int x3, int x4)
{ int m = x1;
  if (x2 < m)  m = x2;
  if (x3 < m)  m = x3;
  if (x4 < m)  m = x4;
  return m;
}

static int max(int x1, int x2, int x3, int x4)
{ int m = x1;
  if (x2 > m)  m = x2;
  if (x3 > m)  m = x3;
  if (x4 > m)  m = x4;
  return m;
}
}
```

5.5   By replacing 10 with 25 in the program in Example 5.3 on page 90, we get the output

```
f(0)  = 1
f(1)  = 1
f(2)  = 2
f(3)  = 6
f(4)  = 24
f(5)  = 120
f(6)  = 720
f(7)  = 5040
f(8)  = 40320
f(9)  = 362880
f(10) = 3628800
f(11) = 39916800
f(12) = 479001600
f(13) = 6227020800
f(14) = 87178291200
f(15) = 1307674368000
f(16) = 20922789888000
f(17) = 355687428096000
f(18) = 6402373705728000
f(19) = 121645100408832000
f(20) = 2432902008176640000
f(21) = -4249290049419214848
f(22) = -1250660718674968576
f(23) = 8128291617894825984
f(24) = -7835185981329244160
```

From this, we can see that integer overflow first occurs with f(21).

5.6
```
public class Problem0506
{ public static void main(String[] args)
  { for (int i = 0; i < 9; i++)
    { for (int j = 0; j <= i; j++)
        System.out.print(p(i, j) + "\t");
      System.out.println();
    }
  }

  static long p(int n, int k)
  { long p = 1;
    while (k-- > 0)
      p *= n--;
    return p;
  }
}
```

5.7
```
public class Problem0507
{ public static void main(String[] args)
  { for (int i = 0; i < 9; i++)
    { for (int j = 0; j <= i; j++)
        System.out.print(c(i, j) + "\t");
      System.out.println();
    }
  }

  static long c(int n, int k)
  { return f(n)/(f(k)*f(n-k));
  }

  static long f(int n)
  { long f = 1;
    while (n > 1)
      f *= n--;
    return f;
  }
}
```

5.8
```
public class Problem0508
{ public static void main(String[] args)
  { for (int i = 0; i < 9; i++)
    { for (int j = 0; j <= i; j++)
        System.out.print(c(i, j) + "\t");
      System.out.println();
    }
  }

  static long c(int n, int k)
  { long c = 1;
    for (int j = 1; j <= k; j++)
    { c *= n--;
      c /= j;
    }
    return c;
  }
}
```

5.9 This test driver shows that the implementation `c2()` from Example 5.8 is much better than the implementation `c1()` from Example 5.7. The `c1()` version computes $c(n,n/2)$ correctly only for $0 \le n \le 20$; the `c2()` version computes $c(n,n/2)$ correctly for $0 \le n \le 61$.
```
public class Problem0509
{ public static void main(String[] args)
  { for (int i = 0; i < 64; i++)
      System.out.println("\t" + i + "\t" + c1(i, i/2) + "\t"
        + c2(i, i/2));
  }

  static long c1(int n, int k)
  { return f(n)/(f(k)*f(n-k));
  }

  static long f(int n)
  { long f = 1;
    while (n > 1)
      f *= n--;
    return f;
  }
```

```
         static long c2(int n, int k)
         { long c = 1;
           for (int j = 1; j <= k; j++)
           { c *= n--;
             c /= j;
           }
           return c;
         }
      }
```

5.10
```
      public class Problem0510
      { public static void main(String[] args)
        { for (int n = -3; n < 7; n++)
            System.out.println(pow(2.0, n));
        }

        static double pow(double x, int n)
        { double p = 1.0;
          for (int i = 0; i < n; i++)
            p *= x;
          for (int i = 0; i < -n; i++)
            p /= x;
          return p;
        }
      }
```

5.11
```
      public class Problem0511
      { public static void main(String[] args)
        { Random random = new Random();
          for (int i = 0; i < 9; i++)
          { float x = random.nextFloat();
            int m = Math.round(100*x);
            x = random.nextFloat();
            int n = Math.round(100*x);
            int g = gcd(m, n);
            System.out.println("gcd(" + m + ", " + n + ") = " + g
              + "  \t" + m + "/" + g + " = " + m/g
              + "  \t" + n + "/" + g + " = " + n/g);
          }
        }

        static int gcd(int m, int n)
        { while (m > 0)
          { if (m < n)
            { int temp = m;
              m = n;
              n = temp;
            }
            m -= n;
          }
          return n;
        }
      }
```

5.12

```
import java.util.Random;
public class Problem0512
{ public static void main(String[] args)
  { Random random = new Random();
    for (int i = 0; i < 9; i++)
    { float x = random.nextFloat();
      int m = Math.round(100*x);
      x = random.nextFloat();
      int n = Math.round(100*x);
      int y = lcm(m, n);
      System.out.println("gcd(" + m + ", " + n + ") = " + y
        + "  \t" + y + "/" + m + " = " + y/m
        + "  \t" + y + "/" + n + " = " + y/n);
    }
    try { System.in.read(); }
    catch (Exception e) {}
  }

  static int lcm(int m, int n)
  { return m*n/gcd(m,n);
  }

  static int gcd(int m, int n)
  { while (m > 0)
    { if (m < n)
      { int temp = m;
        m = n;
        n = temp;
      }
      m -= n;
    }
    return n;
  }
}
```

5.13

```
import java.util.Random;
public class Problem0513
{ public static void main(String[] args)
  { Random random = new Random();
    float x = random.nextFloat();
    System.out.println("x = " + x);
    x = ((float)6.5536E4)*(x - 0.5);
    System.out.println("x = " + x + "\tfloor(x) =       "
      + floor(x));
    System.out.println("x = " + x + "\tMath.floor(x) = "
      + Math.floor(x));
    try { System.in.read(); }
    catch (Exception e) {}
  }
```

```
        static short floor(float x)
        { short min = Short.MIN_VALUE;
          short max = Short.MAX_VALUE;
          if (x < min) return min;
          if (x >= max) return max;
          short mid = 0;
          int width = 0;
          short i = 0;
          do
          { mid = (short)((min + (int)max)/2);
            width = max - min;
            System.out.println(i++ + "\t" + min + "\t" + mid
              + "        \t" + max + "      \t" + width);
            if (mid <= x && x < mid + 1) return mid;
            if (x < mid) max = mid;
            else min = mid;
          } while (width > 1);
          return mid;
        }
      }
```

5.14
```
      public class Problem0514
      { public static void main(String[] args)
        { Random random = new Random();
          float x = random.nextFloat();
          long n = Math.round(10000000000L*x);
          System.out.println("digit 9 of " + n + " is " + digit(n,9));
          System.out.println("digit 8 of " + n + " is " + digit(n,8));
          System.out.println("digit 7 of " + n + " is " + digit(n,7));
          System.out.println("digit 2 of " + n + " is " + digit(n,2));
          System.out.println("digit 1 of " + n + " is " + digit(n,1));
          System.out.println("digit 0 of " + n + " is " + digit(n,0));
        }

        static int digit(long n, int k)
        { for (int i = 0; i < k; i++)
            n /= 10;
          return (int)n%10;
        }
      }
```

5.15 This prints the first 17 Fibonacci numbers, like Example 4.5 on page 69:
```
      public class Problem0515
      { public static void main(String[] args)
        { for (int i = 0; i < 17; i++)
            System.out.print(fib(i) + " ");
          try { System.in.read(); }
          catch (Exception e) {}
        }

        static long fib(int n)
        { if (n < 2) return n;
          return fib(n-1) + fib(n-2);
        }
      }
```

5.16
```
      import java.util.Random;
      public class Problem0516
      { public static void main(String[] args)
        { Random random = new Random();
```

```
      for (int i = 0;  i < 9;  i++)
      { float x = random.nextFloat();
        long m = Math.round(100*x);
        x = random.nextFloat();
        long n = Math.round(100*x);
        long g = gcd1(m, n);
        System.out.println("gcd(" + m + ", " + n + ") = " + g
          + "   \t" + m + "/" + g + " = " + m/g
          + "   \t" + n + "/" + g + " = " + n/g);
        g = gcd2(m, n);
        System.out.println("gcd(" + m + ", " + n + ") = " + g
          + "   \t" + m + "/" + g + " = " + m/g
          + "   \t" + n + "/" + g + " = " + n/g);
      }
    }

    static long gcd1(long m, long n)
    { while (m > 0)
      { if (m < n)
        { long temp = m;
          m = n;
          n = temp;
        }
        m -= n;
      }
      return n;
    }

    static long gcd2(long m, long n)
    { if (m < 1) return n;
      if (m < n) return gcd2(n, m);
      return gcd2(m-n,n);
    }
  }
```

5.17
```
  public class Problem0517
  { public static void main(String[] args)
    { for (int n = -3; n < 7; n++)
      System.out.println("\t" + n + "\t" + pow(2.0, n)
        + "\t" + Math.pow(2.0,n));
    }

    static double pow(double x, int n)
    { if (n == 0) return 1.0;
      if (n < 0) return pow(1.0/x, -n);
      return x*pow(x, n-1);
    }
  }
```

5.18
```
  public class Problem0518
  { public static void main(String[] args)
    { for (int i = 0; i < 10; i++)
        System.out.println(i + "\t" + t(i));
      try { System.in.read(); }
      catch (Exception e) {}
    }

    static long t(int n)
    { if (n < 2) return n;
      return t(n-1) + n;
    }
  }
```

5.19   ```
public class Problem0519
{ public static void main(String[] args)
  { for (int i = 0; i < 10; i++)
      System.out.println(i + "\t" + s(i));
  }

  static long s(int n)
  { if (n < 2) return n;
    return s(n-1) + 2*n - 1;
  }
}
```

**5.20**     ```
public class Problem0520
{ public static void main(String[] args)
  { for (int i = 0; i < 10; i++)
      System.out.println("\tc(" + i + ") = " + c(i)
      + " = " + f(i));
  }

  static long c(int n)
  { if (n < 2) return 1;
    long c = 0;
    for (int i=0; i < n; i++)
      c += c(i)*c(n-i-1);
    return c;
  }

  static long f(int n)
  { return c(2*n,n)/(n+1);
  }

  static long c(int n, int k)
  { long c = 1;
    for (int j = 1; j <= k; j++)
    { c *= n--;
      c /= j;
    }
    return c;
  }
}
```

5.21   ```
public class Problem0521
{ public static void main(String[] args)
  { for (int i = 0; i < 10; i++)
      System.out.println("\tb(" + i + ") = " + b(i)
      + " = " + f(i));
  }

  static long b(int n)
  { if (n < 1) return 41;
    return b(n-1) + 2*n;
  }

  static long f(int n)
  { return n*n + n + 41;
  }
}
```
```

5.22

```
public class Problem0522
{ public static void main(String[] args)
  { for (int i = 0; i < 100; i++)
      if (isTriangular(i))
        System.out.println(i + " is triangular.");
  }

  static boolean isTriangular(long n)
  { long sum = 0;
    long i = 1;
    while (sum < n)
    { sum += i;
      ++i;
    }
    return (sum == n);
  }
}
```

5.23

```
public class Problem0523
{ public static void main(String[] args)
  { for (int i = 0; i < 200; i++)
      if (isSquare(i)) System.out.println(i + " is square.");
    try { System.in.read(); }
    catch (Exception e) {}
  }

  static boolean isSquare(long n)
  { long sum = 0;
    long i = 1;
    while (sum < n)
    { sum += i;
      i += 2;
    }
    return (sum == n);
  }
}
```

Chapter 6

Classes

6.1 CLASSES

A *Java program* is a collection of one or more text files that contains Java classes, at least one of which is `public` and contains a method named `main()` that has this form:

```
public static void main(String[] args)
{ // program statements go here
}
```

The program is compiled and run at the command line by executing the commands

```
javac Xxxx.java
java Xxxx
```

where `Xxxx` is the name of the class that contains the `main()` method to be executed, and `Xxxx.java` is the name of the file that contains that class. For example, the following two commands would compile and run the program shown in Example 4.13 on page 78:

```
javac Example0413.java
java Example0413
```

A *Java class* is a specific category of objects, similar to a Java *type* (*e.g.*, `short`), which is a specific category of variables. Just as a Java type specifies the range of values (*e.g.*, −32768 to 32767 for `short`) that variables of that type can have, a Java class specifies the range of data that objects of that class can have. The data that an object has is called it *state*.

There are three essential features that distinguish classes from types in Java:

1. classes can be defined by the programmer;
2. class objects can contain variables, including references to other objects;
3. classes can contain methods which give their objects the ability to act.

There are also other important features of classes, such as inheritance and packages, that make the Java language so powerful.

Object-oriented programming means writing programs that define classes whose methods carry out the program's instructions. The programs are designed by deciding what objects will be used and what actions they will perform. The classes for the program are then defined to satisfy those decisions. Object-oriented programs are designed by deciding first what classes will be needed and then defining methods for those classes that solve the problem.

Suppose you need to write a program about plane geometry. In that case, the objects are pretty obvious: points, lines, triangles, circles, *etc*. We can "abstract" these geometric elements by defining classes whose objects will represent them. Example 6.1 abstracts the idea of a point in the cartesian plane and Example 6.2 on page 114 abstracts the idea of a line. We know that points are used to define lines, so we use the `Point` class to define our `Line` class. This "reusing" of software is an essential feature of object-oriented programming.

110

EXAMPLE 6.1 A `Point` Class

This class uses its `main()` method as a test driver:

```
public class Point
{ // Objects represent points in the cartesian plane

    private double x, y;   // the point's coordinates

    public Point(double a, double b)
    { x = a;
      y = b;
    }

    public double x()
    { return x;
    }

    public double y()
    { return y;
    }

    public boolean equals(Point p)
    { return (x == p.x && y == p.y);
    }

    public String toString()
    { return new String("(" + x + ", " + y + ")");
    }

    public static void main(String[] args)
    { Point p = new Point(2,3);
      System.out.println("p.x() = " + p.x() + ", p.y() = " + p.y());
      System.out.println("p = " + p);
      Point q = new Point(7,4);
      System.out.println("q = " + q);
      if (q.equals(p)) System.out.println("q equals p");
      else System.out.println("q does not equal p");
      q = new Point(2,3);
      System.out.println("q = " + q);
      if (q.equals(p)) System.out.println("q equals p");
      else System.out.println("q does not equal p");
    }
}
```

The output is

```
p.x() = 2.0, p.y() = 3.0
p = (2.0, 3.0)
q = (7.0, 4.0)
q does not equal p
q = (2.0, 3.0)
q equals p
```

The class has two fields, `x` and `y`, whose values are the coordinates of the point that the object represents. The first line in the `main()` method is

```
Point p = new Point(2,3);
```

This does three things. First, it declares p to be a reference to Point
objects. Then it applies the new operator to create a Point object with
values 2 and 3 for the fields x and y. Then it initializes the reference p
with this new object. You can visualize the result like the picture here. The
result is two things: the reference p and the object to which it refers. The

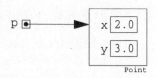

actual value of the variable is whatever information the operating system needs to access the object. Note
that, technically, objects do not have names. Instead, they have references. Nevertheless, it is common and
convenient to refer to the object as if the reference were its name, as in "the Point object p," or more
simply, "the point p."

The second line in main() invokes the two methods x() and y() to obtain the values of p's
fields so that the println() method can print the first line of output, confirming that the values of p's
fields really are 2.0 and 3.0. Note that three methods are invoked in this statement: x(), y(), and
println(). The first two are members of the Point class and are bound to the Point object p. The
println() method is a member of the System class and is bound to the System object out.
Every action in a Java program is performed by some method that is defined in some class.

The third line invokes the toString() method. This is a special method in Java. In any class
Xxxx, if this method's definition conforms to the syntax

```
public String toString()
```

then the method will be invoked whenever a reference to an object of that class is passed to the
println() method, as in

```
System.out.println("p = " + p);
```

In other words, this statement is equivalent to

```
System.out.println("p = " + p.toString());
```

This is a nice shorthand feature that makes the code more readable, so it is usually a good idea to include
the toString() method in each class you define.

The next two lines repeat the
previous steps for the object   q
representing the point (7,4). After
they execute, the situation looks
like this:

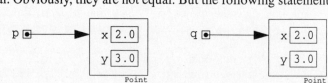

Next, the   if   statement
invokes the equals() method
to determine whether the two objects are equal. Obviously, they are not equal. But the following statement

```
q = new Point(2,3);
```

does make them equal. After it
executes, the situation looks like
the picture here. However, something subtle has occurred. The
new operator invoked the Point
class constructor which created a new object, and now q refers to that object. The fact is that this is a different object. It didn't just change the fields of the other object; it created a new one. The old one is gone.
The bytes that it was occupying in memory have been returned to the *free store* (also called *the heap*).
That means that those bytes can be used for another purpose; *e.g.*, storage for another variable or object.

The last if statement confirms that these two objects are equal.

Note that equality does not imply identity. The two objects are still distinct: separate, but equal.

Java is different from some other modern programming languages (*e.g.*, C and C++) because
of the way it disposes of "dead" objects:

Rule: an object exists only as long as it has a reference.

We saw this happen in Example 6.1. When the reference q was assigned to a new object, the old object died. Unlike other programming languages, Java requires the operating system to take responsibility for disposing of the old object properly and returning its memory storage to the free store. This process has the technical name "garbage collection." Programming languages that do not require the operating system to do this leave the responsibility to the programmer. The Java advantage is obvious: it leaves the programmer with less to worry about. There is no risk of a "memory leak." The disadvantage is that Java programs tend to run more slowly.

6.2 DECLARATIONS

The purpose of a declaration is to introduce an identifier to the compiler. It provides all the information that the compiler needs in order to compile statements which use the identifier that is being declared. In Java, all classes, fields, local variables, constructors, and methods must be declared. (A *field* is a variable that is declared as a member of a class; a *local variable* is declared as a variable that is local to a constructor or method.)

The syntax for a simple *class declaration* is

```
modifiers class class-name
{ body
}
```

where the optional `modifiers` may be one or more of the three keywords {`public`, `abstract`, `final`}, *class-name* is any valid identifier, and *body* is a sequence of declarations of variables, constructors, and methods. For example, the `Point` class declared in Example 6.1 contains two variable declarations (`x` and `y`), one constructor declaration (`Point()`), and six method declarations (`x()`, `y()`, `equals()`, `toString()`, `translate()`, and `main()`).

The syntax for a simple *field* is

```
modifiers type-name variable-name;
```

where the optional `modifiers` may be one or more of the seven keywords {`static`, `final`, `transient`, `volatile`, `public`, `protected`, `private`}, *type-name* is one of the eight keywords {`boolean`, `byte`, `char`, `short`, `int`, `long`, `float`, `double`}, and *variable-name* is any valid identifier. Several variables can be declared together, as `x` and `y` are in Example 6.1.

The syntax for a simple *local variable declaration* is the same as that for a field declarations, except that `final` is the only allowable modifier.

The syntax for a simple *constructor declaration* is

```
modifier class-name(parameter-list)
{ body
}
```

where the optional *modifier* may be one of the three keywords {`public`, `protected`, `private`}, *class-name* is the name of the class in which the constructor is declared, *parameter-list* is a sequence of parameter declarations, and *body* is a sequence of declarations and statements to be executed by the constructor after it creates the object. For example, the declaration

```
public Point(double a, double b)
{ x = a;
  y = b;
}
```

declares a constructor for the `Point` class in Example 6.1. The *modifier* is "public", the *class-name* is "Point", the *parameter-list* is "double a, double b", and the *body* is "x = a; y = b;". When the constructor is invoked, it creates a `Point` object and then assigns the values 2 and 3 to its fields.

The syntax for a simple *method declaration* is

```
modifiers return-type method-name(parameter-list)
{ body
}
```

where the optional *modifiers* may be one or more of the eight keywords {static, abstract, final, native, synchronized, public, protected, private}, *return-type* is any class name or one of the nine keywords {void, boolean, byte, char, short, int, long, float, double}, *method-name* is any valid identifier, *parameter-list* is a sequence of parameter declarations, and *body* is a sequence of declarations and statements to be executed by the method. For example, every Java program must include at least one class that has a `main()` method, declared as

```
public static void main(String[] args)
{
}
```

Here, the *modifiers* are "public static", the *return-type* is "void", the *method-name* is "main", and the *parameter-list* is "String args[]".

Note that unlike methods, constructors have no return type.

EXAMPLE 6.2 A `Line` Class

```
class Line
{ // Objects represent lines in the cartesian plane

    private Point p0;  // a point on the line
    private double m;  // the slope of the line

    public Line(Point p, double s)
    { p0 = p;
      m = s;
    }

    public double slope()
    { return m;
    }

    public double yIntercept()
    { return (p0.y() - m*p0.x());
    }

    public boolean equals(Line line)
    { return (slope() == line.slope()
            && yIntercept() == line.yIntercept());
    }

    public String toString()
    { return new String("y = " + (float)m + "x + "
        + (float)yIntercept());
    }
```

```
    public static void main(String[] args)
    { Point p = new Point(5,-4);
      Line line1 = new Line(p,-2);
      System.out.println("\nThe equation of the line 1 is " + line1);
      System.out.println("Its slope is " + line1.slope()
         + " and its y-intercept is " + line1.yIntercept());
      Line line2 = new Line(p,-1);
      System.out.println("\nThe equation of the line 2 is " + line2);
      System.out.println("Its slope is " + line2.slope()
         + " and its y-intercept is " + line2.yIntercept());
      if (line2.equals(line1)) System.out.println("They are equal.");
      else System.out.println("They are not equal.");
      Point q = new Point(2,2);
      line2 = new Line(q,-2);
      System.out.println("\nThe equation of the line 2 is " + line2);
      System.out.println("Its slope is " + line2.slope()
         + " and its y-intercept is " + line2.yIntercept());
      if (line2.equals(line1)) System.out.println("They are equal.");
      else System.out.println("They are not equal.");
    }
  }
```

The output is

```
The equation of the line 1 is y = -2.0x + 6.0
Its slope is -2.0 and its y-intercept is 6.0

The equation of the line 2 is y = -1.0x + 1.0
Its slope is -1.0 and its y-intercept is 1.0
They are not equal.

The equation of the line 2 is y = -2.0x + 6.0
Its slope is -2.0 and its y-intercept is 6.0
They are equal.
```

This program begins by creating two objects: the `Point` object p and `Line` object line1. The `Point` object has two fields: x and y, both with type double, with values 5 and –4. The `Line` object also has two fields: p0 which references the `Point` object p, and m which has type double and value –2. These represent a point p_0 on the line and the slope m of the line. After creating the objects p and line1, the program tests the `toString()`, `slope()`, and `yIntercept()` methods, similar to Example 6.1 on page 111. (The y-intercept b of a line is given by the formula

$$b = y_0 - m \cdot x_0,$$

where (x_0, y_0) is a point on the line and m is its slope.)

Then the program creates another `Line` object, line2, which refers to the same `Point` object but has slope value –1. The `toString()` method is invoked to print that line, and then the `equals()` method is invoked to see that the two lines are not equal.

The last part of the program creates a second `Point` object and a third `Line` object. It declares the new reference variable `q` to refer to the new `Point` object, and it assigns the existing reference variable `line2` to refer to the new `Line` object. This dereferences the previous `Line` object to which `line2` referred, which kills it. Now there are four objects, as shown in this picture.

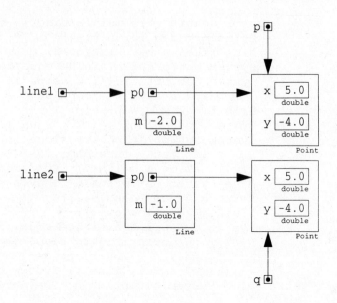

The last if statement invokes the `equals()` method to discover that these two lines are equal. Note that this `equals()` method tests whether the two objects represent the same line, not whether the objects themselves are the same. This `Line` class allows different objects to represent the same line. That design flaw is corrected in Example 6.8 on page 131.

The `x()` and `y()` methods in Example 6.1 and the `slope()` method in Example 6.2 are called *accessor methods* because they simply provide public access to the objects' `private` fields. They are *read-only* methods because they only allow the outside world to read what's inside. In contrast, *read-write* methods that allow the public to change the internal state of the object are called *mutator methods*.

6.3 MODIFIERS

The following tables summarize the modifiers that can appear in the declarations of classes, fields, local variables, constructors, and methods.

Class Modifiers

Modifier	Meaning
public	It is accessible from all other classes.
abstract	The class cannot be instantiated.
final	No subclasses can be declared.

Constructor Modifiers

Modifier	Meaning
public	It is accessible from all classes.
protected	It is accessible only from within its own class and its subclasses.
private	It is accessible only from within its own class.

Field Modifiers

Modifier	Meaning
public	It is accessible from all classes.
protected	It is accessible only from within its own class and its subclasses.
private	It is accessible only from within its own class.
static	Only one value of the field exists for all instances of the class.
transient	It is not part of the persistent state of an object.
volatile	It may be modified by asychronous threads.
final	It must be initialized and cannot be changed.

Local Variable Modifiers

Modifier	Meaning
final	It must be initialized and cannot be changed.

Method Modifiers

Modifier	Meaning
public	It is accessible from all classes.
protected	It is accessible only from within its own class and its subclasses.
private	It is accessible only from within its own class.
abstract	It has no body and belongs to an abstract class.
final	No subclasses can override it.
static	It is bound to the class itself instead of an instance of the class.
native	Its body is implemented in another programming language.
synchronized	It must be locked before a thread can invoke it.

The three *access modifiers*, public, protected, and private, are used to specify where the declared entity (class, field, constructor, or method) can be used. If none of these is specified, then the entity has *package access*, which means that it can be accessed from any class in the same package.

The modifier static is used to specify that a method is a class method. Without it, the method is an instance method. An *instance method* is a method that can be invoked only when bound to an object of the class. That object is called the *implicit argument* of the method. For example, the method x() in Example 6.1 on page 111 is an instance method. It is invoked in the second statement in main() as p.x(). In that invocation, the method x() is bound to the object p, so p is the implicit argument. A *class method* is a method that is invoked without being bound to any specific object of the class. For example, the print() method in Example 6.1 is a class method because it is declared to be static. It is invoked in the fourth statement in main() as print(p,q1). Its two arguments, p and q1, are both explicit arguments.

The modifier final has three different meanings, depending upon which kind of entity it modifies. If it modifies a class, it means that the class cannot have subclasses. (See Chapter 7.) If it modifies a field or a local variable, it means that the variable must be initialized and cannot be changed (*i.e.*, it is a constant). If it modifies a method, it means that the method cannot be overridden in any subclass.

6.4 CONSTRUCTORS

Classes can have three kinds of members: fields, methods, and constructors. A *field* is a variable that is declared as a member of a class. Its type may be any of the eight primitive types (boolean, char, byte, short, int, long, float, double) or a reference to an object. A *method* is a function that is used to perform some action for instances of the class. A *constructor* is a special kind of function whose only purpose is to create the class's objects. This is called *instantiating* the class, and the objects are called *instances* of the class.

Class constructors are different from class methods in three distinct ways:

1. Constructors have the same name as the class itself.
2. Constructors have no return type.
3. Constructors are invoked by the new operator.

Every variable has a *name* and a *type* which are specified when the variable is declared. For example, the declaration

```
    int n;
```

declares a variable named n with type int. Similarly, the declaration

```
    Point p;
```

declares the variable named p with type "reference to objects of the Point class."

An object cannot live without a reference to it. So the reference must be declared before the object can be created. The reference may be declared separately, as p is above. Then the objects can be created, like this:

```
    p = new Point(2,3);
```

Here, the new operator invokes the Point class constructor, passing the arguments 2 and 3 to it, allowing it to create the Point object that represents the geometric point (2,3).

Alternatively, we can declare the reference and initialize it by invoking the class constructor to create the new object at the same time, as we did in Example 6.1 on page 111:

```
    Point p = new Point(2,3);
```

Every class has at least one constructor to instantiate it. If you do not declare any constructors in your class, the compiler will automatically declare one with no arguments. This is called the *default constructor*. (See Section 6.6 on page 122.) But you will usually want to declare your own class constructors so that you can control how its objects are initialized.

In Example 6.1 on page 111, we declared the following constructor for the Point class:

```
    public Point(double a, double b)
    { x = a;
      y = b;
    }
```

This simply initializes the two Point class fields x and y with the two values passed to it.

In Example 6.2 on page 114, we declared the following constructor for the Line class:

```
    public Line(Point p, double s)
    { p0 = p;
      m = s;
    }
```

This initializes the two Line class fields p0 and m with the two values passed to it.

The next example adds two more constructors to the Line class. Since all constructors in the same class must have the same name (*viz.*, the name of the class itself), there must be some other way for the compiler to be able to distinguish them. The only other way is for them to have distinct parameter lists.

Rule: The sequence of parameter types must be different for each overloaded constructor or method.

Recall (page 31) that "overloading" refers to having different constructors or different methods with the same signature.

EXAMPLE 6.3 A Line Class with Three Constructors

```
public class Line
{ // Objects represent lines in the cartesian plane

  private Point p0;   // a point on the line
  private double m;   // the slope of the line

  public Line(Point p, double s)
  { p0 = p;
    m = s;
  }

  public Line(Point p, Point q)
  { p0 = p;
    m = (p.y() - q.y())/(p.x() - q.x());
  }

  public Line(double a, double b)
  { p0 = new Point(0,b);
    m = -b/a;
  }

  public double slope()
  { return m;
  }

  public double yIntercept()
  { return (p0.y() - p0.x()*m);
  }

  public boolean equals(Line line)
  { return (slope() == line.slope()
          && yIntercept() == line.yIntercept());
  }

  public String toString()
  { return new String("y = " + (float)m + "x + "
      + (float)yIntercept());
  }
```

```
public static void main(String[] args)
{ Point p1 = new Point(5,-4);
  Line line1 = new Line(p1,-2);
  System.out.println("The equation of the line 1 is " + line1);
  Point p2  = new Point(-1,2);
  Line line2 = new Line(p1,p2);
  System.out.println("The equation of the line 2 is " + line2);
  if (line2.equals(line1)) System.out.println("They are equal.");
  else System.out.println("They are not equal.");
  Line line3 = new Line(3,6);
  System.out.println("The equation of the line 3 is " + line3);
  if (line3.equals(line1)) System.out.println("They are equal.");
  else System.out.println("They are not equal.");
}
}
```

The output is

```
The equation of the line 1 is y = -2.0x + 6.0
The equation of the line 2 is y = -1.0x + 1.0
They are not equal.
The equation of the line 3 is y = -2.0x + 6.0
They are equal.
```

This program creates the five objects shown here: the two points p1 and p2, and the three lines line1, line2, and line3. It uses their classes' toString() methods to print their identifying features, and then uses the Line class's equals() methods to test the Line objects for equality. That test confirms that line1 and line3 are equal, since they have the same equation $y = -2x + 6$. (But note that the two objects do have different data: their p0 fields refer to different objects.).

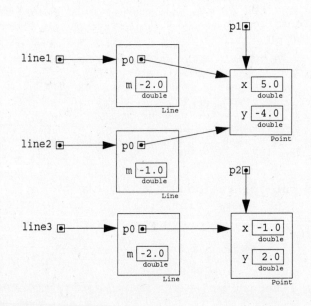

The first constructor has the parameter type list (Point, double). This is the same constructor as in Example 6.2 on page 114. It simply initializes the object's two fields, p0 and m, with the arguments passed to it. These represent a point on the line and the slope of the line. So the line represented by line1 contains the point $p_1 = (5,-4)$ and has the slope $m = -2$.

The second constructor has the parameter type list (Point, Point). Its two arguments represent two points on the line. So the line represented by line2 contains the points $p_1 = (5,-4)$ and $p_2 = (-1,2)$. This constructor then has to compute the slope m for these two points from the formula

$$m = \frac{\Delta y}{\Delta x} = \frac{y_2 - y_1}{x_2 - x_1}$$

It initializes m with the value of this difference quotient, and it initializes p0 with the first point passed.

The third constructor has the parameter type list `(double, double)`. Its two arguments represent the line's *x*-intercept *a* and *y*-intercept *b*. That means that the line contains the two points (*a*,0) and (0,*b*). It then computes the slope *m* from the formula

$$m = \frac{\Delta y}{\Delta x} = \frac{0-b}{a-0} = \frac{-b}{a}$$

It initializes `m` with the value of this difference quotient, and it initializes `p0` to refer to a new point that represents (0,*b*).

6.5 COPY CONSTRUCTORS

The simplest kind of constructor that a class can have is the one that has no parameters. This is called the *default constructor* or the *no-arg constructor* (needs no arguments).

Another simple kind is the constructor whose only parameter is a reference to an object of the same class to which the constructor belongs. This form is usually used to duplicate an existing object of the class, so it is called the *copy constructor*.

EXAMPLE 6.4 Duplicating a `Point` Object

```
public class Point
{ // Objects represent points in the cartesian plane

   private double x, y;

   public Point(double a, double b)
   { x = a;
     y = b;
   }

   public Point(Point p)   // copy constructor
   { x = p.x;
     y = p.y;
   }

   public double x()
   { return x;
   }

   public double y()
   { return y;
   }

   public boolean equals(Point p)
   { return (x == p.x && y == p.y);
   }

   public String toString()
   { return new String("(" + x + ", "  + y + ")");
   }
```

```
public static void main(String[] args)
{ Point p = new Point(2,3);
  System.out.println("p = " + p);
  Point q = new Point(p);
  System.out.println("q = " + q);
  if (q.equals(p)) System.out.print("q equals p");
  else System.out.print("q does not equal p");
  if (q == p) System.out.println(", and q == p");
  else System.out.println(", but q != p");
}
}
```

The output is

```
p = (2.0, 3.0)
q = (2.0, 3.0)
q equals p, but q != p
```

The line
```
Point p = new Point(2,3);
```
uses the constructor
```
public Point(double a, double b)
{ x = a;
  y = b;
}
```
to create the point p, just as it did in Example 6.1 on page 111.

The line
```
Point q = new Point(p);
```
uses the copy constructor
```
public Point(Point p)   // copy constructor
{ x = p.x;
  y = p.y;
}
```
to create the point q. This makes the object q a duplicate of the object p. They are distinct objects but they have the same data. The equals() method confirms that they are equal. But the condition (q == p) is false because q and p refer to distinct objects.

6.6 DEFAULT CONSTRUCTORS

In Java, every class field is automatically initialized to the default initial value for its type. Those values for the eight primitive types and the reference type are listed in the following table.

Default Initial Values for Class Fields

Type	Initial Value
boolean	false
char	'\u0000'
integer	0
floating point	0.0
reference	null

The `char` value `'\u0000'` is the character whose Unicode is 0. This character, called the NUL character, is not detectable when printed. The reference value `null` is the special value that every reference has to indicate that it has not yet been assigned to an object.

If your class has no explicitly declared constructors, then objects can be created only by means of the class's (implicit) default constructor. It automatically initializes all the objects' fields with their default initial values, as listed in the table above. That is what happens in Example 6.5 below with the declaration

```
Purse purse = new Purse();
```

This creates a `Purse` object and initializes all four of its fields to 0.0.

If your class does have some explicitly declared constructors, as do the `Point` and `Line` classes defined in the previous examples, then the compiler will not automatically declare a default constructor. So, for example, the analogous declaration

```
Point p = new Point();
```

would not compile.

EXAMPLE 6.5 A Class to Represent Coin Purses

This class illustrates the use of the implicitly declared default constructor.

```
public class Purse
{ // An object represents a coin purse

    private int pennies;
    private int nickels;
    private int dimes;
    private int quarters;

    public float dollars()
    { int p = pennies + 5*nickels + 10*dimes + 25*quarters;
      return (float)p/100;
    }

    public void insert(int p, int n, int d, int q)
    { pennies += p;
      nickels += n;
      dimes += d;
      quarters += q;
    }

    public void remove(int p, int n, int d, int q)
    { pennies -= p;
      nickels -= n;
      dimes -= d;
      quarters -= q;
    }

    public String toString()
    { return new String(quarters + " quarters + "
                  + dimes + " dimes + "
                  + nickels + " nickels + "
                  + pennies + " pennies = $"
                  + dollars());
    }
```

```
public static void main(String[] args)
{ Purse purse = new Purse();   // invokes the default constructor
  System.out.println(purse);
  purse.insert(3,0,2,1);
  System.out.println(purse);
  purse.insert(3,1,1,3);
  System.out.println(purse);
  purse.remove(3,1,0,2);
  System.out.println(purse);
  purse.remove(0,0,0,4);
  System.out.println(purse);
}
}
```

The output is

```
0 quarters + 0 dimes + 0 nickels + 0 pennies = $0.0
1 quarters + 2 dimes + 0 nickels + 3 pennies = $0.48
4 quarters + 3 dimes + 1 nickels + 6 pennies = $1.41
2 quarters + 3 dimes + 0 nickels + 3 pennies = $0.83
-2 quarters + 3 dimes + 0 nickels + 3 pennies = $-0.17
```

The first line declares the reference `purse` and then calls the default constructor to create an empty `Purse` object to which it refers. The output from the second line confirms that the object has been initialized to the *zero state*: all fields are zero. The third line invokes the `insert()` method to insert 48 cents into the purse: 3 pennies 2 dimes and a quarter, as confirmed by the next `println()` statement. The picture illustrates the state of the purse object after this first insertion. Another test is made to the `insert()` method, and the `remove()` method is tested twice.

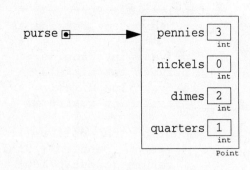

This class obviously has some design faults. They are remedied in Example 6.7 on page 129.

6.7 CLASS INVARIANTS

The design faults recognized in the `Line` class in Example 6.3 on page 119 and the `Purse` class in Example 6.5 above are due to the propensity of their objects to obtain *inconsistent states*. Different `Line` objects could represent the same line, and different `purse` states could total the same dollar amount. These anomalies cannot occur with primitive types. Variables of type `int` that have different values represent different integers. To make classes behave more like primitive types, it is important to ensure that their objects' representations are unique. This can be achieved by specifying and enforcing class invariants.

A *class invariant* is a condition imposed on the fields of the all instances of the class. The most common objective of a class invariant is to guarantee uniqueness of representation.

EXAMPLE 6.6 A Class to Represent Days of the Week

This class illustrates the use of a class invariant to guarantee that each object represents a unique day of the week.

```
public class Day
{ // An instance represents a unique day of the week
  // Class invariant: 0 <= dayNumber < 7

  private final String DAYS = "SUMOTUWETHFRSA";
  private int dayNumber;

  public Day()  // default constructor
  { dayNumber = 0;
  }

  public Day(Day d)  // copy constructor
  { dayNumber = d.dayNumber;
  }

  public Day(String s)
  { String ab = s.substring(0,2).toUpperCase();  // 2-char abbrev.
    dayNumber = DAYS.indexOf(ab)/2;
  }

  public String toString()
  { switch (dayNumber)
    { case 0: return "Sunday";
      case 1: return "Monday";
      case 2: return "Tuesday";
      case 3: return "Wednesday";
      case 4: return "Thursday";
      case 5: return "Friday";
      default:  return "Saturday";
    }
  }


  public void advance(int n)
  { dayNumber = (dayNumber + n)%7;
  }

  public Day prev()
  { int n = (dayNumber+6)%7;  // day number for previous day
    String ab = DAYS.substring(2*n, 2*n+2);  // 2-char abbrev.
    return new Day(ab);
  }

  public static void main(String[] args)
  { Day today = new Day("Wed");
    System.out.println("Today is " + today
      + ", and yesterday was " + today.prev());
    Day heute = new Day(today);
    today.advance(4);
    System.out.println("In 4 days, today will be " + today
      + ", and yesterday will have been " + today.prev());
    System.out.println("But today is still " + heute
      + ", and yesterday was " + heute.prev());
  }
}
```

The output is

```
Today is Wednesday, and yesterday was Tuesday
In 4 days, today will be Sunday, and yesterday will have been Saturday
But today is still Wednesday, and yesterday was Tuesday
```

The String literal DAYS contains the first two letters of each of the seven days of the week. It is used as a device for computing the dayNumber for a given day name.

The first line of main() uses the third constructor to create the today object to represent Wednesday. Here's how it works. The argument "Wed" is passed to the parameter s. The invocation s.substring(0,2) returns the anonymous temporary String object "We". The first argument 0 means to begin with character number 0 (the 'W'). The second argument 2 means to end with the character (the 'e') that precedes character number 2 (the 'd'). The invocation toUpperCase() that is bound to that temporary String object returns the anonymous temporary String object "WE". That then is used to initialize the String object ab. The second line then passes this argument to the indexOf() method bound to the String object DAYS, which returns the number 6 because the substring "WE" begins at character number 6 in the string "SUMOTUWETHFRSA". This number is divided by 2 (because the abbreviations here have 2 characters), resulting in the number 3 being assigned to the dayNumber field.

The second line invokes the toString() method which prints the literal string "Wednesday" for the day. The second part of that println() statement invokes the prev() method bound to the today object which returns the Day object representing Tuesday. That invokes the toString() method again which prints the literal string "Tuesday".

Here's how the prev() method works. First it evaluates the expression (dayNumber+6)%7 as (3+6)%7 = 9%7 = 2, and initializes the variable n with that value which represents Tuesday. Then it passes the arguments 2*n = 4 and 2*n + 2 = 6 to the toString() method bound to the string "SUMOTUWETHFRSA". That returns the substring "TU" which initializes the ab object. That is then passed to the third constructor which creates an anonymous String object representing Tuesday. The prev() method returns that object.

The String object heute is created by the copy constructor. It is a copy of the today object.

On the fifth line, the advance() method bound to the today object is invoked with the argument 4. This changes dayNumber field in the today object to (3+4)%7 = 7%7 = 0 so that it represents Sunday. The next println() statement confirms that and that its previous day is Saturday.

The last println() statement shows that the duplicate object heute was not changed. It is an independent object.

The picture here shows how the three objects look at the end of the program.

The class invariant is the condition that the field dayNumber always be one of the seven integers 0 through 6. (Note that this means there are only 7 different possible objects for the class.) The invariant is enforced by means of the remainder operator %: the reduction %7 is always performed before an integer is assigned to dayNumber.

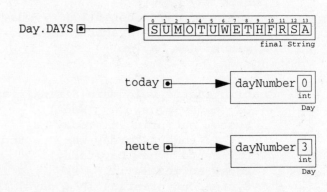

Note that this class has no accessor function. There is no need for the public to know that the days are being represented by an integer or that the specific integer for Wednesday is 3.

6.8 IDENTITY, EQUALITY, AND EQUIVALENCE

"You are sad," the Knight said in an anxious tone: "let me sing you a song to comfort you."

"Is it very long?" Alice asked, for she had heard a good deal of poetry that day.

"It's long," said the Knight, "but it's very, very beautiful.
Everybody that hears me sing it–either it brings the tears into their eyes, or else–"

"Or else what?" said Alice, for the Knight had made a sudden pause.

"Or else it doesn't, you know. The name of the song is called 'Haddocks' Eyes.' "

"Oh, that's the name of the song, is it?" Alice said, trying to feel interested.

"No, you don't understand," the Kinght said, looking a little vexed.

"That's what the name is called. The name really is 'The Aged Aged Man.'"

"Then I ought to have said, 'That's what the song is called'?" Alice corrected herself.

"No, you oughtn't: that's another thing.
The song is called 'Ways and Means': but that's only what it's called, you know!"

"Well, what is the song, then?" said Alice, who was by this time completely bewildered.

"I was coming to that," the Knight said.

"The song really is 'A sitting on a Gate': and the tune's my own invention."

—*Through the Looking Glass*, Chapter VII, by Lewis Carroll

Most people don't give much thought to the distinctions between the name of an object, the object itself, and the thing that the object represents. But in object-oriented programming, those distinctions are important. We saw in Example 6.2 on page 114 that the same object could have different references, and that two distinct objects could represent the same line. In Example 6.3 on page 119, we saw that two different objects could represent the same line. Under what circumstances should we consider two objects equal, and how can we avoid this representation problem?

First consider the distinction between identity and equality. In algebra, we distinguish between an identity such as $x^2 - 1 = (x - 1)(x + 1)$ which is always true, and an equation such as $y = x^2 - 1$ which is sometimes true. "Identically equal" means "different in name only." You can replace one with the other at any time. "President Jefferson" and "Thomas Jefferson" are identically equal because they are only different names for the same person.

In Java, the equality operator "==" is used to determine whether two objects are identically equal. That happens when you assign one reference to another:

```
Point p = new Point(2,3);
Point q = p;                  // q is identically equal to p
boolean ideq = (p2 == p1);   // true: there is only one Point object
```
This is illustrated in the picture on the right:

The point q constructed in Example 6.4 on page 121 was created by the class's copy constructor. This makes a duplicate copy of the object, separate but equal:

```
Point p = new Point(2,3);
Point q = new Point(p);  // q is equal to p
boolean ideq = (q == p); // false: there are two distinct Point objects
```
This is illustrated in the picture on the right:

You can see that there are two distinct Point   objects in this second block of code by the fact that "new Point" appears twice. It only appears once in the first block of code.

These two examples show that the equality operator is not very useful for comparing objects. It only determines whether their references are different. So instead of using the equality operator, we defined our own equals() method to test the contents of the objects themselves:

```
public boolean equals(Point p)
{ return (x == p.x && y == p.y);
}
```

In both cases above, the expression q.equals(p) will be true.

We can define the equals() method any way we want. (The preferred definition is given in Example 7.11 on page 169.) It would seem natural to define it to return true only when all the fields of the two objects are equal. But that can lead to incorrect results if any of the fields are references. For example, in the Line class, the field p0 is a reference to Point objects. We have just seen that the equality operator to references will be false unless they refer to the same object. So in a situation like that illustrated here, the condition (line1.p0 == line2.p0) will be false, even though both fields are equal. That problem can be avoided by using the Point.equals() method instead:

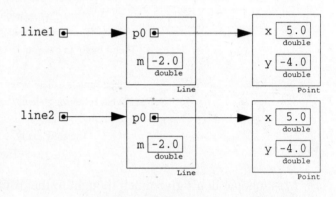

```
public boolean equals(Line line)
{ return (p0.equals(line.p0)) && (m == line.m));
}
```

This version would be quite satisfactory if it weren't for the design flaw in our Line class. As it is, this version of the equals() method will give incorrect results when we have two different objects that represent the same line, as in Example 6.3 on page 119. Here are two Line objects, line1 and line3, that represent the same line: $y = -2x + 6$. But the equals() method shown here will find them not equal because their p0 fields are different. That is why we defined the equals() method differently.

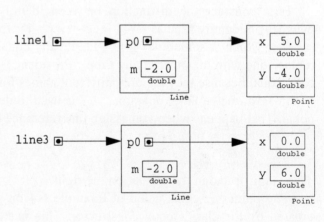

In both Example 6.2 and Example 6.3, we used the declaration

```
public boolean equals(Line line)
{ return (slope() == line.slope()
        && yIntercept() == line.yIntercept());
}
```

This is based upon the more familiar geometric definition: two lines are equal if they have the same slope and the same y-intercept.

That solves the problem of defining equality for the `Line` class. But the source of the problem remains: two objects with different data can represent the same line. That uniqueness problem can be solved by imposing a class invariant, as described in the next section.

Warning: If your class does not declare its own `equals()` method, it will inherit a default version that is equivalent to the equality operator.

6.9 MORE CLASS INVARIANTS

The next two examples show how we can use class invariants to eliminate the possibility that two different objects represent the same thing.

EXAMPLE 6.7 An Unambiguous `Purse` Class

This is a modification of the class defined in Example 6.5 on page 123. It assumes that a purse always exchanges coins to minimize the total number of coins for a given dollar amount. The `reduce()` method enforces this constraint. That method is called by the other methods that can change the contents of the purse: the `insert()` and `remove()` methods. The only information that they need is the total dollar amount inserted or removed, so that is the only parameter that each has.

```
public class Purse
{ // An object represents a coin purse
  // Class invariant: the sum of the field values is minimal and >= 0;
  //                  enforced by the reduce() method

  private int pennies;
  private int nickels;
  private int dimes;
  private int quarters;

  private int cents()
  { return pennies + 5*nickels + 10*dimes + 25*quarters;
  }

  public float dollars()
  { return (float)cents()/100;
  }

  public void clear()
  { pennies = nickels = dimes = quarters = 0;
  }

  private void reduce()
  { pennies = cents();
    if (pennies < 0)
    { clear();
      return;
    }
    quarters = pennies/25;
    pennies %= 25;
    dimes = pennies/10;
    pennies %= 10;
    nickels = pennies/5;
    pennies %= 5;
  }
```

```
public void insert(double dollars)
{ pennies += 100*dollars;
  reduce();
}

public void remove(double dollars)
{ int p = cents() - (int)Math.round(100.0*dollars);
  clear();
  pennies = p;
  reduce();
}

public String toString()
{ return new String(quarters + " quarters + "
              + dimes + " dimes + "
              + nickels + " nickels + "
              + pennies + " pennies = $"
              + dollars());
}

public static void main(String[] args)
{ Purse purse = new Purse();
  System.out.println(purse);
  purse.insert(0.48);
  System.out.println(purse);
  purse.insert(0.93);
  System.out.println(purse);
  purse.remove(0.57);
  System.out.println(purse);
  purse.remove(1.00);
  System.out.println(purse);
}
}
```

The output is

```
0 quarters + 0 dimes + 0 nickels + 0 pennies = $0.0
1 quarters + 2 dimes + 0 nickels + 3 pennies = $0.48
5 quarters + 1 dimes + 1 nickels + 1 pennies = $1.41
3 quarters + 0 dimes + 1 nickels + 4 pennies = $0.84
0 quarters + 0 dimes + 0 nickels + 0 pennies = $0.0
```

The private cents() method is a utility method, used only by other methods in the Purse class. It simply returns the value of money in the purse as an equivalent number of pennies.

The insert() method converts the dollar value 0.48 into the integer 48 which is used to initialize the local variable pennies. Then it invokes the reduce() method which computes and assigns the correct numbers to the object's four fields.

The reduce() method enforces the *class invariant* requirement that the purse always contains the minimal number of coins for its given dollar value. It first computes the equivalent number of pennies, assigning that integer value to the pennies field. If that numerical value is negative, then the purse is emptied by invoking the clear() method and then aborting the reduce() method with the return statement. Otherwise, it computes the correct numbers for the four fields by dividing by 25, 10, and 5. The assignment quarters = pennies/25 changes quarters to 1 and the assignment pennies %= 25 changes pennies to 23. Similarly, the assignment dimes = pennies/10 changes dimes to 2 and the assignment pennies %= 10 changes pennies to 3. When reduce() returns to insert(), the purse fields have the correct values, as shown in the picture above.

The remove() method is called to remove the dollar value 0.57. It first computes the integer number of pennies that would result from subtracting that dollar value from the dollar value of the purse's current contents. It initializes the local variable p with that integer and then calls the reduce() method to compute the correct minimal number of coins.

The reduce() method is our first example of a method with the modifier private instead of public. It is declared to be private because it is a *utility method,* used only by other methods in the Purse class.

EXAMPLE 6.8 An Unambiguous Line Class

This example modifies the class defined in Example 6.3 on page 119. The most significant improvement is the class invariant that guarantees that each line has a unique object to represent it. Other improvements include the methods that return the *x*- and *y*-intercepts and the boolean methods that determine whether the line is horizontal or vertical. It also includes the private print() method for debugging purposes.

```
public class Line
{ // Objects represent lines in the cartesian plane
  // Class invariant: either p0.x() == 0 or p0.y() == 0
  //                   enforced by the normalize() method

  private Point p0;   // a point on the line
  private double m;   // the slope of the line

  public Line(Point p, double s)
  { p0 = p;
    m = s;
    normalize();
  }

  public Line(Point p, Point q)
  { p0 = p;
    m = (p.y() - q.y())/(p.x() - q.x());
    normalize();
  }

  public Line(double a, double b)
  { p0 = new Point(0,b);
    m = -b/a;
    normalize();
  }

  public double slope()
  { return m;
  }
```

```
public double xIntercept()
{ return (p0.x() - p0.y()/m);
}

public double yIntercept()
{ return (p0.y() - p0.x()*m);
}

public boolean equals(Line line)
{ return (m == line.m && yIntercept() == line.yIntercept());
}

public boolean isHorizontal()
{ return (m == 0.0);
}

public boolean isVertical()
{ return (m == Double.POSITIVE_INFINITY
        || m == Double.NEGATIVE_INFINITY);
}

public String toString()
{ float a = (float)xIntercept();
  float b = (float)yIntercept();
  float fm = (float)m;
  if (isHorizontal()) return new String("y = " + b);
  if (isVertical()) return new String("x = " + a);
  if (yIntercept() == 0) return new String("y = " + fm + "x");
  return new String("y = " + fm + "x + " + yIntercept());
}

private void normalize()
{ // enforces class invariant
  if (isHorizontal()) p0 = new Point(0,yIntercept());
  else if (isVertical()) p0 = new Point(xIntercept(),0);
  else if (yIntercept() == 0) p0 = new Point(1,m);
  else p0 = new Point(0,yIntercept());
}

public static void main(String[] args)
{ Point p1 = new Point(5,-4);
  Point p2  = new Point(1,4);
  Line line1 = new Line(p1,-2);
  Line line2 = new Line(p1,p2);
  Line line3 = new Line(3,6);
  print(line1, line2);
  print(line1, line3);
  print(line2, line2);
}

private static void print(Line line1, Line line2)
{ System.out.print("Lines (" + line1 + ") and (" + line2);
  if (line1.equals(line2)) System.out.println(") are equal.");
  else System.out.println(") are not equal.");
}
}
```

The output is

```
Lines (y = -2.0x + 6.0) and (y = -2.0x + 6.0) are equal.
Lines (y = -2.0x + 6.0) and (y = -2.0x + 6.0) are equal.
Lines (y = -2.0x + 6.0) and (y = -2.0x + 6.0) are equal.
```

Three lines are created each using a different constructor. Then they are compared pairwise to test the equals() method.

The equals() method invokes the yIntercept() method which computes the y-intercept b from the formula $b = (y_0 - x_0) \cdot m$, where $(x_0, y_0) = p_0$, which is the Point field.

The slope of a vertical line is infinity (∞). Fortunately, this value and $-\infty$ are represented in Java. They are constants POSITIVE_INFINITY and NEGATIVE_INFINITY defined in the Double class. (See Section 6.10 below.) Java allows ordinary arithmetic and comparisons on these two fields. (See Appendix D.) For example, 2.0/0.0 evaluates to POSITIVE_INFINITY, and 4.4/POSITIVE_INFINITY evaluates to 0.0. So the expressions involving m in these methods will work correctly for vertical lines.

6.10 WRAPPER CLASSES

Each of Java's eight primitive types (boolean, byte, char, short, int, long, float, and double) has a corresponding class, called a *wrapper class*, that generalizes the type. These wrapper classes are defined in the java.lang package, so you can use them without an import statement. The eight wrapper classes are named Boolean, Byte, Character, Short, Integer, Long, Float, and Double. (Note that the class names Character and Integer are not abbreviated like the types char and int). They are called wrapper classes because each encapsulates a primitive type so that a variable can be represented by an object when necessary. They also provide the minimum and maximum values of the type, and the two floating-point classes define the constants POSITIVE_INFINITY, NEGATIVE_INFINITY, and NaN.

This diagram shows the six conversion methods that you can use to convert between the type short and the classes Short and String. Similar methods exist for the other seven wrapper classes.

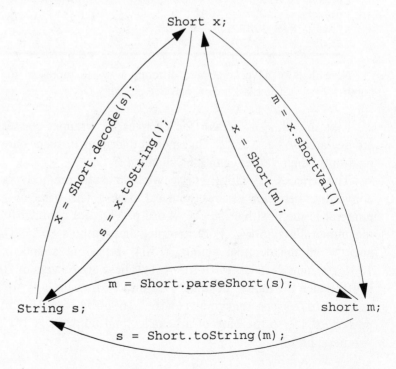

EXAMPLE 6.9 Testing the short Class

This program illustrates the conversion between a variable of short type, an instance of the Short class, and an instance of the String class. It also prints the values of the constants values MIN_VALUE and MAX_VALUE that are defined in the Short class.

```
public class TestShort
{ public static void main(String[] args)
  { short m = 22;
    System.out.println("short m = " + m);
    Short x = new Short(m);                    // converts short to Short
    System.out.println("Short x = " + x);
    String s = x.toString();                   // converts Short to String
    System.out.println("String s = " + s);
    m = Short.parseShort(s);                   // converts String to short
    System.out.println("short m = " + m);
    s = Short.toString(m);                     // converts short to String
    System.out.println("String s = " + s);
    x = Short.decode(s);                       // converts String to Short
    System.out.println("Short x = " + x);
    m = x.shortValue();                        // converts Short to short
    System.out.println("short m = " + m);
    System.out.println("Short.MIN_VALUE = " + Short.MIN_VALUE);
    System.out.println("Short.MAX_VALUE = " + Short.MAX_VALUE);
  }
}
```

The output is
```
short m = 22
Short x = 22
String s = 22
short m = 22
String s = 22
Short x = 22
short m = 22
Short.MIN_VALUE = -32768
Short.MAX_VALUE = 32767
```

Note that we have here three different ways to represent the number 22: a short, a Short, and a String.

Like the String class (see Chapter 2), wrapper classes are declared to be final. That means that their instances are read-only: their values cannot be changed.

The Integer wrapper classes include useful methods for converting between various numeral bases. The base of a numeral is the positive integer whose powers are counted by the numeral's symbols. For example, the symbols "5", "0", and "4" in the decimal numeral "504" represent counts of 100s, 10s, and 1s ($5 \cdot 100 + 0 \cdot 10 + 4 \cdot 1$). These are powers of 10, so the base of a decimal numeral is 10 (hence the name "decimal"). Similarly, the symbols "d", "7", and "b" in the hexadecimal numeral "d7b" represent counts of 16^2s, 16^1s, and 16^0s ($13 \cdot 256 + 7 \cdot 16 + 11 \cdot 1 = 3451$). These are powers of 16, so the base of a hexadecimal numeral is 16. The word *radix* is a synonym for "numeral base."

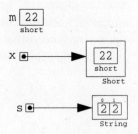

EXAMPLE 6.10 Using the `Integer` Class for Radix Conversion

```
public class TestRadix
{ public static void main(String[] args)
  { int n = 59;
    System.out.println("Decimal:\t" + Integer.toString(n));
    System.out.println("Binary: \t" + Integer.toBinaryString(n));
    System.out.println("Octal:  \t" + Integer.toOctalString(n));
    System.out.println("Hexadecimal:\t" + Integer.toHexString(n));
    System.out.println("Ternary:\t" + Integer.toString(n,3));
    System.out.println("Dodecimal:\t" + Integer.toString(n,12));
    System.out.println("Bigesimal:\t" + Integer.toString(n,20));
    System.out.println("Character.MIN_RADIX = "
      + Character.MIN_RADIX);
    System.out.println("Character.MAX_RADIX = "
      + Character.MAX_RADIX);
    n = Integer.parseInt("d7b",16);
    System.out.println("d7b (base 16) = " + n);
  }
}
```

The output is

```
Decimal:      59
Binary:       111011
Octal:        73
Hexadecimal: 3b
Ternary:      2012
Dodecimal:    4b
Bigesimal:    2j
Character.MIN_RADIX = 2
Character.MAX_RADIX = 36
d7b (base 16) = 3451
```

This program prints the integer 59 in seven different radixes: 10, 2, 8, 16, 3, 12, and 20. The radixes 2, 8, and 16 have the special conversion methods `toBinaryString()`, `toOctalString()`, and `toHexadecimalString()`. The general `toString()` method can be used to convert a decimal numeral to any radix in the range 2 to 36.

The last two statements convert the hexadecimal numeral "d7b" into its equivalent decimal value 3451. Note that the `Integer.parseInt()` method takes two arguments, the `String` object that represents the hexadecimal numeral and an `int` which is the radix of the numeral, and returns the equivalent decimal value as an `int`.

Note that all of the methods invoked in this example are class methods (declared `static`), not instance methods. They are bound to the class itself, not one of its instances.

Review Questions

6.1 What is a class's state?

6.2 What is the difference between a field and a local variable?

6.3 What advantage is there in including a `toString()` method that has zero parameters and returns a `String` object?

6.4 How is the `Point.equals()` method in Example 6.1 on page 111 fundamentally different from the `Line.equals()` method in Example 6.2 on page 114?

6.5 What is the difference between a constructor and a method?

6.6   What is the difference between a class method and an instance method?

6.7   What is an implicit argument?

6.8   Why is it illegal for a `static` method to invoke a non-`static` method?

6.9   What is the difference between equality of objects and equality of the references that refer to them?

6.10   What is the difference between a `public` member and a `private` member of a class?

6.11   Would it be better to make the `clear()` method `private` in the `Purse` class (Example 6.7 on page 129)? Why, or why not?

6.12   Why does the compiler automatically create a default constructor for the `Purse` class (Example 6.5 on page 123) but not for the `Point` class (Example 6.1 on page 111) or the `Line` class (Example 6.2 on page 114)?

6.13   What is the difference between an accessor method and a mutator method?

6.14   What is a class invariant?

6.15   What is a default constructor?

6.16   How many constructors can a class have?

6.17   How many default constructors can a class have?

6.18   What is a copy constructor?

6.19   What is the difference between invoking a copy constructor and using an assignment?

6.20   Why wouldn't the following declaration compile if included in Example 6.1 on page 111?
```
Point p = new Point();
```

6.21   Explain the difference between the output from
```
String s;
System.out.println("s = " + s);
```
and
```
String s = new String();
System.out.println("s = " + s);
```

6.22   What is the purpose of declaring a field `private` and declaring a mutator method that allows the public to change it. Wouldn't it be just as good to just make it `public`?

Programming Problems

6.1   Add and test the following method to the `Point` class defined in Example 6.1 on page 111:
```
public void translate(double dx, double dy)
// shifts the point dx units to the right and dy units up
```
For example, `p.translate(5,1)` would change the point `p` in Example 6.1 to (7,4).

6.2   Add and test the following method to the `Point` class defined in Example 6.1 on page 111:
```
public void rotate(double theta)
// rotates the point theta radians counter-clockwise
```
For example, `p.rotate(Math.PI/2)` would change the point `p` to (–3,2) in Example 6.1. Use the following trigonometric transformation equations:

$$x_2 = x_1 \cos\theta - y_1 \sin\theta$$

$$y_2 = x_1 \sin\theta + y_1 \cos\theta$$

6.3   Modify the `Point` class defined in Example 6.1 on page 111 so that it represents 3-dimensional points in space.

6.4 Add and test the following method to the `Line` class defined in Example 6.2 on page 114:
```
public boolean isParallelTo(Line line)
// returns true iff this is parallel to line
```

6.5 Add and test the following method to the `Line` class defined in Example 6.2 on page 114:
```
public boolean isPerpendicularTo(Line line)
// returns true iff this is perpendicular to line
```

6.6 Add and test the following method to the `Line` class defined in Example 6.2 on page 114:
```
public void translate(double dx, double dy)
// shifts every point in the line by (dx,dy)
```

6.7 Add and test the following method to the `Line` class defined in Example 6.2 on page 114:
```
public void rotate(theta)
// rotates the line counter-clockwise theta radians
```
For example, `p.rotate(Math.PI/2)` would change the object `line` to $y = 0.5x + 3$ in Example 6.2. Use the following trigonometric identity and the fact that the slope of a curve is equal to $\tan\alpha$, where α is the acute angle between the line and the x-axis:

$$\tan(\alpha + \theta) = \frac{\tan\alpha + \tan\theta}{1 - \tan\alpha\tan\theta}$$

6.8 Modify and test the `Purse` class defined in Example 6.5 on page 123 so that `Purse` objects can also contain half dollar coins.

6.9 Convert and test the `Purse` class defined in Example 6.5 on page 123 into a `Wallet` class whose objects represent wallets that contain the lower denomination U.S. dollar bills: $1, $2, $5, $10, $20, and $50.

6.10 Add and test the following method to the `Day` class defined in Example 6.6 on page 124:
```
public Day next();
// returns a Day object that represents the next day
```

6.11 Add and test the following method to the `Day` class defined in Example 6.6 on page 124:
```
public boolean isWeekday();
// returns true iff this is a weekday (Monday through Friday)
```

6.12 Add and test a `copy()` method to the `Line` class defined in Example 6.2 on page 114.

6.13 Add and test a copy constructor to the `Line` class defined in Example 6.2 on page 114.

6.14 Test the `Line` class (Example 6.8 on page 131) on various horizontal and vertical lines. Check that the correct equations are produced.

6.15 You don't have to create `Point` objects explicitly in order to use the `Line` class constructors (Example 6.8 on page 131). You can create an implicit anonymous `Point` object and pass it as an argument to the constructor like this
```
Line line4 = new Line(new Point(2,2), new Point(-1,8))
```
Try this on both constructors that have `Point` parameters.

6.16 Modify the program in Example 6.9 on page 134 so that it tests the `Integer` class the same way.

6.17 Implement a class that is similar to the `Day` class in Example 6.6 on page 124 whose objects represent months.

6.18 Implement a class whose objects represent circles in the cartesian plane.

6.19 Implement the `Point` class using the radial magnitude r and the angular amplitude θ as the class fields instead of the rectangular coordinates x and y. Enforce the class invariant that either $r = \theta = 0$, or $r > 0$ and $0 \le \theta < 2\pi$.

Supplementary Programming Problems

6.20   Add and test the following method to the `Point` class defined in Example 6.1 on page 111:
```
static double distance(Point p1, Point p2);
// returns the distance between the two points
```
Use the following formula for the distance between two points $P_1 = (x_1, y_1)$ and $P_2 = (x_2, y_2)$:

$$\sqrt{(x_1 - x_2)^2 + (y_1 - y_2)^2}$$

6.21   Add and test the following method to the `Line` class defined in Example 6.2 on page 114:
```
boolean contains(Point p);
// returns true iff the point p is on this line
```

6.22   Implement the `Line` class using the coefficients a, b, and c of the equation $ax + by + c = 0$ that represents the line as the class fields. Enforce the class invariant that either a or b is nonzero and c is either 0 or 1.

6.23   Implement the `Line` class using two points on the line as the class fields. Enforce the class invariant that either $x_1 = 0$ and $x_2 = 1$ or $x_1 = x_2$ and $y_1 = 0$ and $y_2 = 1$, where (x_1, y_1) and (x_2, y_2) are the two points.

6.24   Implement a class whose objects represent ratios of integers. Enforce the class invariant that the two integers are relatively prime (*i.e.*, they have no common factors other than 1) and that the denominator is positive. Use the Euclidean Algorithm (Example 4.8 on page 72) to reduce the ratios.

Answers to Review Questions

6.1   A class's *state* is the set of values that is fields have at the current moment.

6.2   A *field* is a variable that is a data member of a class. A *local variable* is a variable that is declared local in a method. For example, in Example 6.1 on page 111, `x` is a field of the `Point` class, and `p` is a local variable in the `main()` method. Note that, as a variable, `p` has type reference. We may say "the `Point` object p," but we really mean "the reference `p` that refers to the `Point` object." Technically, objects themselves do not have names (or types); their references are their handles.

6.3   When declared as
```
String toString()
```
the `toString()` method is given special treatment by the `println()` method, allowing you to abbreviate the syntax `+ x.toString()` with the simpler `+ x` as part of the argument passed to `println()`. (See Example 6.1 on page 111.)

6.4   The `Point.equals()` method in Example 6.1 returns true only if the two objects have the same data. The `Line.equals()` method in Example 6.2 returns true even if the two objects have different data, if they represent the same line. This ambiguity, resolved in Example 6.8 on page 131, is due to the fact the a line is determined by its slope and any point on it, but not uniquely.

6.5   A *constructor* is a member function of a class that is used to create objects of that class. It has the same name as the class itself, has no return type, and is invoked using the `new` operator. A *method* is an ordinary member function of a class. It has its own name, a return type (which may be `void`), and is invoked using the dot operator.

6.6   A *class method* is declared `static` and is invoked using the class name; for example,
```
double y = Math.abs(x);
```
invokes the class method `abs()` that is defined in the `Math` class. An *instance method* is declared without the `static` modifier and is invoked using the name of the object to which it is bound. For example,
```
double x = random.nextDouble();
```

invokes the class method `nextDouble()` that is defined in the `Random` class and is bound to the object `random` which is an instance of that class.

6.7 An *implicit argument* of the invocation of a class instance method is an object to which the method is bound. For example, in the invocation `q.equals(p)`, `q` is the implicit argument and `p` is an explicit argument.

6.8 A `static` method is not bound to any specific object; it has no implicit argument. So within a `static` method, there is no implicit object to which a non-`static` method would be bound.

6.9 Two objects are equal if they have the same data values. Two references are equal if the refer to the same object. The condition `(p == q)` tests equality of the references `p` and `q`, not the equality of the objects to which they refer. You can declare a method `equals()` to test equality of objects, as in Example 6.1 on page 111.

6.10 A `public` class member can be accessed from methods of other classes. A `private` class member can only be accessed from methods of the same class.

6.11 The `clear()` method in the `Purse` class (Example 6.5 on page 123) should not be made `private`, because if it were it could not be invoked from outside the class. It should be accessible outside the class because it allows others to empty the purse.

6.12 The compiler automatically creates a default constructor for the `Purse` class because it has no constructors declared explicitly. The `Point` class and the `Line` class constructors are declared explicitly.

6.13 An *accessor method* returns the current value of one of the class's fields; it is read-only. A *mutator method* allows the method's invoker to change the class's state; it is read-write.

6.14 A *class invariant* is a condition on the fields of the class. For example, the condition that `dayNumber` be between 0 and 6 inclusive is a class invariant on the `Day` class in Example 6.6 on page 124.

6.15 A *default constructor* is a constructor that has no parameters.

6.16 There is no limit (imposed by the language) to the number of constructors a class may have.

6.17 A class can have only one default constructor.

6.18 A *copy constructor* is a constructor that replicates an existing object. It has the signature
```
X(X x);
```
where `X` is the name of the class. For example, the method
```
public Day(Day d);
```
is the copy constructor for the `Day` class in Example 6.6 on page 124.

6.19 Invoking a copy constructor, like this
```
X y = new X(x);
```
creates a new object that is a duplicate of the object passed to it. Using an assignment, like this
```
X z = x;
```
merely declares another reference (*i.e.*, a synonym) for the existing object.

6.20 The declaration `Point p = new Point();` would not compile in Example 6.1 because no default constructor exists for the `Point` class. If the constructor that is declared had been omitted, then a default constructor would exist and the declaration would compile.

6.21 The output from the code
```
String s;
System.out.println("s = " + s);
```
is
```
s = null
```
The output from the code
```
String s = new String();
System.out.println("s = " + s);
```
is
```
s =
```
In the first case, the reference `s` is initialized by default to be `null`; there is no `String` object. In the second case, `s` is initialized to refer to the empty `String` object.

6.22 The advantage of forcing the public to use a mutator method to change a field is that you can control how the field is changed.

Solutions to Programming Problems

6.1
```
public void translate(double a, double b)
{ x += a;
  y += b;
}
```

6.2
```
public void rotate(double theta)
  { double temp = x*Math.cos(theta) - y*Math.sin(theta);
    y = x*Math.sin(theta) + y*Math.cos(theta);
    x = temp;
  }
```

6.3
```
public class Point
{ // Objects represent points in space

  private double x, y, z;

  public Point(double a, double b, double c)
  { x = a;
    y = b;
    z = c;
  }

  public double x()
  { return x;
  }

  public double y()
  { return y;
  }

  public double z()
  { return z;
  }

  public boolean equals(Point p)
  { return (x == p.x && y == p.y && z == p.z);
  }

  public String toString()
  { return new String("(" + x + ", "  + y + ", "  + z + ")");
  }

  public void translate(double a, double b, double c)
  { x += a;
    y += b;
    z += c;
  }
  public static void main(String[] args)
  { Point p = new Point(2,3,-1);
    System.out.println("p.x() = " + p.x() + ", p.y() = " + p.y()
      + ", p.z() = " + p.z());
    System.out.println("p = " + p);
    p.translate(-3,1,2);   // now p = (-1,4,1)
    System.out.println("p = " + p);
    Point q = new Point(7,4,1);
    System.out.println("q = " + q);
    if (p.equals(q)) System.out.println("p equals q");
    else System.out.println("p does not equal q");
    q.translate(-8,0,0);   // now q = (-1,4,1)
    System.out.println("q = " + q);
```

```
                  if (p.equals(q)) System.out.println("p equals q");
                  else System.out.println("p does not equal q");
               }
       }
6.4    public boolean isParallelTo(Line line)
       { return (m == line.m);
       }
6.5    public boolean isPerpendicularTo(Line line)
       { return (m == -1.0/line.m);
       }
6.6    public void translate(double dx, double dy)
          { p0.translate(dx,dy);
       }
6.7    public void rotate(double theta)
       { p0.rotate(theta);
         m = (m + Math.tan(theta))/(1 - m*Math.tan(theta));
       }
6.8    public class Purse
       { // An object represents a coin purse
         // Class invariant: the sum of field values is minimal and >= 0;
         //                  enforced by the reduce() method

         private int pennies;
         private int nickels;
         private int dimes;
         private int quarters;
         private int halves;

         public float dollars()
         { int p = pennies + 5*nickels + 10*dimes + 25*quarters
                    + 50*halves;
           return (float)p/100;
         }

         public void clear()
         { pennies = nickels = dimes = quarters = halves = 0;
         }

         private void reduce()
         { pennies += 5*nickels + 10*dimes + 25*quarters + 50*halves;
           if (pennies < 0)
           { clear();
             return;
           }
           halves = pennies/50;
           pennies %= 50;
           quarters = pennies/25;
           pennies %= 25;
           dimes = pennies/10;
           pennies %= 10;
           nickels = pennies/5;
           pennies %= 5;
         }

         public void insert(double dollars)
         { pennies += 100*dollars;
           reduce();
         }
```

```
public void remove(double dollars)
{ int p = (int)(100.0*(dollars() - dollars));
  clear();
  pennies = p;
  reduce();
}

public String toString()
{ return new String(halves + " halves + "
                + quarters + " quarters + "
                + dimes + " dimes + "
                + nickels + " nickels + "
                + pennies + " pennies = $"
                + dollars());
}

public static void main(String[] args)
{ Purse purse = new Purse();
  System.out.println(purse);
  purse.insert(0.48);
  System.out.println(purse);
  purse.insert(0.93);
  System.out.println(purse);
  purse.remove(0.57);
  System.out.println(purse);
  purse.remove(1.00);
  System.out.println(purse);
}
}
```

6.9
```
public class Wallet
{ // An object represents a coin purse
  // Class invariant: the sum of field values is minimal and >= 0;
  //                     enforced by the reduce() method

  private int ones, twos, fives, tens, twenties, fifties;

  public int dollars()
  { return ones + 2*twos + 5*fives + 10*tens + 20*twenties
              + 50*fifties;
  }

  public void clear()
  { ones = twos = fives = tens = twenties = fifties = 0;
  }

  private void reduce()
  { ones += 2*twos + 5*fives + 10*tens + 20*twenties + 50*fifties;
    if (ones < 0)
    { clear();
      return;
    }
    fifties = ones/50;
    ones %= 50;
    twenties = ones/20;
    ones %= 20;
    tens = ones/10;
    ones %= 10;
    fives = ones/5;
    ones %= 5;
    twos = ones/2;
    ones %= 2;
  }
```

```
          public void insert(int dollars)
          { ones += dollars;
            reduce();
          }

          public void remove(int dollars)
          { int n = dollars() - dollars;
            clear();
            ones = n;
            reduce();
          }

          public String toString()
          { return new String( fifties + " fifties + "
              + twenties + " twenties + " + tens + " tens + "
              + fives + " fives + " + twos + " twos + "
              + ones + " ones = $" + dollars());
          }

          public static void main(String[] args)
          { Wallet wallet = new Wallet();
            System.out.println(wallet);
            wallet.insert(48);
            System.out.println(wallet);
            wallet.insert(93);
            System.out.println(wallet);
            wallet.remove(57);
            System.out.println(wallet);
            wallet.remove(100);
            System.out.println(wallet);
          }
        }
```

6.10
```
     public Day next()
     { return new Day((dayNumber + 1)%7);
     }
```
6.11
```
     public boolean isWeekday()
     { return (dayNumber > 0 && dayNumber < 6);
     }
```
6.12
```
     public Line copy()
     { Line temp = new Line(p0,m);
       return temp;
     }
```
6.13
```
     public Line(Line line)  // copy constructor
     { p0 = line.p0;
       m = line.m;
     }
```
6.14
```
     public class Line
     { // include here code from Example 6.8

       public static void main(String[] args)
       { Point p0 = new Point(0,0);
         Point px = new Point(0,1);
         Point py = new Point(1,0);
         Point p1 = new Point(1,1);
         Line linex = new Line(p0,px);
         Line liney = new Line(p0,py);
         Line line0 = new Line(p0,p1);
         Line line1 = new Line(px,p1);
         Line line2 = new Line(py,p1);
         Line line3 = new Line(px,py);
```

```
          print(linex);
          print(liney);
          print(line0);
          print(line1);
          print(line2);
          print(line3);
        }

      private static void print(Line line)
      { System.out.print("Line (" + line + ") is ");
        if (line.isHorizontal()) System.out.println("horizontal.");
        else if (line.isVertical()) System.out.println("vertical.");
        else System.out.println("neither horizontal nor vertical.");
      }
    }
```

6.15
```
    public class Line
    { // include here code from Example 6.8

      public static void main(String[] args)
      { Line line = new Line(new Point(3,0), new Point(5,1));
        System.out.println(line);
        line = new Line(new Point(1,-1), new Point(2,1));
        System.out.println(line);
        System.out.println(new Line(new Point(0,4), new Point(3,1)));
      }
    }
```

6.16
```
    public class TestInteger
    { public static void main(String[] args)
      { int n = 66;
        System.out.println("int n = " + n);
        Integer x = new Integer(n);   // convert int to Integer
        System.out.println("Integer x = " + x);
        String s = x.toString();   // convert Integer to String
        System.out.println("String s = " + s);
        n = Integer.parseInt(s);   // convert String to int
        System.out.println("int n = " + n);
        s = Integer.toString(n);   // convert int to String
        System.out.println("String s = " + s);
        x = Integer.decode(s);   // convert String to Integer
        System.out.println("Integer x = " + x);
        n = x.intValue();   // convert Integer to int
        System.out.println("int n = " + n);
        System.out.println("Integer.MIN_VALUE = "
          + Integer.MIN_VALUE);
        System.out.println("Integer.MAX_VALUE = "
          + Integer.MAX_VALUE);
      }
    }
```

6.17
```
    public class Month
    { // An instance represents a unique month of the year
      // Class invariant: 0 <= dayNumber < 12

      private final String MONTHS = "JANFEBMARAPRMAYJUN"
        + "JULAUGSEPOCTNOVDEC";
      private int monthNumber;

      public Month()  // default constructor
      { monthNumber = 0;
      }
```

```
        public Month(Month m)   // copy constructor
        { monthNumber = m.monthNumber;
        }

        public Month(String s)
        { String ab = s.substring(0,3).toUpperCase();   // 3-char abbrev.
          monthNumber = MONTHS.indexOf(ab)/3;
        }

        public String toString()
        { switch (monthNumber)
          { case 0: return "January";
            case 1: return "February";
            case 2: return "March";
            case 3: return "April";
            case 4: return "May";
            case 5: return "June";
            case 6: return "July";
            case 7: return "August";
            case 8: return "September";
            case 9: return "October";
            case 10: return "November";
            default: return "December";
          }
        }

        public void advance(int n)
        { monthNumber = (monthNumber + n)%12;
        }

        public Month prev()
        { int n = (monthNumber+11)%12;
          String ab = MONTHS.substring(3*n, 3*n+3);   // 3-char abbrev.
          return new Month(ab);
        }

        public static void main(String[] args)
        { Month now = new Month("June");
          System.out.println("This month is " + now
            + ", and last month was " + now.prev());
          Month summer = new Month(now);
          now.advance(7);
          System.out.println("In 7 months, now will be " + now
            + ", and last month will have been " + now.prev());
          System.out.println("But this month is still " + summer
            + ", and last month was " + summer.prev());
        }
    }
```

6.18
```
    public class Circle
    { // Objects represent circles in the cartesian plane
      // Class invariant: r > 0

        private Point p0;   // the center of the circle
        private double r;   // the radius of the circle

        public Circle(Point p, double radius)
        { p0 = p;
          r = radius;
          normalize();
        }
```

```
        public Circle(Circle c)   // copy constructor
        { p0 = c.p0;
          r = c.r;
        }

        public Point center()
        { return p0;
        }

        public double radius()
        { return r;
        }

        public double area()
        { return Math.PI*r*r;
        }

        public boolean equals(Circle c)
        { return (p0.equals(c.p0) && r == c.r);
        }

        public Circle copy()
        { Circle temp = new Circle(p0,r);
          return temp;
        }

        public void translate(double dx, double dy)
        { p0.translate(dx,dy);
        }

        public void rotate(double theta)
        { p0.rotate(theta);
        }

        public String toString()
        { return new String("(x - " + p0.x() + ")^2 = (y - "
            + p0.y() + ")^2 = " + r*r);
        }

        private void normalize()
        { // enforces class invariant
          if (r <= 0) r = 1.0;
        }

        public static void main(String[] args)
        { Point p = new Point(5,-4);
          Circle circle = new Circle(p,2);
          System.out.println("The circle is: " + circle);
          System.out.println("Its area is " + circle.area());
          circle = new Circle(p,-1);
          System.out.println("The circle is: " + circle);
          System.out.println("Its area is " + circle.area());
        }
    }
```

6.19
```
    public class Point
    { // An instance represents a point in the cartesian plane
      // Implementation: polar coordinates
      // Invariant: either r = 0 and theta = 0,
      //                 or r > 0 and 0 < theta < 2*pi

        private double r;      // radial distance from origin
        private double theta;  // radian measure of amplitude
```

```
      private void normalize()
      { // enforces the class invariant
        if (r == 0.0) theta = 0.0;
        if (r < 0)
        { r = -r;
          theta += Math.PI;
        }
        theta %= 2*Math.PI;
        if (theta == 0) r = 0;
      }

      public Point(double a, double b)
      { r = Math.sqrt(a*a + b*b);
        theta = Math.atan2(a,b);
        normalize();
      }

      public double x()
      { return r*Math.cos(theta);
      }

      public double y()
      { return r*Math.sin(theta);
      }

      public void move(double a, double b)
      { r = Math.sqrt(a*a + b*b);
        theta = Math.atan2(a,b);
        normalize();
      }

      public void shift(double h, double k)
      { double x = h + x();
        double y = k + y();
        r = Math.sqrt(x*x + y*y);
        theta = Math.atan2(x,y);
        normalize();
      }

      public String str()
      { return new String("(" + (float)x() + ", " + (float)y() + ")");
      }

      public static void main(String[] args)
      { Point p = new Point(4,4);
        System.out.println("The point p is at " + p.str());
        p.shift(6,6);
        System.out.println("The point p is now at " + p.str());
        p.move(2,-2);
        System.out.println("The point p is now at " + p.str());
      }
}
```

Chapter 7

Composition and Inheritance

One of the features of object-oriented programming that makes it so powerful is the ease with which you can "re-use" implementations for different purposes. This is done through composition and inheritance.

7.1 COMPOSITION

Composition is the creation of one class using another class for its component data. We used composition in the definition of the `Line` class in Example 6.2 on page 114. It was composed of the `Point` class.

The most widely used component class is the `String` class, as the first example illustrates.

EXAMPLE 7.1 A `Name` Class

```
class Name
{ // Objects represent names of people

    protected String first;    // e.g., "William"
    protected String middle;   // e.g., "Jefferson"
    protected String last;     // e.g., "Clinton"

    Name()  // default constructor
    {
    }

    Name(String first, String last)
    { this.first = first;
      this.last = last;
    }

    Name(String first, String middle, String last)
    { this(first,last);
      this.middle = middle;
    }

    String first()
    { return first;
    }

    String middle()
    { return middle;
    }

    String last()
    { return last;
    }
```

148

```
    void setFirst(String first)
    { this.first = first;
    }

    void setMiddle(String middle)
    { this.middle = middle;
    }

    void setLast(String last)
    { this.last = last;
    }

    public String toString()
    { String s = new String();
      if (first != null) s += first + " ";
      if (middle != null) s += middle + " ";
      if (last != null) s += last + " ";
      return s.trim();
    }
}
```

Here is a test driver:

```
class TestName
{ // Test driver for Name class
  public static void main(String[] args)
  { Name tr = new Name("Theodore", "Roosevelt");
    Name fc = new Name("Francis", "Harry Compton", "Crick");
    System.out.println(fc + " won the 1962 Nobel in Physiology.");
    System.out.println("His first name was " + fc.first());
    System.out.println(tr + " won the 1906 Nobel Peace Prize.");
    System.out.println("His middle name was " + tr.middle());
  }
}
```

Its output is

```
Francis Harry Compton Crick won the 1962 Nobel in Physiology.
His first name was Francis
Theodore Roosevelt won the 1906 Nobel Peace Prize.
His middle name was null
```

The five objects in this program can be visualized as shown here. The Name object referenced by tr is created explicitly when the new operator invokes the two-argument Name() constructor on the first line of main(). Its two arguments, first and last, are references to String objects, so that constructor implicitly invokes the String constructor twice to create the objects tr.first and tr.last. The keyword this stands for the implicit argument tr. Note that the reference tr.middle has no referent, so that field remains null.

The second line of main() has a similar effect on the reference fc. But it

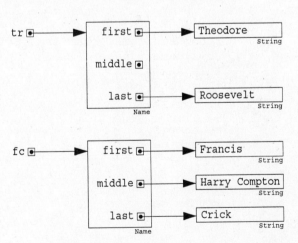

invokes the three-argument constructor, so in addition to another `Name` object, three more `String` objects are created.

The `Name` class is defined to have three fields, three constructors, and eight methods. The first three methods are *accessor methods*: each simply returns one of the fields. The next three methods are *mutator methods*: they allow other methods outside the class to modify the fields. The last two methods are the usual `toString()` for displaying the object as a string, and the `main()` method which serves as a test driver for the class.

The keyword `this` can be used inside an instance method to refer to the *implicit argument*; that is, the object to which the method is bound when it is invoked. It was used in the constructors in the `Name` class in Example 7.1 as a prefix to the class field names so that they could be distinguished from the constructor's parameters. The two-argument constructor could have been declared as

```
public Name(String string1, String string2)
{ first = string1;
  last = string2;
}
```

But this version is not as clear as the other.

EXAMPLE 7.2 A `Person` Class

This class uses the `Name` class from Example 7.1.

```
class Person
{ // Objects represent people

  protected Name name;
  protected char sex;    // 'M' or 'F'
  protected String id;   // e.g., Social Security number

  Person(Name name, char sex)
  { this.name = name;
    this.sex = sex;
  }

  Person(Name name, char sex, String id)
  { this.name = name;
    this.sex = sex;
    this.id = id;
  }

  Name name()
  { return name;
  }

  char sex()
  { return sex;
  }

  String id()
  { return id;
  }
  void setId(String id)
  { this.id = id;
  }
```

```
   public String toString()
   { String s = new String(name + " (sex: " + sex);
     if (id != null) s += "; id: " + id;
     s += ")";
     return s;
   }
}
```

The test driver is

```
class TestPerson
{ // Test driver for the Person class:
   public static void main(String[] args)
   { Name bobsName = new Name("Robert", "Lee");
     Person bob = new Person(bobsName, 'M');
     System.out.println("bob: " + bob);
     bob.name.setMiddle("Edward");
     System.out.println("bob: " + bob);
     Person ann = new Person(new Name("Ann", "Baker"), 'F');
     System.out.println("ann: " + ann);
     ann.setId("053011736");
     System.out.println("ann: " + ann);
   }
}
```

Its output is

```
bob: Robert Lee (sex: M)
bob: Robert Edward Lee (sex: M)
ann: Ann Baker (sex: F)
ann: Ann Baker (sex: F; id: 053011736)
```

The 10 objects created in this program are illustrated here. Note that the four composite objects (the two Person objects and the two Name objects) are created explicitly with the new operator, while the six String objects are created implicitly.

The Person class has three fields: a Name reference, a char, and a String reference. Note that, in general, reference fields can be null. But in this case, the name field cannot be null because there is no constructor that allows that field (or the sex field) to be omitted. Also note that this class has no default

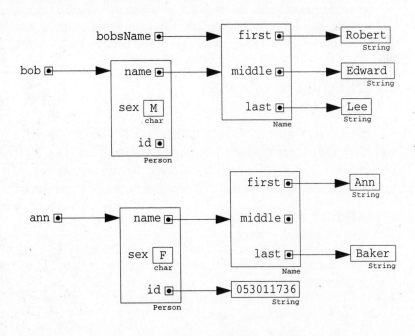

constructor. We don't want any nameless or sexless Person objects. Since we require the name and sex fields at construction time, the only mutator method declared is one to change the id field. This means that the name and sex fields cannot be changed.

The first line in main() creates the Name object bobsName. Then the Person object bob is created on the second line, passing the Name object and the char 'M' to the two-argument Person constructor. Notice that leaves the id reference null in that object. (We don't know Robert E. Lee's I.D. number.)

The third line passes the bob reference to the println() method. This automatically invokes the Person class's toString() method which prints the output in the form shown here.

The fourth line invokes the setMiddle() mutator method which creates a duplicate of the string "Edward" and assigns it to the String reference bob.name.middle. Then the println() method prints the second line of output shown above.

Two objects are created when the sixth line executes. The anonymous Name object with fields "Ann" and "Baker" is created by the two-argument constructor declared in the Name class (Example 7.1 on page 148). This constructor is activated by the new operator as the first argument passed to the two-argument Person constructor. So that Name object is created "on the fly." It is passed, along with the char 'F' to the two-argument Person constructor which creates the ann object.

On the second line, the println() method invokes the Person.toString() method to print the ann object. That method invokes one of the String constructors to create the string s:

    String s = new String(name + " (sex: " + sex);
The String class actually has four one-argument constructors. This one has a String parameter. The String object passed to it is

    name + " (sex: " + sex
which is formed by concatenating an anonymous String object with the string literal " (sex: " and the char 'F' (which is converted into a 1-character string). The anonymous String object is produced by the Name.toString() method when the object name is detected in this concatenation. So the first line of output is the result of both the Person.toString() and the Name.toString() methods.

After the object ann is created, the setId() method is invoked to change its id field from null to the string passed. Thence this object represents a female person named "Ann Baker" with identification number 053011736. (The Name object that represents Ann's name is anonymous.)

7.2 RECURSIVE CLASSES

A recursive method is one which invokes itself. These are described in Section 5.4. A *recursive class* is one which is composed with itself; *i.e.*, it has a reference field that refers to objects of the class to which it belongs. Recursive classes provide a powerful technique for building linked structures that can represent complex relationships very efficiently.

EXAMPLE 7.3 Family Trees

This version of the Person class defined in Example 7.2 on page 150 adds the four fields mother, father, twoBlanks, and tab, and it modifies the toString() method:

```
class Person
{ // Objects represent people
    protected Name name;
    protected char sex;    // 'M' or 'F'
    protected String id;   // e.g., Social Security number
    protected Person mother;
    protected Person father;
    private static final String twoBlanks = "  ";
    private static String tab = "";
```

```
     Person(Name name, char sex)
     { this.name = name;
       this.sex = sex;
     }

     Person(Name name, char sex, String id)
     { this.name = name;
       this.sex = sex;
       this.id = id;
     }

     Name name()
     { return name;
     }

     // The sex() and id() accessor methods are the same as in Example 7.2

     void setId(String id)
     { this.id = id;
     }

     void setMother(Person mother)
     { this.mother = mother;
     }

     void setFather(Person father)
     { this.father = father;
     }

     public String toString()
     { String s = new String(name + " (" + sex + ")");
       if (id != null) s += "; id: " + id;
       s += "\n";
       if (mother != null)
       { tab += twoBlanks;                    // adds two blanks
         s += tab + "mother: " + mother;
         tab = tab.substring(2);              // removes two blanks
       }
       if (father != null)
       { tab += twoBlanks;                    // adds two blanks
         s += tab + "father: " + father;
         tab = tab.substring(2);              // removes two blanks
       }
       return s;
     }
   }
```

The test driver is

```
   class TestPerson
   { // Test driver for the Person class:
     public static void main(String[] args)
     { Person ww = new Person(new Name("William", "Windsor"), 'M');
       Person cw = new Person(new Name("Charles", "Windsor"), 'M');
       Person ds = new Person(new Name("Diana", "Spencer"), 'F');
       Person es = new Person(new Name("Edward", "Spencer"), 'M');
       Person ew = new Person(new Name("Elizabeth", "Windsor"), 'F');
       Person pm = new Person(new Name("Philip", "Mountbatten"), 'M');
```

```
        Person eb = new Person(new Name("Elizabeth", "Bowes-Lyon"), 'F');
        Person gw = new Person(new Name("George", "Windsor"), 'M');
        ww.setFather(cw);
        ww.setMother(ds);
        ds.setFather(es);
        cw.setMother(ew);
        cw.setFather(pm);
        ew.setMother(eb);
        ew.setFather(gw);
        System.out.println(ww);
    }
}
```

The output is

```
 William Windsor (M)
   mother: Diana Spencer (F)
     father: Edward Spencer (M)
   father: Charles Windsor (M)
     mother: Elizabeth Windsor (F)
       mother: Elizabeth Bowes-Lyon (F)
       father: George Windsor (M)
     father: Philip Mountbatten (M)
```

The program creates the eight Person objects shown here. (Some of the details of the objects are omitted. Each of the 16 name fields is actually a reference to a distinct Name object.)

This version of the Person class is recursive because its mother and father fields are references to Person objects.

The main() method first creates the eight objects. Then it invokes the setMother() and setFather() methods to link them. The result is the linked tree structure shown below.

The two static fields blanks and tab are used only in the toString() method. They produce the tabbed formatting in the output shown above. Each time the toString() method prints a line with "mother:" or "father:," it appends two blanks to the tab string, prints that first, and then removes the two blanks. Since that field is declared to be static, it remains unchanged throughout the life of the program except when changed by the toString() method. So the effect is to tab over $2n$ blanks, where n is the current level of recursion. For example, the string "father: George Windsor (M)" is tabbed over 6 blanks because it is printed in a level 3 recursive call: ww.toString() invokes cw.toString() which invokes ew.toString() which invokes gw.toString(). This mechanism makes it easy to see from the output who is who's parents.

EXAMPLE 7.4 A Telephone List

This class maintains a list of friends' telephone numbers:

```
class Friend
{ // Objects represent my friends

    protected String name;          // e.g., "Bill Ross"
    protected String telephone;     // e.g., "283-9104"
    protected Friend next;          // next object in list
    static Friend list;             // linked list of friends
```

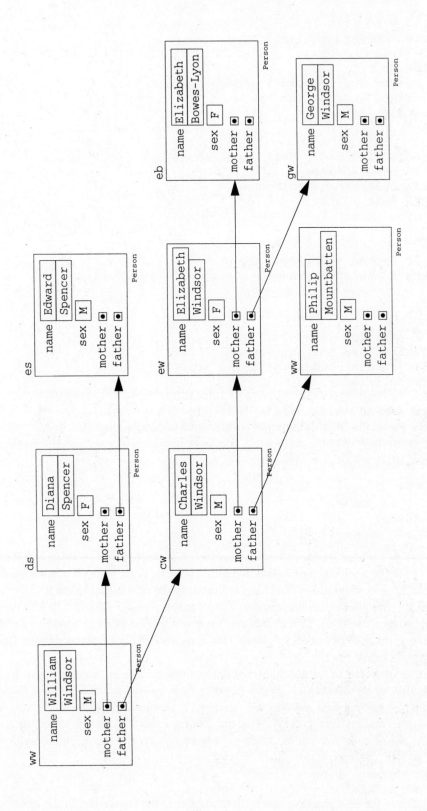

```
        static void print()
        { Friend friend = list;
          if (friend == null) System.out.println("The list is empty.");
          else do
          { System.out.println(friend);
            friend = friend.next;
          } while (friend != null);
        }

        Friend(String name, String telephone)
        { this.name = name;
          this.telephone = telephone;
          this.next = list;
          list = this;
        }

        public String toString()
        { return new String(name + ":\t" + telephone);
        }
    }
```

The test driver is

```
 class TestFriend
 { // Test driver for the Friend class:
   public static void main(String args[])
   { Friend.print();
     new Friend("Martin Ryle", "388-1095");
     new Friend("Bill Ross", "283-9104");
     new Friend("Nat Withers", "217-5912");
     Friend.print();
   }
 }
```

The output is

```
 The list is empty.
 Nat Withers:     217-5912
 Bill Ross:       283-9104
 Martin Ryle:     388-1095
```

The list consists of a sequence of linked `Friend` objects. Each object has three data fields: `name`, `telephone`, and `next`. The `next` field is a reference to the next object in the list.

The `static` modifier in the declaration of the variable `list` identifies it as a *class variable* (as opposed to an instance variable). That means that there is only one of these variables for the entire class (as opposed to one for each object of the class). This class variable is a reference to the first object in the list. (See the picture below.)

The `static` modifier in the declaration of the method `print()` identifies it as a *class method*. It prints the entire list, or reports that it is empty. It works by following the `next` links in the objects.

The `main()` method first invokes the `print()` method while the list is still empty. Then it creates three objects and invokes `print()` again. The list looks like the picture below.

The objects are inserted into the list when the constructor creates them. That is achieved by the two lines

```
        this.next = list;
        list = this;
```

The first line assigns the new object's `next` field to refer to the first object in the existing list, which is what the class variable `list` refers to. The second line reassigns that class variable to refer to the new object, thereby placing it at the beginning of the list. Note that before any objects are created, the `list` variable is `null`, which means that the list is empty. So when the first object is inserted into the list, the first of the two lines above assigns `null` to that first object's `next` field. Then since all other objects are inserted at the beginning of the list, that first object remains the last in the list. Thus the end of the list is identified by the fact that its last object's next field is `null`.

The `print()` method traverses the list, invoking the `println()` method (which invokes the `toString()` method) on each object. Each time the `do...while` loop iterates, the statement

        friend = friend.next;

advances the local reference variable `friend` to the next object in the list. When it is referring to the last object, this statement assigns `null` to it, thereby stopping the loop.

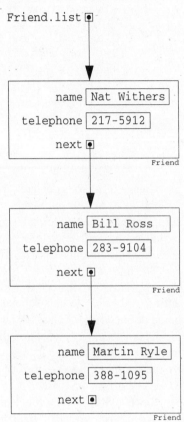

Linked structures like the tree created in Example 7.3 and the list created in Example 7.4 are powerful data structures, widely used in large software applications. But the incautious use of links can lead to confusion and run-time errors that are difficult to track down. These are usually due to assigning references or testing their equality. Java helps avoid these problems by providing the special `clone()` and `equals()` methods described in Section 7.10 on page 168.

7.3 INHERITANCE

Inheritance is the creation of one class by extending another class so that instances of the new class automatically inherit the fields and methods of its parent class. This chapter describes how to do that in Java.

EXAMPLE 7.5 Subclass `ClassY` Inherits the `protected` Field `m` from Class `ClassX`

This defines a trivial class with one field and one method:

```
class ClassX
{ // A trivial class:
  protected int m;

  public String toString()
  { return new String("(" + m + ")");
  }
}
```

Note that the field `m` is declared to have `protected` instead of `private` access.

Here is a second class, defined to extend the first class:

```
public class ClassY extends ClassX
{ // A trivial subclass of ClassX:
  private int n;

  public String toString()
  { return new String("(" + m + "," + n + ")");
  }
}
```

Note that its `toString()` method has the same signature as the `toString()` method declared in `ClassX`.

Here is the test driver program:
```
class TestClassY
{ // Test driver for ClassY:
  public static void main(String[] args)
  { ClassX x = new ClassX();
    System.out.println("x = " + x);
    ClassY y = new ClassY();
    System.out.println("y = " + y);
  }
}
```
Its output is
```
x = (0)
y = (0,0)
```

Class `ClassX` declares the single `int` field `m` and the single method `toString()`. Since `ClassX` has no explicit constructor, the compiler produces a default constructor for it. That default constructor initializes the field `m` to 0 for every instances of `ClassX`. So the object `x` created in the first line of `main()` looks like the picture shown here.

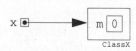

The line
```
public class ClassY extends ClassX
```
defines `ClassY` to be a subclass of `ClassX`. The keyword `extends` is used to specify that the class being defined is a subclass of the other class.

Class `ClassY` declares the single `int` field `n` and the single method `toString()`. Its default constructor is also produced implicitly by the compiler. So the object `y` created in the third line of `main()` looks like the picture shown here.

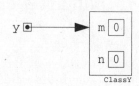

Since `ClassY` is a subclass of `ClassX`, every instance of `ClassY` has two fields: the `int` field `m` that it inherits from `ClassX`, and the field `n` that it declared explicitly.

The field `m` in `ClassX` is declared to be `protected` instead of `private`. Recall (page 116) that the `protected` field modifier means that the field is accessible from any subclass, whereas `private` means that it is accessible only from within the class itself.

Here is an equivalent definition of `ClassY` without using inheritance:
```
public class ClassY
{ // A trivial class:
  private int m, n;

  public String toString()
  { return new String("(" + m + "," + n + ")");
  }
}
```

EXAMPLE 7.6 Subclasses Do Not Inherit `private` Fields

These definitions are identical to those in Example 7.5 except that the field `m` in `ClassX` is declared to have `private` access instead of `protected`:
```
class ClassX
{ // A trivial class:
  private int m;
```

```
    public String toString()
    { return new String("(" + m  + ")");
    }
}

public class ClassY extends ClassX
{ // A trivial subclass of ClassX:
  private int n;

  public String toString()
  { return new String("(" + m  + "," + n + ")");  // ERROR: no field m
  }
}

class TestClassY
{ // Test driver for ClassY:
  public static void main(String[] args)
  { ClassX x = new ClassX();
    System.out.println("x = " + x);
    ClassY y = new ClassY();
    System.out.println("y = " + y);
  }
}
```

This <u>program will not compile</u> because the ClassY.toString() method is attempting to access the field ClassX.m which is declared private.

When a second class inherits from another class, we call the first class the *superclass* or *parent class* of the second, and the second class a *subclass* or *child class* of the first. For example, in Example 7.5, ClassX is the superclass and ClassY is the subclass. A subclass extends the definition of its superclass by adding fields and methods. This makes instances of the subclass more specialized than instances of its parent class. Every instance of the subclass has all the characteristics of instances of the superclass. So the set of all instances of the subclass is essentially a subset of the set of all instances of the superclass:

$$\{y : \text{object } y \text{ is an instance of ClassY}\} \subseteq \{x : \text{object } x \text{ is an instance of ClassX}\}$$

That is why ClassY is called a "subclass" of ClassX.

7.4 OVERRIDING FIELDS AND METHODS

An instance y of ClassY is "essentially" the same as being an instance of ClassX with more data and functionality. But not exactly. If both classes declare a method g() with the same signature, the method y.g() will invoke the method declared in ClassY, not the one declared in ClassX. In this case, the method y.g() is said to *override* the method x.g(). Overriding is similar to overloading: different methods have the same name. Overriding is different because the methods have the same signature (same name, same parameter type list) and they are declared in different classes. They must also have the same return types, and the overriding method must has access that is as wide as the overridden method. So a public method can be overridden only by another public method.

Overriding fields is similar to overriding methods: they have the same declarations but in different classes.

EXAMPLE 7.7 Overriding Fields and Methods

This example is similar to Example 7.6 on page 158. It illustrates how a subclass's fields and methods override those of its superclass. Here is a trivial class with two `protected` fields and three methods:

```
class ClassX
{ // A trivial class:
  protected int m;
  protected int n;

  void f()
  { System.out.println("Now in ClassX.f().");
    m = 22;
  }
  void g()
  { System.out.println("Now in ClassX.g().");
    n = 44;
  }

  public String toString()
  { return new String( "{ m=" + m  + ", n=" + n + " }" );
  }
}
```

Here is a subclass:

```
public class ClassY extends ClassX
{ // A trivial subclass of ClassX:
  private double n;                        // overrides the field ClassX.n

  void g()                               // overrides the method ClassX.g()
  { System.out.println("Now in ClassY.g().");
    n = 3.1415926535897932;
  }

  public String toString()    // overrides the method ClassX.toString()
  { return new String( "{ m=" + m  + ", n=" + n + " }" );
  }
}
```

Its field `n` and methods `g()` override the members of `ClassX` with the same name.

Here is a test driver:

```
class TestClassY
{ // Test driver for ClassY:
  public static void main(String[] args)
  { ClassX x = new ClassX();
    x.f();
    x.g();
    System.out.println("x = " + x);
    ClassY y = new ClassY();          //  y "is a" ClassY
    y.f();            // polymorphism: y also "is a" ClassX
    y.g();
    System.out.println("y = " + y);
  }
}
```

Its output is

```
Now in ClassX.f().
Now in ClassX.g().
x = { m=22, n=44 }
```

```
Now in ClassX.f().
Now in ClassY.g().
y = { m=22, n=3.141592653589793 }
```

The ClassX object x has fields x.m and x.n and methods x.f(), x.g(), and x.toString(). The ClassY object y has fields y.m and y.n and methods y.f(), y.g(), and y.toString(). The field y.m and method y.f() are declared in its superclass ClassX. The field y.n and methods y.g() and y.toString() are declared in its own class ClassY, overriding the declarations of n, g(), and toString() in ClassX.

You can tell which declarations were used for the field y.n and method y.g() by the output of the test driver. The field y.n has type double, assigned to be 3.141592653589793 in the method y.g() that is declared in ClassY.

The statement

```
y.f();              // polymorphism: y also "is a" ClassX
```

in main() is an example of *polymorphism* ("capable of many forms"). Although the implicit argument y is a ClassY object, it can take the form of a ClassX object in order to invoke the method ClassX.f(). This works for both implicit and explicit arguments to methods of superclasses.

7.5 THE super KEYWORD

Java uses the keyword super to refer to members of the parent class. When used in the form super(), it invokes the superclass's constructor. When used in the form super.f(), it invokes the function f() declared in the superclass. This allows you to override the override.

EXAMPLE 7.8 A Student Subclass of the Person Class

Here is a subclass of the Person class (Example 7.2 on page 150):

```
class Student extends Person
{ // Objects represent students
   protected int credits;  // credit hours earned
   protected double gpa;    // grade-point average

   Student(Name name, char sex, int credits, double gpa)
   { super(name, sex);            // invokes the Person class constructor
     this.credits = credits;
     this.gpa = gpa;
   }

   int credits()
   { return credits;
   }

   double gpa()
   { return gpa;
   }
```

```
public String toString()
{ String s;
  s = new String(super.toString());          // invokes Person.toString()
  s += "\n\tcredits: " + credits;
  s += "\n\tgpa:      " + gpa;
  return s;
}
}
```

Here is a test driver:

```
class TestStudent
{ public static void main(String[] args)
  { Name annsName = new Name("Ann", "Baker");
    Student ann = new Student(annsName, 'F', 16, 3.5);
    System.out.println("ann: " + ann);
  }
}
```

Its output is

```
ann: Ann Baker (sex: F)
    credits: 16
    gpa:      3.5
```

The first line in the test driver creates the Name object annsName. The second line creates the Student object ann, just as in Example 7.2 on page 150, except here it is an instance of the Student class instead of the Person class. But the first line of the Student constructor is

```
super(name, sex);    // invokes the constructor in the Person class
```

The keyword super refers to the superclass of the current class. Since that is the Person class, the arguments name and sex are passed to the Person class constructor which executes its code on the Student object ann. This has the same effect as if the Student class constructor had been declared as

```
Student(Name name, char sex, int credits, double gpa)
{ this.name = name;
  this.sex = sex;
  this.credits = credits;
  this.gpa = gpa;
}
```

We used the indirect method instead here just to illustrate the use of the super keyword.

The objects in this program can be visualized as shown in the following picture.

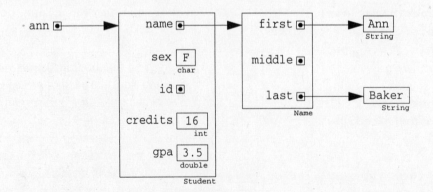

7.6 INHERITANCE VERSUS COMPOSITION

Inheritance means specialization. A subclass specializes by inheriting all the fields and methods of its superclass and adding more. The extra fields and methods make the subclass more restrictive, more special. The set of all subclass objects is a subset of the set of all its superclass objects. The set of all students is a subset of the set of all persons. Students are specialized persons.

Note that the essential criterion for class Y to be a subclass of class X is that class Y include all fields of class X. That means that the set of fields of a subclass is a superset of the set of fields of its superclass! That seems contradictory until you realize that specialization to a smaller group results from a larger set of criteria, because criteria are restrictions and more restrictions lead to smaller groups.

Inheritance means specialization, while composition means aggregation. The Student class is a specialization of the Person class, while it is an aggregate of the Name and String classes (and the char, int, and double types). Programmers often use the phrases "is a" and "has a" to distinguish inheritance from composition. A student "is a" person, while a student "has a" name.

The clear distinction between the "is a" and "has a" relationships can help you avoid making the mistake of defining a subclass when it should not be a subclass. That design error sometimes occurs when one assumes that inheritance simply means adding fields. For example, we could define a general Circle class with a single field for the radius of a circle. Then recognizing that cylinders are also geometric objects with radii, we might think that a general Cylinder class should be defined as a subclass of the Circle class, adding a second field for the height of a cylinder. But cylinders are not specialized circles. They don't even have the same dimension. Extending a Circle class to a Cylinder class is a misuse of inheritance.

7.7 CLASS HIERARCHIES

A class can have more than one subclass. For example, in addition to the Student class, we could also define the following subclasses of the Person class: Tailor, Butcher, Baker, CandleStickMaker, Lawyer, Judge, etc. Also, subclasses can have subclasses. For example, the subclass Student could have the subclass CollegeStudent (see Problem 7.12 on page 172), and that subclass could have the subclass GradStudent (see Problem 7.13). These relationships lead to a natural tree hierarchy of classes, as shown in the diagram at the top of the next page.

In a class hierarchy like this, we say that class *Y* is a *descendant* of class *X* if there is a sequence of classes beginning with *Y* and ending with *X* within which each class is the superclass of the one before it. For example, in the hierarchy shown above, the UnderGrad class is a descendant of the Person class because of the sequence UnderGrad → CollegeStudent → Student → Person. Also, if class *Y* is a descendant of class *X*, then we also say that class *X* is a *ancestor* of class *Y*. So, in the example above, the Person class is an ancestor of the UnderGrad class. The words "subclass" and "extension" are used transitively in Java, so they are also synonyms for the word "descendant:" the Person class is a subclass of the UnderGrad class.

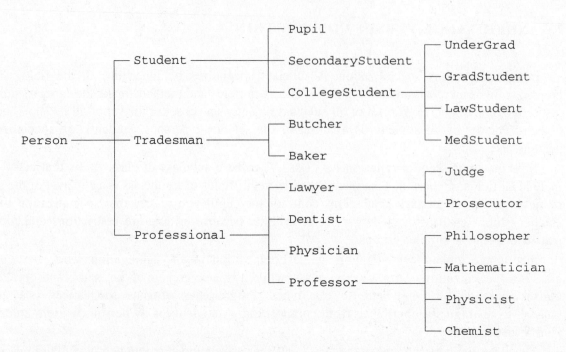

Within a class hierarchy, there are two special kinds of classes: abstract classes and final classes. These are identified by the `abstract` and `final` modifiers.

An *abstract class* is a class that has at least one abstract method. An *abstract method* is a method that is declared with only its signature; it has no implementation. Since it has at least one abstract method, an abstract class cannot be instantiated. Classes and methods are declared to be abstract by means of the `abstract` modifier.

EXAMPLE 7.9 An `abstract` Class

This example defines three classes: the `abstract` class `Shape`, and the two (concrete) classes `Circle` and `Square`. The latter are both subclasses of the former.

```
abstract class Shape
{ // Objects represent geometric shapes in the cartesian plane

    abstract Point center();

    abstract double diameter();
    abstract double area();
}
```

The abstract class `Shape` has three abstract methods: `center()`, `diameter()`, and `area()`. As abstract methods, they are declared with only their prototypes.

```
class Circle extends Shape
{ // Objects represent circles in the cartesian plane

    private Point center;
    private double radius;

    Circle(Point center, double radius)
    { this.center = center;
      this.radius = radius;
    }
```

```
      Point center()
      { return center;
      }

      double diameter()
      { return 2*radius;
      }

      double area()
      { return Math.PI*radius*radius;
      }

      public String toString()
      { return new String("{ center = " + center
          + ", radius = " + radius + "}");
      }
   }
```

The `Circle` class has two fields, one constructor, and four methods. The fields specify the circle's center and radius. The three (concrete) methods `center()`, `diameter()`, and `area()` implement the corresponding abstract methods declared in the superclass.

```
   class Square extends Shape
   { // Objects represent squares in the cartesian plane

      private Point northWestCorner;
      private double side;

      Square(Point northWestCorner, double side)
      { this.northWestCorner = northWestCorner;
        this.side = side;
      }

      Point center()
      { Point c = new Point(northWestCorner);
        c.translate(side/2, -side/2);
        return c;
      }

      double diameter()
      { return side*Math.sqrt(2.0);
      }

      double area()
      { return side*side;
      }

      public String toString()
      { return new String("{northWestCorner = " + northWestCorner
          + ", side = " + side + "}");
      }
   }
```

The `Square` class also has two fields, one constructor, and four methods. The fields specify the square's location and size. The three (concrete) methods `center()`, `diameter()`, and `area()` implement the corresponding abstract methods declared in the superclass.

Here is a test driver for the `Circle` class:

```
class TestCircle
{ // Test driver for the Circle class
   public static void main(String[] args)
    { Circle circle = new Circle(new Point(3,1),2.0);
      System.out.println("The circle is " + circle);
      System.out.println("Its center is " + circle.center());
      System.out.println("Its diameter is " + circle.diameter());
      System.out.println("Its area is " + circle.area());
    }
}
```

Its output is

```
The circle is: { center = (3.0, 1.0), radius = 2.0}
Its center is (3.0, 1.0)
Its diameter is 4.0
Its area is 12.566370614359172
```

Here is a test driver for the `Square` class:

```
class TestSquare
{ // Test driver for the Square class
   public static void main(String[] args)
    { Square square = new Square(new Point(1,5),3.0);
      System.out.println("The square is: " + square);
      System.out.println("Its center is " + square.center());
      System.out.println("Its diameter is " + square.diameter());
      System.out.println("Its area is " + square.area());
    }
}
```

Its output is

```
The square is {northWestCorner = (1.0, 5.0), side = 3.0}
Its center is (2.5, 3.5)
Its diameter is 4.242640687119286
Its area is 9.0
```

Note that the *diameter* of a geometric shape is defined to be the length of the longest line segment inside the shape. In the case of the circle, that is its diagonal length.

The circle and square objects and their reference location points look like the picture here in the cartesian plane.

An `abstract` method can be regarded as an outline or a specification contract. It specifies what its subclasses have to implement, but leaves the actual implementations up to them. For example, the abstract `area()` method is declared in the `Shape` class above, because we want every subclass to have a complete method that returns the areas of its instances, and we want all those methods to have the same signature:

```
double area()
```

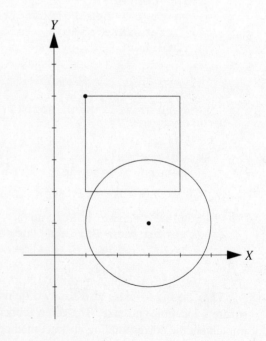

The abstract method in the abstract superclass enforces that specification.

An `abstract` method is one that is intended to be overridden in each of a whole family of subclasses. A `final` method is just the opposite: a method that cannot be overridden in any subclass. The main reason for declaring a method to be `final` is to guarantee that it cannot be changed.

An `abstract` class is one that has at least one `abstract` method. Similarly, a `final` class is one that has at least one `final` method.

7.8 THE `Object` CLASS

Java defines one special class, the `Object` class, which is the ancestor of every other class. It declares twelve members: a constructor and eleven methods. Since every class is a subclass of the `Object` class, every object can invoke these methods. Four of them, `clone()`, `hashCode()`, `equals()`, and `toString()`, are intended to be overridden. (See Section 7.10 on page 168.)

If you do not use the `extends` keyword explicitly to make your new class a subclass of another class, then it is automatically made a subclass of the `Object` class. So for example, the following two definitions are equivalent:

```
class Point
{ double x, y;
}

class Point extends Object
{ double x, y;
}
```

```
Object
    ├─AbstractCollection
    │   └─AbstractList
    │       └─AbstractSequentialList
    │           └─LinkedList
    ├─Boolean
    ├─Character
    ├─Class
    ├─Component
    │   ├─Container
    │   │   └─Window
    │   │       └─Frame
    │   └─TextComponent
    ├─Date
    ├─Math
    ├─Number
    │   ├─Byte
    │   ├─Double
    │   ├─Float
    │   ├─Integer
    │   ├─Long
    │   └─Short
    ├─Random
    ├─String
    ├─StringBuffer
    ├─System
    ├─Thread
    ├─Throwable
    │   ├─Exception
    │   │   ├─RuntimeException
    │   │   │   ├─ArithmeticException
    │   │   │   ├─IllegalArgumentException
    │   │   │   ├─IndexOutOfBoundsException
    │   │   │   └─NullPointerException
    │   │   ├─InterruptedException
    │   │   └─IOException
    │   │       ├─FileNotFoundException
    │   │       └─EOFException
    │   └─Error
    └─Vector
        └─Stack
```

7.9 THE JAVA CLASS HIERARCHY

This diagram above shows a very small part (less than 3%) of the class hierarchy in the Java class libraries (JDK 1.2 Beta). It shows, for example, that the `LinkedList` class is the great-great-grandchild of the `Object` class in the class genealogy. It also shows that most of the classes that we have been using so far (*e.g.*, the `Math` class, the `Random` class, the `String` class, the `System` class) are first-generation subclasses of the `Object` class. Note that the six wrapper classes for the numeric types (see Section 6.10 on page 133) are subclasses of the `Number` class, which is an abstract class (see page 167).

The subclasses of the `Throwable` class are the classes used for handling run-time errors in Java. They are described in Chapter 10.

The `Vector` class encapsulates the features of arrays, described in Chapter 8.

The subclasses of the `Component` class are the classes used for building graphical user interfaces. They are described in Chapter 9.

7.10 THE `clone()` AND `equals()` METHODS

The `clone()` and `equals()` methods are two of the twelve methods declared in the `Object` class. They are declared there to encourage you to override them in your own classes, thereby providing clean and consistent facilities for duplicating objects and determining when they are the same.

EXAMPLE 7.10 An `equals()` Method for the `Point` Class

Here is the `Point` class from Section 6.1:

```
class Point
{ // Objects represent points in the cartesian plane

  double x, y;  // the point's coordinates

  Point(double a, double b)
  { x = a;
    y = b;
  }

  boolean equals(Point p)
  { return (x == p.x && y == p.y);
  }

  public String toString()
  { return new String("(" + x + ", "  + y + ")");
  }
}
```

This local version of the `equals()` method to guarantee that `q.equals(p)` would not be false unless the two `Point` objects really did represent different points. Without this local version, this expression would invoke the `Object.equals()` method which would return false if the `Point` objects were distinct but equal.

The `equals()` method defined above does <u>not</u> override the `Object.equals()` method because their signatures are not quite the same. The signature of the former is `equals(Point)`; the signature of the latter is `equals(Object)`. So, here is the correct way to override the `equals()` method:

```
public boolean equals(Object p)
{ if (!(p instanceof Point)) return false;
  return (x == ((Point)p).x && y == ((Point)p).y);
}
```

The test driver in Example 6.1 works the same way with this corrected version.

EXAMPLE 7.11 The Preferred Overrides of the `clone()` and `Point` Methods

At last, here is the preferred version of our `Point` class:

```
class Point
{ // Objects represent points in the cartesian plane

  double x, y;  // the point's coordinates

  Point(double a, double b)
  { x = a;
    y = b;
  }

  public Object clone()
  { return new Point(x,y);
  }

  public boolean equals(Object p)
  { if (!(p instanceof Point)) return false;
    return (x == ((Point)p).x && y == ((Point)p).y);
  }

  public String toString()
  { return new String("(" + x + ", "  + y + ")");
  }
}
```

The test driver

```
class TestPoint
{ public static void main(String args[])
  { Point p = new Point(2,3);
    System.out.println("p = " + p);
    Point q = (Point)p.clone();
    System.out.println("q = " + q);
    if (q == p) System.out.println("q == p");
    else System.out.println("q != p");
    if (q.equals(p)) System.out.println("q equals p");
    else System.out.println("q does not equal p");
  }
}
```

has output

```
p = (2.0, 3.0)
q = (2.0, 3.0)
q != p
q equals p
```

The `Point.clone()` method creates a `Point` object with the same coordinates as its implicit argument, and then returns it. But, to override the `Object.clone()` method, the `Point.clone()` method must return an instance of the `Object` class. So the `Point` object being returned is recast as an `Object` object as it is returned. Then the statement

```
Point q = (Point)p.clone();
```
recasts it back to a `Point` object and then initializes `q` with it.

To override the `Object.equals()` method, the `Point.equals()` method must have a single parameter of the `Object` class. But that means that `p.equals(x)` could be invoked on an object `x` of <u>any</u> class since all classes are subclasses of the `Object` class. So it is the responsibility of the method itself to determine first whether its argument really is an instance of the `Point` class. That is done by the `instanceof` operator.

The condition `(x == ((Point)p).x && y == ((Point)p).y)` looks a little strange because of the `(Point)` cast. This is necessary because `p` is an instance of the `Object` class. So even though `p` has the proper `x` and `y` fields, they cannot be accessed from `p` directly. Java is a *strongly typed language*, so the *dot operator* (`.`) requires that the operand on its left be an instance of the class to which the member on the right belongs: `p` is an instance of the `Object` class, but `(Point)p` is an instance of the `Point` class.

Now we have two distinct `Point` objects that have the same data, one produced by cloning the other. So the equality operator `==` finds them unequal, while the `equals()` method finds them equal, just as before in the example on page 127. These overrides of the `clone()` and `equals()` methods are consistent with those in all the Java standard library classes.

Review Questions

7.1 What is the difference between composition and inheritance?

7.2 In Example 7.2 on page 150, how many objects will die if the statement
```
ann = new Person(new Name("Ann","Landers"), 'F');
```
executes after the others?

7.3 In Example 7.2 on page 150, how many objects will die if the statement
```
bob = new Person(new Name("Robert","Bruce"), 'M');
```
executes after the others?

7.4 Why wouldn't the `tab` field work properly in Example 7.3 on page 152 if it were not declared to be `static`?

7.5 What would go wrong in Example 7.4 on page 154 if the two lines
```
this.next = list;
list = this;
```
in the constructor were reversed?

7.6 In the `print()` method in Example 7.4 on page 154, why is it necessary to use the local variable `friend`, instead of using the `list` field directly?

7.7 Delete the `toString()` method from `ClassY` in Example on page 160 and then rerun it. The output is
```
Now in ClassX.f().
Now in ClassX.g().
x = { m=22, n=44 }
Now in ClassX.f().
Now in ClassY.g().
y = { m=22, n=0 }
```

Explain this different result.

7.8   What is the difference between overriding and overloading a method?

7.9   What is polymorphism?

Programming Problems

7.1   Modify the `Name` class defined in Example 7.1 on page 148 by adding the following three fields:

```
protected String prefix;  // e.g., "Dr."
protected String suffix;  // e.g., "Jr."
protected String nick;    // e.g., "Bill"
```

7.2   Implement an `Address` class for representing postal mailing addresses.

7.3   Implement a `Phone` class for representing telephone numbers.

7.4   Implement an `Email` class for representing email addresses.

7.5   Implement a `Url` class for representing Internet Uniform Resource Locator addresses.

7.6   Modify the `Person` class defined in Example 7.2 on page 150 by adding the following six fields:

```
protected Phone phone;    // home telephone number
protected Email email;    // Internet email address
protected Url url;        // Internet home page URL
```

7.7   Implement a class for celestial bodies (the sun, the planets, their moons, *etc.*). Include the following fields:

```
private String name;
private double mass;         // in grams
private double diameter;     // in kilometers
private double period;       // in earth days
private CelestialBody orbits;
private CelestialBody next;
static CelestialBody list;
```

The list field maintains a linked list of all the objects created, similar to that in Example 7.4 on page 154.

7.8   Modify the `Person` class defined in Example 7.3 on page 152 by adding these fields:

```
protected int number;         // the number of the object
protected static int count;   // number of Person objects in tree
```

Add to each constructor a statement that increments the counter, and modify the `toString()` method so that it prints the current count. Then test your modified class. If run on the same data as in Example 7.3, the output should look like this:

```
William Windsor (M) #1
  mother: Diana Spencer (F) #2
    father: Edward Spencer (M) #4
  father: Charles Windsor (M) #3
    mother: Elizabeth Windsor (F) #5
      mother: Elizabeth Bowes-Lyon (F) #7
      father: George Windsor (M) #8
    father: Philip Mountbatten (M) #6
```

This shows, for example, that the `Charles` object was created third.

7.9   Write an `insert()` method of the `Friend` class defined in Example 7.4 on page 154 so that the objects are inserted into the list in alphabetical order. Use the `compareTo()` method that is defined in the `String` class to determine the alphabetical ordering of two strings `p` and `q` like this::

```
(p.name.compareTo(q.name) < 0) // means that p precedes q
(p.name.compareTo(q.name) == 0) // means that p equals q
(p.name.compareTo(q.name) > 0) // means that p follows q
```

7.10 Modify the `Friend` class in Example 7.4 on page 154 so that it is a subclass of the `Person` class.

7.11 Add the following method to the `Student` class defined in Example 7.8 on page 161:

```
void update(int credit, char grade);
// Updates the student's credits and gpa by adding the new credit
// and recomputing the gpa based upon the new grade
```

For example, if `ann` has the data shown in Example 7.8, then the action

```
ann.update(4,'B');
```

would change `ann.credit` to 20 and `ann.gpa` to 3.4. Use the formula

$$newgpa = \frac{credits \times gpa + credit \times points}{credits + credit}$$

where points is the numerical equivalent (4, 3, 2, or 1) of the letter grade (A, B, C, or D).

7.12 Extend the `Student` class (Example 7.8 on page 161) to a subclass named `CollegeStudent` with a field named `year` for the year of the student's college graduation.

7.13 Extend the `CollegeStudent` class (Problem 7.12) to a subclass named `GradStudent` with a field named `degree` for the student's undergraduate degree.

7.14 Extend the `abstract` `Shape` class (Example 7.9 on page 164) to a concrete subclass named `Triangle` whose instances represent triangles in the cartesian plane. For the area() method, use the formula $\pm(x_1 y_2 + x_2 y_3 + x_3 y_1 - y_1 x_2 - y_2 x_3 - y_3 x_1)/2$ for the area of the triangle with vertices at (x_1, y_1), (x_2, y_2), and (x_3, y_3). You may also want to use a `private static` utility method that implements the following formula for the distance between two points (x_1, y_1) and (x_2, y_2):

$$\sqrt{(x_1 - x_2)^2 + (y_1 - y_2)^2}$$

(See Problem 6.20 on page 138.)

Answers to Review Questions

7.1   Composition is where one class is a component of another class. For example, the `Name` class is a component of the `Person` class. Inheritance is where one class extends another class. For example, the `Student` class extends the `Person` class. Composition is a "has a" relationship, while inheritance is an "is a" relationship. A person "has a" name, while a student "is a" person.

7.2   This statement removes the reference `ann` from its current referent, thereby killing that `Person` object. Since it itself has two non-null references, their referents (a `Name` object and a `String` object) are also killed. Also, the two `String` objects that are referenced by fields in that `Name` object die. So the net carnage is five dead objects.

7.3   This dereferences only the single `Person` object. The `Name` object (and its three affiliated `String` objects) survives because it retains its independent reference `bobsName`.

7.4   If it were not declared to be `static` in Example 7.3 on page 152, there would be a separate `tab` field in each `Person` object instead of just one for the entire class. Declaring it `static` makes it a *class field* instead of an *instance field*.

7.5   If the two lines
```
    this.next = list;
    list = this;
```
in the constructor were reversed in Example 7.4 on page 154, then the class variable `list` would be reassigned before its existing value is saved. But that value refers to the first object in the list. When all references to an object are removed, the objects dies. So in this case, the whole list would be lost. Also, if the first line above follows the second, it will make the object refer to itself.

7.6   If we used the `list` field directly in Example 7.4 instead of the local variable `friend`, it would empty the list! Each time the assignment
```
    list = list.next;
```
executes, the object to which `friend` refers would be dereferenced, killing that object.

7.7   With the `ClassY.toString()` method deleted, the statement
```
    System.out.println("y = " + y);
```
invokes the `ClassX.toString()` method instead.

7.8   A method is *overloaded* when another method with the same name but different parameter type list is declared in the same class. A method is *overridden* when another method with the same signature is declared in a subclass. For example, in Example 7.1 on page 148, the constructor `Name()` is overloaded twice in the `Name` class, and in Example 7.7 on page 160 the method `g()` declared in `ClassY` overrides the method `g()` declared in `ClassX`.

7.9   In object-oriented programming, the term "polymorphism" refers to the ability of objects to take the form objects of different classes. For example, in Example 7.7 on page 160, the object `y` is an instance of `ClassY` but is able to take the form of a `ClassX` object when it invokes the method `ClassX.f()`.

Solutions to Programming Problems

7.1
```
class Name
{ // Objects represent names of people

    protected String prefix;   // e.g., "Mr."
    protected String first;    // e.g., "William"
    protected String middle;   // e.g., "Jefferson"
    protected String last;     // e.g., "Clinton"
    protected String suffix;   // e.g., "Jr."
    protected String nick;     // e.g., "Bill"

    Name()  // default constructor
    {
    }

    Name(String nick)
    { this.nick = nick;
    }

    Name(String first, String last)
    { this.first = first;
      this.last = last;
    }
    Name(String first, String middle, String last)
    { this(first,last);
      this.middle = middle;
    }
    Name(String first, String middle, String last,
               String nick)
    { this(first,middle,last);
      this.nick = nick;
    }
```

```
Name(String prefix, String first, String middle,
          String last, String suffix)
{ this(first,middle,last);
  this.prefix = prefix;
  this.suffix = suffix;
}

Name(String prefix, String first, String middle,
          String last, String suffix, String nick)
{ this(prefix,first,middle,last,suffix);
  this.nick = nick;
}

String prefix()
{ return prefix;
}

String first()
{ return first;
}

String middle()
{ return middle;
}

String last()
{ return last;
}

String suffix()
{ return suffix;
}

String nick()
{ return nick;
}

void setPrefix(String prefix)
{ this.prefix = prefix;
}

void setFirst(String first)
{ this.first = first;
}

void setMiddle(String middle)
{ this.middle = middle;
}

void setLast(String last)
{ this.last = last;
}

void setSuffix(String suffix)
{ this.suffix = suffix;
}

void setNick(String nick)
{ this.nick = nick;
}
```

```
        public String toString()
        { String s = new String();
          if (prefix != null) s += prefix + " ";
          if (first != null) s += first + " ";
          if (middle != null) s += middle + " ";
          if (last != null) s += last + " ";
          if (suffix != null) s += suffix + " ";
          if (nick != null) s += "(\"" + nick + "\")";
          return s.trim();
        }
    }

    class TestName
    { public static void main(String[] args)
        { Name mlk = new Name("Dr.", "Martin", "Luther", "King", "Jr.");
          System.out.println(mlk + " won the 1964 Nobel Peace Prize.");
        }
    }
```

7.2
```
    class Address
    { // Objects represent mailing addresses

        private String street;
        private String city;
        private String state;
        private String zip;
        private String country;

        Address()
        {
        }

        Address(String city)
        { this.city = city;
        }
        Address(String street, String city)
        { this(city);
          this.street = street;
        }

        Address(String street, String city, String state)
        { this(street,city);
          this.state = state;
        }

        Address(String street, String city, String state,
                      String zip)
        { this(street,city,state);
          this.zip = zip;
        }

        Address(String street, String city, String state,
                      String zip, String country)
        { this(street,city,state,zip);
          this.country = country;
        }

        void setStreet(String street)
        { this.street = street;
        }
```

```
    void setCity(String city)
    { this.city = city;
    }

    void setState(String state)
    { this.state = state;
    }

    void setZip(String zip)
    { this.zip = zip;
    }

    void setCountry(String country)
    { this.country = country;
    }
    public String toString()
    { String s = new String();
      if (street != null) s += street + "\n";
      if (city != null) s += city + ", ";
      if (state != null) s += state + " ";
      if (zip != null) s += zip + "\n";
      if (country != null) s += country + " ";
      return s.trim();
    }
  }

  class TestAddress
  { public static void main(String[] args)
    { Name bg = new Name("William", "H.", "Gates", "Bill");
      Address bga = new Address("One Microsoft Way", "Redmond",
        "WA", "98052");
      System.out.println("The world's richest person is " + bg
        + ".\nHis address is:\n" + bga);
    }
  }
```

7.3
```
  class Phone
  { // Objects represent telephone numbers in the United States

    private String area;
    private String number;

    Phone()
    {
    }

    Phone(String s)
    { if (s.length() == 13)          // e.g., s = "(012)345-6789"
      { area = s.substring(1,4);     // e.g., "012"
        s = s.substring(5,13);       // e.g., "345-6789"
      }
      if (s.length() == 10)          // e.g., s = "0123456789"
      { area = s.substring(0,3);     // e.g., "012"
        s = s.substring(3,10);       // e.g., "3456789"
      }
      setNumber(s);
    }

    void setArea(String area)
    { this.area = area;
    }
```

```
    void setNumber(String s)
    { if (s.length() == 8)              // e.g., s = "345-6789"
        number = s.substring(0,3) +  s.substring(4,8);
      if (s.length() == 7)             // e.g., s = "3456789"
        number = s;
    }

    public String toString()
    { String s = new String();
      if (area != null) s += "(" + area + ")";
      if (number != null)
        s += number.substring(0,3) + "-"
           + number.substring(3,7);
      return s;
    }
}
class TestPhone
{ public static void main(String[] args)
  { Name bg = new Name("William", "H.", "Gates", "Bill");
    Address bga = new Address("One Microsoft Way", "Redmond",
      "WA", "98052");
    Phone bgp = new Phone("(425)882-8080");
    Phone bgf = new Phone("4259367329");
    System.out.println("The world's richest person is " + bg
      + ".\nHis address is:\n" + bga + "\nPhone: " + bgp
      + "\nFax: " + bgf);
  }
}
```

7.4

```
class Email
{ // Objects represent Internet email addresses
  private String username;
  private String hostname;

  Email()
  {
  }

  Email(String s)
  { int i = s.indexOf('@');
    if (i > -1)              // e.g., s = "jhubbard@richmond.edu"
    { username = s.substring(0,i);   // e.g., "jhubbard"
      hostname = s.substring(i+1);   // e.g., "richmond.edu"
    }
  }

  void setUsername(String username)
  { this.username = username;
  }

  public String toString()
  { String s = new String();
    if (username != null && hostname != null)
      s += username + "@" + hostname;
    return s;
  }
}
```

```
class TestEmail
{ public static void main(String[] args)
  { Name bg = new Name("William", "H.", "Gates", "Bill");
    Address bga = new Address("One Microsoft Way", "Redmond",
      "WA", "98052");
    Phone bgp = new Phone("(425)882-8080");
    Phone bgf = new Phone("4259367329");
    Email bge = new Email("bgates@microsost.com");
    System.out.println("The world's richest person is " + bg
      + ".\nHis address is:\n" + bga + "\nPhone: " + bgp
      + "\nFax: " + bgf + "\nEmail: " + bge);
  }
}
```

7.5
```
class Url
{ // Objects represent Internet web page addresses
  // e.g., "http://www.dell.com/products/dim/xpsr/index.htm"
  private String service;    // e.g., "http"
  private String host;       // e.g., "www.dell.com"
  private String path;       // e.g., "products/dim/xpsr"
  private String file;       // e.g., s = "index.html"

  Url()
  {
  }

  Url(String url)
  { setUrl(url);
  }

  String service()
  { return service;
  }

  String host()
  { return host;
  }

  String path()
  { return path;
  }

  String file()
  { return file;
  }

  void setUrl(String s)
  { // e.g., "http://www.dell.com/products/dim/xpsr/index.htm"
    int i = s.indexOf("://");          // e.g., i = 4
    if (i < 0) service = "http";       // not found
    else service = s.substring(0,i);   // e.g., "http"
    s = s.substring(i+3);
    // e.g., s = "www.dell.com/products/dim/xpsr/index.htm"
    i = s.indexOf('/');                // e.g., i = 13
    if (i < 0) return;                 // not found
    host = s.substring(0,i);           // e.g., "www.dell.com"
    s = s.substring(i+1);
    // e.g., s = "products/dim/xpsr/index.htm"
    i = s.lastIndexOf('/');            // e.g., i = 17
    if (i < 0) return;                 // not found
    path = s.substring(0,i);           // e.g., "products/dim/xpsr"
    file = s.substring(i+1);           // e.g., s = "index.html"
  }
```

```
        public String toString()
        { String s = new String();
          if (host != null)
          { if (service == null) s += "http://" + host + "/";
            else s += service + "://" + host + "/";
            if (path != null) s += path + "/";
            if (file != null) s += file;
          }
          return s;
        }
      }
      class TestUrl
      { public static void main(String[] args)
        { String s = "http://www.dell.com/products/dim/xpsr/index.htm";
          Url url = new Url(s);
          System.out.println("service = " + url.service());
          System.out.println("host = " + url.host());
          System.out.println("path = " + url.path());
          System.out.println("file = " + url.file());
          System.out.println("url = " + url);
          s = "http://gum.richmond.edu/~hubbard/books/pwj.html";
          url = new Url(s);
          System.out.println("service = " + url.service());
          System.out.println("host = " + url.host());
          System.out.println("path = " + url.path());
          System.out.println("file = " + url.file());
          System.out.println("url = " + url);
        }
      }
```

7.6
```
      class Person
      { // Objects represent people

        protected Name name;
        protected char sex;    // 'M' or 'F'
        protected String id;  // e.g., Social Security number
        protected Phone phone;     // home telephone number
        protected Email email;     // Internet email address
        protected Url url;         // Internet home page URL

        Person(Name name, char sex)
        { this.name = name;
          this.sex = sex;
        }

        Person(Name name, char sex, String id)
        { this.name = name;
          this.sex = sex;
          this.id = id;
        }
```

COMPOSITION AND INHERITANCE

```
    Name name()
    { return name;
    }

    char sex()
    { return sex;
    }

    String id()
    { return id;
    }

    Phone phone()
    { return phone;
    }

    Email email()
    { return email;
    }

    Url url()
    { return url;
    }

    void setId(String id)
    { this.id = id;
    }

    void setPhone(Phone phone)
    { this.phone = phone;
    }

    void setEmail(Email email)
    { this.email = email;
    }

    void setUrl(Url url)
    { this.url = url;
    }

    public String toString()
    { String s = new String(   "\n\t   name: " + name
                          + "\n\t    sex: " + sex);
      if (id != null)    s += "\n\t     id: " + id;
      if (phone != null) s += "\n\t  phone: " + phone;
      if (email != null) s += "\n\t  email: " + email;
      if (url != null)   s += "\n\t    url: " + url;
      return s;
    }
}

class TestPerson
{ // Test driver for the Person class:
  public static void main(String args[])
  { Person ann = new Person(new Name("Ann", "Baker"), 'F');
    System.out.println("ann: " + ann);
    ann.setId("053011736");
    System.out.println("ann: " + ann);
    ann.setPhone(new Phone("8043790610"));
    System.out.println("ann: " + ann);
    ann.setEmail(new Email("abaker@richmond.com"));
    System.out.println("ann: " + ann);
```

```
            ann.setUrl(new Url("www.richmond.edu/~abaker/index.html"));
            System.out.println("ann: " + ann);
        }
    }
```

7.7   `class CelestialBody`

```
{ // Objects represent celestial bodies: planets, moons, etc.

    private String name;
    private double mass;          // in grams
    private double diameter;      // in kilometers
    private double period;        // in earth days
    private CelestialBody orbits;
    private CelestialBody next;
    static CelestialBody list;

    static void print()
    { CelestialBody cb = list;
      int count = 0;
      while (cb != null)
      { System.out.println("\n" + ++count + ". " + cb);
        cb = cb.next;
      }
    }

    CelestialBody(String name)
    { this.name = name;
      next = list;
      list = this;
    }

    CelestialBody(String name, double mass, double diameter,
                  double period)
    { this.name = name;
      this.mass = mass;
      this.diameter = diameter;
      this.period = period;
      next = list;
      list = this;
    }

    CelestialBody(String name, double mass, double diameter,
                  double period, CelestialBody orbits)
    { this(name, mass, diameter, period);
      this.orbits = orbits;
    }

    public String toString()
    { String s = new String(      "\t     name: " + name);
      if (mass > 0.0) s += "\n\t     mass: " + mass + " grams";
      if (diameter > 0.0)
        s += "\n\t diameter: " + diameter + " kilometers";
        if (period > 0.0)   s += "\n\t   period: " + period + " days";
        if (orbits != null) s += "\n\t   orbits: " + orbits.name;
        return s;
    }
}

class TestCelestialBody
{ // Test driver for the CelestialBody class:
  public static void main(String args[])
  { CelestialBody sun
      = new CelestialBody("Sol", 1.99E33, 1.392E6, 8.218E10);
```

```
      CelestialBody mars
        = new CelestialBody("Mars", 6.418E28, 6.7938E3, 686.98, sun);
      CelestialBody marsMoon1
        = new CelestialBody("Deimos", 2E18, 15, 1.26244, mars);
      CelestialBody.print();
    }
  }
```

7.8
```
class Person
{ // Objects represent names of people

  private Name name;
  private char sex;         // 'M' or 'F'
  private String id;        // e.g., Social Security number
  private Person mother;
  private Person father;
  private int number;       // the number of the object

  private static final String blanks = "   ";
  private static String tab = "";
  private static int count;  // number of person objects in tree

  Person(Name name, char sex)
  { this.name = name;
    this.sex = sex;
    number = ++count;
  }

  Person(Name name, char sex, String id)
  { this.name = name;
    this.sex = sex;
    this.id = id;
    number = ++count;
  }

  public String toString()
  { String s = new String(name + " (" + sex + ") #" + number);
    if (id != null) s += "; id: " + id;
    s += "\n";
    if (mother != null)
    { tab += blanks;
      s += tab + "mother: " + mother;
      tab = tab.substring(0, tab.length() - 2);
    }
    if (father != null)
    { tab += blanks;
      s += tab + "father: " + father;
      tab = tab.substring(0, tab.length() - 2);
    }
    return s;
  }

  // other methods are the same as in Example 7.3 on page 152
}
```

7.9
```
class Friend
{ // Objects represent my friends

  private String name;       // e.g., "Bill Ross"
  private String telephone;  // e.g., "283-9104"
  private Friend next;       // next object in list
  static Friend list;
```

```
     static void print()
     { Friend friend = list;
       if (friend == null) System.out.println("The list is empty.");
       else do
       { System.out.println(friend);
         friend = friend.next;
       } while (friend != null);
     }

     Friend(String name, String telephone)
     { this.name = name;
       this.telephone = telephone;
       if (list == null) list = this;
       else if (list.name.compareTo(name) > 0)
       { next = list;
         list = this;
       }
       else
       { Friend p = list;
         Friend q = p.next;
         while (q != null && q.name.compareTo(name) < 0)
         { p = q;
           q = q.next;
         }
         p.next = this;
         next = q;
       }
     }

     public String toString()
     { return new String(name + ":\t" + telephone);
     }
   }

   class TestFriend
   { // Test driver for the Friend class:
     public static void main(String args[])
     { Friend.print();
       new Friend("Ryle, Martin", "388-1095");
       new Friend("Ross, Bill", "283-9104");
       new Friend("Withers, Nat", "217-5912");
       new Friend("Anderson, Gene", "283-4490");
       new Friend("Tarver, Jerry", "379-0226");
       new Friend("Martin, Erika", "217-8451");
       Friend.print();
       try { System.in.read(); }
       catch (Exception e) {}
     }
   }
```

7.10
```
   class Friend extends Person
   { // Objects represent my friends
     protected String telephone;  // e.g., "283-9104"
     protected Friend next;        // next object in list
     static Friend list;
     static void print()
     { Friend friend = list;
       if (friend == null) System.out.println("The list is empty.");
       else do
       { System.out.println(friend);
         friend = friend.next;
       } while (friend != null);
     }
```

```
    static void insert(Friend f)
    { f.next = list;
      list = f;
    }

    Friend(String name, char sex, String telephone)
    { super(null,sex);
      int i = name.indexOf(' ');
      String firstName = name.substring(0,i);
      String lastName = name.substring(i+1);
      this.name = new Name(firstName,lastName);
      this.telephone = telephone;
    }

    public String toString()
    { return new String(name + ":\t" + telephone);
    }
  }

class TestFriend
{ // Test driver for the Friend class:
  public static void main(String args[])
  { Friend.print();
    Friend.insert(new Friend("Clarence Jung", 'M', "388-1905"));
    Friend.insert(new Friend("Rob James", 'M', "217-6143"));
    Friend.insert(new Friend("Dick Dunsing", 'M', "217-5192"));
    Friend.print();
  }
}
```

7.11
```
class Student extends Person
{ // Objects represent students

  protected int credits;   // credit hours earned
  protected double gpa;     // grade-point average

  Student(Name name, char sex)
  { super(name, sex);
  }

  int credits()
  { return credits;
  }

  double gpa()
  { return gpa;
  }

  void setCredits(int credits)
  { if (credits < 0 || credits > 200) this.credits = 0;
    else this.credits = credits;
  }

  void setGpa(double gpa)
  { if (gpa < 0.0 || gpa > 4.0) this.gpa = 0.0;
    else this.gpa = gpa;
  }
```

```
        void update(int credit, char grade)
        // Updates the studentís credits and gpa by adding the
        // new credit and recomputing the gpa
        { int points = 0;
          switch (grade)
          { case 'A': ++points;
            case 'B': ++points;
            case 'C': ++points;
            case 'D': ++points;
          }
          double num = credits*gpa + credit*points;
          credits += credit;
          gpa = num/credits;
        }

        public String toString()  // overrides Person.toString()
        { String s = new String(super.toString());
          if (credits > 0) s += "\n\tcredits: " + credits;
          if (gpa > 0.0) s += "\n\tgpa:      " + gpa;
          return s;
        }
      }

      class TestStudent
      { public static void main(String args[])
        { Name annsName = new Name("Ann", "Baker");
          Student ann = new Student(annsName, 'F');
          ann.setCredits(16);
          ann.setGpa(3.5);
          System.out.println("ann: " + ann);
          ann.update(4,'A');
          System.out.println("ann: " + ann);
        }
      }
```

7.12
```
      class CollegeStudent extends Student
      { // Objects represent college students

        protected String year;   // year of graduation

        CollegeStudent(Name name, char sex, int credits, double gpa,
                      String year)
        { super(name, sex, credits, gpa);
          this.year = year;
        }

        String year()
        { return year;
        }

        public String toString()
        { String s = new String(super.toString());
          s += "\n\tyear:     " + year;
          return s;
        }
      }
```

```
class TestCollegeStudent
{ public static void main(String args[])
   { Name annsName = new Name("Ann", "Baker");
     CollegeStudent ann
        = new CollegeStudent(annsName, 'F', 16, 3.5, "2002");
     System.out.println("ann: " + ann);
   }
}
```

7.13
```
class GradStudent extends CollegeStudent
{ // Objects represent college students

   protected String degree;    // undergraduate degree

   GradStudent(Name name, char sex, int credits, double gpa,
                 String year, String degree)
   { super(name, sex, credits, gpa, year);
     this.degree = degree;
   }

   String degree()
   { return degree;
   }

   public String toString()
   { String s = new String(super.toString());
     s += "\n\tdegree:  " + degree;
     return s;
   }
}
```

```
class TestGradStudent
{ public static void main(String args[])
   { Name annsName = new Name("Ann", "Baker");
     GradStudent ann
        = new GradStudent(annsName, 'F', 16, 3.5, "2002", "A.B.");
     System.out.println("ann: " + ann);
   }
}
```

7.14
```
class Triangle extends Shape
{ // Objects represent triangle in the cartesian plane

   private Point a, b, c;

   Triangle(Point a, Point b, Point c)
   { this.a = a;
     this.b = b;
     this.c = c;
   }

   Point center()
   { double x = (a.x + b.x + c.x)/3;
     double y = (a.y + b.y + c.y)/3;
     return new Point(x,y);
   }

   private static double d(Point p, Point q)
   { double dx = p.x - q.x;
     double dy = p.y - q.y;
     return Math.sqrt(dx*dx + dy*dy);
   }
```

```
      double diameter()
      { double diam = d(a,b);
        if (d(b,c) > diam) diam = d(b,c);
        if (d(c,a) > diam) diam = d(c,a);
        return diam;
      }

      double area()
      { double d = a.x*b.y + b.x*c.y + c.x*a.y
                 - a.y*b.x - b.y*c.x - c.y*a.x;
        return 0.5*( d>0 ? d : -d );
      }

      public String toString()
      { return new String("{a= = " + a + ", b = " + b
          + ", c = " + c + "}");
      }
    }

    class TestTriangle
    { // Test driver for the Triangle class
      public static void main(String[] args)
      { Point a = new Point(2,1);
        Point b = new Point(4,-1);
        Point c = new Point(5,4);
        Triangle triangle = new Triangle(a,b,c);
        System.out.println("The triangle is: " + triangle);
        System.out.println("Its center is " + triangle.center());
        System.out.println("Its diameter is " + triangle.diameter());
        System.out.println("Its area is " + triangle.area());
      }
    }
```

Chapter 8

Arrays and Vectors

An *array* is an object that consists of a sequence of numbered elements that have the same type. The elements are numbered beginning with 0 and can be referenced by their number using the *subscript operator* []. Arrays are widely used because of their efficiency.

8.1 CHARACTER ARRAYS

One of the simplest kinds of arrays are those whose element type is char. We saw in Chapter 2 that strings are nearly the same as character arrays. Here is part of the program from Example 2.1 on page 20 again:

EXAMPLE 8.1 A Simple String Object

This program prints some of the properties of a String object named alphabet.

```
public class TestStringProperties
{ // tests String properties
  public static void main(String[] args)
  { String alphabet = "ABCDEFGHIJKLMNOPQRSTUVWXYZ";
    System.out.println(alphabet);
    System.out.println("This string contains " + alphabet.length()
      + " characters.");
    System.out.println("The character at index 4 is "
      + alphabet.charAt(4));
    System.out.println("The index of the character Z is "
      + alphabet.indexOf('Z'));
  }
}
```

The output is

```
ABCDEFGHIJKLMNOPQRSTUVWXYZ
This string contains 26 characters.
The character at index 4 is E
The index of the character Z is 25
```

The object named alphabet is declared on the third line to be an instance of the String class and is initialized with the string literal value "ABCDEFGHIJKLMNOPQRSTUVWXYZ". It looks like this:

Technically, alphabet is not the name of the object; it is the name of a reference variable that refers to instances of the String class, and currently refers to one that represents the string "ABCDEFGHIJKLMNOPQRSTUVWXYZ". That is a result of the third line of code which does both the declaration of the reference and its initialization. They could also have been done separately, like this:

```
String alphabet;         // declares alphabet to be a String reference
alphabet = "ABCDEFGHIJKLMNOPQRSTUVWXYZ";  // initializes the reference
```

But the single line of code works just is well and so is preferred.

188

A `String` object is an instance of the `String` class. A *character array* is an array object whose elements have type `char`. The next example illustrates the differences between `String` objects and `char` arrays.

EXAMPLE 8.2 Comparing a `String` Object with a `char` Array

```
class TestCharArrays
{ // Tests the String.toCharArray() method and array access
  public static void main(String args[])
  { String s = new String("ABCDEFG");
    char[] a = s.toCharArray();
    System.out.println("s = \"" + s + "\"\t\ta = \"" + a + "\"");
    System.out.println("s.length() = " + s.length()
      + "\t\ta.length = " + a.length);
    for (int i=0; i<s.length(); i++)
      System.out.println("s.charAt(" + i + ") = " + s.charAt(i)
        + "\t\ta[" + i + "] = " + a[i]);
  }
}
```

The output is

```
s = "ABCDEFG"            a = "ABCDEFG"
s.length() = 7           a.length = 7
s.charAt(0) = A          a[0] = A
s.charAt(1) = B          a[1] = B
s.charAt(2) = C          a[2] = C
s.charAt(3) = D          a[3] = D
s.charAt(4) = E          a[4] = E
s.charAt(5) = F          a[5] = F
s.charAt(6) = G          a[6] = G
```

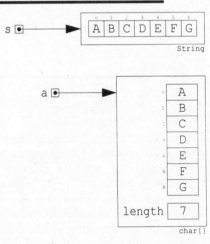

Each line of output compares the way the two objects `s` and `a` handle their respective operations. Both objects represent the 7-letter string "ABCDEFG". The `String` object `s` is created by the `new` operator invoking the `String` constructor that takes a single `char` array argument. It is passed the argument "ABCDEFG" and creates the object `s` shown here. The array object `a` is created by invoking the `String.toCharArray()` method bound to the `String` object `s`. Note that, like `s`, `a` is actually a reference variable; `s` refers to a `String` object, while `a` refers to a `char[]` object.

Array objects have a `public` field named `length` which stores the number of elements in the array. So the expression `a.length` is analogous to the invocation `s.length()`; each evaluates to 7 in this example.

The subscript operator `[]` provides access to the individual elements of the array. The expression `a[i]` is analogous to the invocation `s.charAt(i)`; each returns the character at index number `i`.

Arrays are almost always processed using for loops. The index of the `for` loop matches the array index, both ranging from `0` to `a.length-1`. So the form

```
for (int i=0; i<a.length; i++)
  // ...
```

is the preferred control mechanism.

Warning: Like strings, arrays use *zero-based indexing*. The means the first element has index 0, the second element has index 1, the third element has index 2, *etc*. In general, the ith element has index $i–1$. Consequently, an array of length n has index numbers from 0 to $n–1$. There is no element with index number n. For example, the array a in Example 8.2 has length 7, which means that it contains 7 elements. But any attempt to access a[7] will fail, throwing an exception.

EXAMPLE 8.3 A Method for Removing All Occurrences of a Character from a String

This example tests a method that removes all occurrences of a given character in a given string. It illustrates the use of a character array for string processing.

```
class TestStripMethod
{ // Test driver for the strip() method

  static String strip(String s, char c)
  { int n = s.length();
    char[] a = new char[n];
    int i=0;
    int j=0;
    while (i+j < n)
    { char sc = s.charAt(i+j);// i+j is the current index in s
      if (sc == c) j++;       // j is the number of characters removed
      else a[i++] = sc;       // i characters have been copied into a
    }
    return new String(a,0,i); // duplicates a as a String object
  }

  public static void main(String args[])
  { String s = new String("ABCAAADEAFA");
    System.out.println(s);
    s = strip(s, 'A');
    System.out.println(s);
  }
}
```

The output is
```
ABCAAADEAFA
BCDEF
```

The table at the top of the next page shows a complete trace of the method executing on the string s.

The while loop iterates 11 times, once for each character in s. The index i always locates the current position in the character array a. The counter j always equals the number of occurrences of the character 'A' that have been removed. These two conditions, together with the fact that i+j always locates the current character in the string s, are *loop invariants*: they are true on every iteration of the loop. They guarantee that the method works.

On each iteration of the while loop, the next character in s is compared with the target character c. If they are equal, j is incremented so that i+j will locate the next character in s for the next iteration. This counts that occurrence of c but does not copy it into a. Only when sc is not equal to c will it be copied into a. In

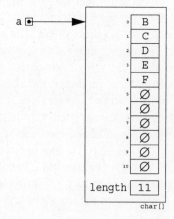

that case, i is post-incremented (*i.e.*, it is incremented after its current value has been used), thereby counting the number of characters copied into a.

When the loop terminates, the array a looks like this: Then the last line in the method invokes one of the String constructors to reproduce the array as a String object to be returned.

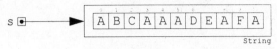

The symbol ∅ is used here to stand for the *null character*. That is the invisible character that produces no discernible effect when displayed or printed. Unlike an ordinary blank, the null character is undetectable. Its Unicode is 0, so it can be expressed in Java source code as '\u0000'. In general, any one of the 65,536 16-bit Unicode characters can be expressed in the form '\unnnn', where each n is one of the 16 hexadecimal numerals. (See Appendixes D and E.) For example, the question mark character '?' is expressed as '\u003F', and the infinity symbol '∞' is expressed as '\u221E'.

i	j	i+j	sc	a[i]
0	0	0	A	
	1	1	B	B
1		2	C	C
2		3	A	
	2	4	A	
	3	5	A	
	4	6	D	D
3		7	E	E
4		8	A	
	5	9	F	F
5		10	A	
	6	11		

8.2 PROPERTIES OF ARRAYS IN JAVA

In Java you can create an array whose element type is any one of the eight primitive types or any reference type. The syntax is

```
element-type[] name;          // declares the array
name = new element-type[n];   // allocates storage for n elements
```

As with single objects, both the declaration and allocation can be combined in a single declaration with initialization:

```
element-type[] name = new element-type[n];
```

Here are some examples:

```
float[] x;      // declares x to be a reference to an array of floats
x = new float[8];  // allocates an array of 8 floats, referenced by x
boolean[] flags = new boolean[1024];
String[] names = new String[32];
Point[] ideal = new Point[1000];
```

Note that when the element type is a reference, *e.g.*, to such as String objects, the allocation is made only to references to objects of that class.

EXAMPLE 8.4 When Are the Elements of an Array Allocated?

```
class TestAllocation
{ // tests the allocation of an array of objects
  public static void main(String args[])
  { String[] name;                    // allocates 1 reference
    name = new String[4];             // allocates 4 references
    System.out.println("name[0] = \"" + name[0] + "\"");
    name[0] = new String("ABC");   // allocates 1 3-char string
```

```
    for (int i=1; i<name.length; i++)
       name[i] = new String();     // allocates 3 0-char strings
    name[3] = "OK";                // allocates 1 8-char string
    for (int i=0; i<name.length; i++)
       System.out.println("name[" + i + "] = \"" + name[i] + "\"");
  }
}
```

The output is
```
name[0] = "null"
name[0] = "ABC"
name[1] = ""
name[2] = ""
name[3] = "OK."
```

The first line of `main()` declares `name` to be a reference to arrays of `String` objects. It allocates storage only for the reference itself. No objects have been created yet. (The `new` operator has not been used yet.) The reference `name` looks like the top picture here.

The second line of `main()` initializes the reference `name` by creating an array object of 4 elements. At this point, the elements are null references. The array object looks like the second picture here.

The third line prints the value of the first element, `name[0]`. It is still null.

The fourth line creates the `String` object that represents "ABC" and assigns `name[0]` to refer to it. Now there exist two objects in the program: the `String[]` object referenced by `name`, and the `String` object referenced by `name[0]`. The third picture here depicts that result.

The `for` loop creates three more `String` objects, and assigns them to the three references `name[1]`, `name[2]`, and `name[3]`. Each of these objects is an empty string. Then the next line replaces the empty string `name[3]` with the `String` object that represents "OK". That result is shown here in the fourth picture. The null string that `name[3]` had been referencing is now dead because it lost its reference to the "OK" string.

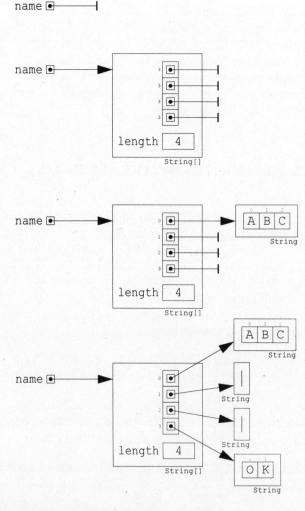

Note that there are five objects at the end of the program: one `String[]` object and four `String` objects. They have the references `name`, `name[0]`, `name[1]`, `name[2]`, and `name[3]`, respectively.

Whenever an array object is allocated (as on the second line of Example 8.4 on page 191), its elements are automatically initialized with their default initial field values. (See page 122.) That is 0 for integer fields (`byte`, `short`, `int`, and `long`), 0.0 for floating-point fields (`float` and `double`), `false` for `boolean`, `'\u0000'` for `char`, and `null` for any reference type.

You can initialize an array explicitly with an *initialization list*, like this:

```
int[] c = {44, 88, 55, 33};
```
This single line is equivalent to the following six lines:
```
int[] c;
c = new int[4];
c[0] = 44;
c[1] = 88;
c[2] = 55;
c[3] = 33;
```
Explicit array initializations are a very nice feature in Java. They should be used regularly.

8.3 COPYING AN ARRAY

EXAMPLE 8.5 Arrays Cannot be Copied by Using the Assignment Operator

This example shows what happens if you try to use the assignment operator to copy an array:
```
class Example0805
{ // tests the effect of assigning an array
  public static void main(String args[])
  { double[] x = {2.2, 4.4};
    print(x, "x");
    double[] y = {1.1, 3.3, 5.5};
    print(y, "y");
    y = x;               // attempts to copy x into y
    print(y, "y");
    x[0] = 8.8;
    print(x, "x");
    print(y, "y");
  }
  static void print(double[] u, String id)
  { for (int i=0; i<u.length; i++)
      System.out.println(id + "[" + i + "] = " + u[i]);
    System.out.println();
  }
}
```
The output is
```
x[0] = 2.2
x[1] = 4.4

y[0] = 1.1
y[1] = 3.3
y[2] = 5.5

y[0] = 2.2
y[1] = 4.4

x[0] = 8.8
x[1] = 4.4
```

```
y[0] = 8.8
y[1] = 4.4
```

The array `x` is initialized to be a two-element array of `doubles` and `y` is initialized to be a different, three-element array of `doubles`. Then the assignment operator is used to attempt to copy `x` into `y`. But, as the output shows, it doesn't work.

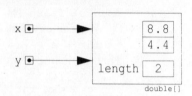

The picture on the right here shows what the problem is. When the assignment statement

```
y = x;
```

executed, the three-element array to which `y` had been referring died because it lost its reference. But the assignment changes only the value of the reference itself, simply reassigning it to refer to the other existing array object. So the result is that now both `x` and `y` refer to the same single array. Thus, when the assignment

```
x[0] = 8.8;
```

changes the first element of `x`, it also changes the first element of `y`, because they are the same element.

Java provides a special universal method for copying arrays. It is a member of the `System` class, declared as

```
public static void arraycopy(Object src, int srcPos,
                             Object dst, int dstPos, int count)
```

It copies elements from the source array `src` into the destination array `dst`. The number of elements to be copied is passed to the parameter `count`. The index position of the first element in the source array to be copied is passed to the parameter `srcPos`, and the location to where it is to be copied in the destination array is passed to the parameter `dstPos`.

Example 8.5 illustrates how to declare an array parameter in a method and how to pass an array argument to a method. Array parameters are declared the same way that array fields are declared, using the subscript operator as a suffix to the element type:

```
static void print(double[] u, String id)
```

And array arguments are passed to methods the same way that ordinary variables are passed, by name:

```
print(x, "x");
```

EXAMPLE 8.6 Using the `System.arraycopy()` Method to Copy an Array

This is the same program as in Example 8.5 except that the array assignment statement has been replaced by the invocation of the `System.arraycopy()` method.

```
class TestArraycopy
{ // tests the System.arraycopy() method
  public static void main(String args[])
  { double[] x = {2.2, 4.4};
    print(x, "x");
    double[] y = {1.1, 3.3, 5.5};
    print(y, "y");
    System.arraycopy(x, 0, y, 0, x.length);  // copies x into y
    print(y, "y");
    x[0] = 8.8;
    print(x, "x");
    print(y, "y");
  }
```

```
     static void print(double[] u, String id)
     { for (int i=0; i<u.length; i++)
         System.out.println(id + "[" + i + "] = " + u[i]);
       System.out.println();
     }
   }
```

The output is

```
x[0] = 2.2
x[1] = 4.4

y[0] = 1.1
y[1] = 3.3
y[2] = 5.5

y[0] = 2.2
y[1] = 4.4
y[2] = 5.5

x[0] = 8.8
x[1] = 4.4

y[0] = 2.2
y[1] = 4.4
y[2] = 5.5
```

The invocation

```
System.arraycopy(x, 0, y, 0, x.length);
```

copies the values of the two elements `x[0]` and `x[1]` into `y[0]` and `y[1]`, respectively. The two arrays remain distinct, as can be seen from the last two blocks of output. They show that the assignment

```
     x[0] = 8.8;
```

changes the first element of `x` but has no effect upon the independent array `y`.

8.4 THE `Vector` CLASS

The element type of an array can be any one of the eight primitive types or a reference type. For primitive types, you declare the array by using the name of the type, like this:

```
   double[] x;  // an array of floating-point numbers
```

For reference types, you declare the array by using the name of the class to which the references refer, like this:

```
   Person[] list;  // a list of people
```

Here, each element of the array is then a reference to objects of that class. But then, by the rules of inheritance, each element can also refer to any object of any subclass of that class. For example:

```
   list = new Person[4];
   list[0] = Person("John Adams");
   list[1] = GradStudent("Ann Baker");
   list[2] = Dentist("Willy Lewis");
   list[3] = Judge("John Marshall");
```

Although each of these elements is, by inheritance, a `Person` object, we really obtain a heterogeneous list this way. This is an example of object-oriented programming feature called *polymorphism*, allowing the array elements to have "many forms."

The most liberal use of the polymorphism described above results when you use the `Object` class, the ultimate superclass, as the array's reference type.

EXAMPLE 8.7 An Array of `Object` Objects

```
class TestObjectArray
{ // tests the Vector class
  public static void main(String args[])
  { Object[] a = new Object[6];
    a[0] = new Point(2,3);
    a[1] = new String("Hello, World!");
    a[2] = new Long(44);
    a[3] = new Name("James","Gosling");
    a[4] = new CelestialBody("Jupiter",18.99E29,142800,4331.7);
    for (int i=0; i<a.length; i++)
      System.out.println("a[" + i + "] = " + a[i]);
  }
}
```
The output is
```
a[0] = (2.0, 3.0)
a[1] = Hello, World!
a[2] = 44
a[3] = James Gosling
a[4] =    name: Jupiter
          mass: 1.899E30 grams
      diameter: 142800.0 kilometers
        period: 4331.7 days
a[5] = null
```

Each element of the array a is `a` reference to an `Object` object. But by inheritance, _every_ object is an `Object` object. So this array can store anything! It is truly a universal array.

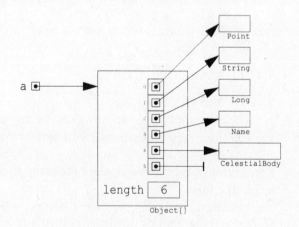

As you should expect by now, every good idea in Java is eventually encapsulated into a class. The idea of a universal array, illustrated in Example 8.7, is encapsulated into the `Vector` class. A `Vector` object is essentially a realizable universal array that is "smart" in the sense that it automatically increases its size when needed. Ordinary arrays can't do that: the `length` field of an array object is `final` (constant).

The `Vector` class is defined in the `java.util` package, so you need to include the `import` statement
```
    import java.util.Vector;
```
to use the `Vector` class.

EXAMPLE 8.8 The Telephone List of Friends Again

Here is the program from Example 7.4 on page 156, done using a `Vector` object:

```java
import java.util.Vector;

class TestFriends
{ // Tests a telephone list of friends
  public static void main(String args[])
  { Vector friends = new Vector();
    friends.addElement(new Friend("Martin", "388-1095"));
    friends.addElement(new Friend("Bill", "283-9104"));
    friends.addElement(new Friend("Nat", "217-5912"));
    System.out.println(friends);
  }
}
```

The output is

```
[Martin: 388-1095, Bill: 283-9104, Nat: 217-5912]
```

The default constructor for the `Vector` class creates the `Vector` object `friends`. We then invoke its `addElement()` method three times to add the `Friend` objects to the list. Then its `toString()` method is invoked implicitly by the `System.out.println()` method to print the entire list.

A `Vector` object in Java is really a dynamic list. Elements can be added or removed from any location in the list. This is achieved using the following methods:

```java
void addElement(Object o)
// adds the object o to the end of the list

boolean contains(Object o)
// returns true iff the object o is in the list

Object elementAt(int i)
// returns the object at position i in the list

Object firstElement()
// returns a reference to the first object in the list

int indexOf(Object o)
// returns the index (or -1) of the first occurrence of the object o

int indexOf(Object o, int i)
// returns the index (or -1) of the first occurrence of the object o,
// searching the list beginning at position i

void insertElementAt(Object o, int i)
// inserts the object o at position i in the list

boolean isEmpty()
// returns true iff the list is empty

Object lastElement()
// returns a reference to the last object in the list

int lastIndexOf(Object o)
// returns the index of the last occurrence of the object o
```

```
int lastIndexOf(Object o, int i)
// returns the index of the last occurrence of the object o,
// searching the list backwards beginning at position i

void removeAllElements()
// removes all the objects in the list;

boolean removeElement(object o)
// removes the first occurrence of the object o in the list;
// returns true iff it was found

void removeElementAt(int i)
// removes the object at position i in the list;

int size()
// returns the number of elements in the list
```
The `addElement()` method was used in Example 8.8.

EXAMPLE 8.9 Rearranging Elements of a Vector

This example expands the program in Example 8.8.
```
import java.util.Vector;

class TestFriends
{ // Tests a telephone list of friends
  public static void main(String args[])
  { Vector friends = new Vector();
    friends.addElement(new Friend("Martin", "388-1095"));
    friends.addElement(new Friend("Bill", "283-9104"));
    friends.addElement(new Friend("Nat", "217-5912"));
    System.out.println(friends);
    friends.insertElementAt(friends.elementAt(2), 0);
    System.out.println(friends);
    friends.removeElementAt(3);
    System.out.println(friends);
  }
}
```
The output is
```
[Martin: 388-1095, Bill: 283-9104, Nat: 217-5912]
[Nat: 217-5912, Martin: 388-1095, Bill: 283-9104, Nat: 217-5912]
[Nat: 217-5912, Martin: 388-1095, Bill: 283-9104]
```

After creating the same list as in Example 8.8, this program uses the `insertElementAt()` and `removeElementAt()` methods to move the third `Friend` object to the front of the list.

8.5 THE SIZE AND CAPACITY OF A `Vector` OBJECT

The *length* of an array is the number of elements that it has. If the element type is a reference type, then some of those elements may be `null`. So the number of objects referenced by the array may be less than its length. For example, the allocated array in Example 8.4 on page 191 has length 4, even though the number of objects referenced changes from 0 to 1 to 4. The `length` of an allocated array is constant.

The situation is different for `Vector` objects. Instead of a length, a vector has a *size*, which is the number of `Object` references it contains. This number is dynamic; it changes each time an object is added to or removed from the vector.

In addition to its size, a vector also has a *capacity*, which is the number of spaces it has allocated to hold `Object` references. This number is always greater than or equal to its size. If they are equal when the `addElement()` method is invoked, the capacity is increased automatically to accommodate the new element. This is illustrated in the next example.

EXAMPLE 8.10 The Size and Capacity of a `Vector` Object

This program processes a list of strings. It prints the current contents, size, and capacity of the list after elements are added.

```java
import java.util.Vector;

class TestSize
{ public static void main(String args[])
  { Vector v = new Vector();
    print(v);
    v.addElement("A");
    print(v);
    v.addElement("B");
    print(v);
    for (int i=0; i<8; i++)   // insert 8 more elements
      v.addElement("C");
    print(v);
    v.addElement("D");
    print(v);
  }

  static void print(Vector v)
  { System.out.println("v = " + v);
    System.out.print("v.size() = " + v.size());
    System.out.println(",\tv.capacity() = " + v.capacity());
    System.out.println();
  }
}
```

The output is

```
v = []
v.size() = 0,    v.capacity() = 10

v = [A]
v.size() = 1,    v.capacity() = 10

v = [A, B]
v.size() = 2,    v.capacity() = 10

v = [A, B, C, C, C, C, C, C, C, C]
v.size() = 10,   v.capacity() = 10

v = [A, B, C, C, C, C, C, C, C, C, D]
v.size() = 11,   v.capacity() = 20v.size() = 11,v.capacity() = 20
```

Initially, the vector is empty, so its size is 0. But its capacity is initialized automatically to 10, which means we can insert up to 10 elements before it will have to be re-allocated, as the output shows. Note that when the vector is re-allocated, its capacity is doubled.

When the capacity of a vector changes, the vector has to be rebuilt. This means that a separate larger block of memory has to be allocated, the complete vector (including all its references, but not the objects to which they refer) is moved to that new location, and then the previously occupied space is de-allocated. This rebuilding process takes time, so it is better to try to minimize the frequency with which it occurs. One way to do that is to allocate enough space by specifying its capacity explicitly. This can be done by passing a capacity number to the constructor when the vector is created or to the `ensureCapacity()` method later.

EXAMPLE 8.11 Setting a Vector's Capacity Explicitly

This program illustrates two ways to set the capacity of a vector: through its constructor, and through the `ensureCapacity()` method. (The actual capacity numbers used here are unrealistically small.)

```java
import java.util.Vector;
class TestCapacity
{ public static void main(String args[])
  { Vector v = new Vector(3);      // set capacity at 3
    for (int i=0; i<7; i++)        // insert 7 elements
    { v.addElement(new Long(9));
      print(v);
    }
    v.ensureCapacity(100);         // reset capacity to 100
    print(v);
  }
  static void print(Vector v)
  { System.out.print("v.size() = " + v.size());
    System.out.println(",\tv.capacity() = " + v.capacity());
  }
}
```

The output is

```
v.size() = 1,v.capacity() = 3
v.size() = 2,v.capacity() = 3
v.size() = 3,v.capacity() = 3
v.size() = 4,v.capacity() = 6
v.size() = 5,v.capacity() = 6
v.size() = 6,v.capacity() = 6
v.size() = 7,v.capacity() = 12
v.size() = 7,v.capacity() = 100
```

The constructor is passed the argument 3 which it uses to set the initial capacity of the vector v. It then gets reset twice, to 6, and then to 12, as more elements are added to the vector. Finally, we reset the capacity to 100.

8.6 CHANGES TO THE `Vector` CLASS IN JAVA 1.2

In Java 1.1, the `Vector` class is a direct subclass of the `Object` class. In Java 1.2 (released in 1998), the `Vector` class has been moved to a subclass of the new `AbstractList` class, which is a subclass of the new `AbstractCollection` class. From those new classes, the `Vector` class inherits 9 new methods and a new field. Java 1.2 has also added 9 other new methods and a

Version 1.1 of Java:
```
Object
 └─Vector
```

Version 1.2 of Java:
```
Object
 └─AbstractCollection
    └─AbstractList
       └─Vector
```

new constructor to the `Vector` class itself, raising its total number of members to 52. Included among these are

```
boolean add(Object o)
// adds the object o to the end of the list

boolean add(int i, Object o)
// adds the object o at position i in the list

void clear()
// removes all the elements from the list

Object get(int i)
// returns the object at position i in the list

Object remove(int i)
// removes the object at position i in the list and returns it

boolean remove(object o)
// removes the first occurrence of the object o in the list;
// returns true iff it was found

void removeRange(int i, int j)
// removes all of the object o from position i to position j-1

Object set(int i, Object o)
// reassigns the reference at position i to object o;
// returns a reference to the dereferenced object
```

Some of these will likely replace existing methods from Java 1.1. After that, newer compilers will report that the obsolete methods have been "deprecated" when you try to use them. For example, the new `clear()` method will "deprecate" the old `removeAll()` method.

See Problems 8.11-8.18 on page 205 for local implementations of these methods.

8.7 TWO-DIMENSIONAL ARRAYS

A *two-dimensional array* is one that uses two subscripts instead of one. We imagine the array as forming a two-dimensional grid of rows and columns, with the first subscript locating the row and the second subscript locating the column. For example,

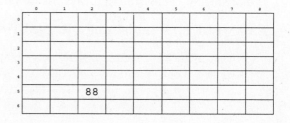

```
int[][] a = new int[7][9];
a[5][2] = 88;
```

would assign the value 88 to the element in row number 5 and column number 2. (Note that this element is actually in the sixth row and third column, due to zero-based indexing.)

A two-dimensional array is actually an array of arrays. Think of each row as a separate array; then the two dimensional array is the same as a one dimensional array of rows, as shown here.

The next example shows that this is how Java regards a two-dimensional array.

EXAMPLE 8.12 An Array of Arrays

This program declares a to be a two-dimensional array of ints with 7 rows and 9 columns:

```
class Test
{ public static void main(String args[])
  { int[][] a = new int[7][9];
    System.out.println("a.length = " + a.length);
    System.out.println("a[0].length = " + a[0].length);
  }
}
```
The output is
```
a.length = 7
a[0].length = 9
```

As an array, the object a has length 7. That's because it is really an array of 7 row arrays. The first of those row arrays is a[0]. Its length is 9. Each row has 9 elements.

A two-dimensional array can be initialized like a one-dimensional array. The only difference is that since it is an array of arrays, its initialization list has to be a list of initialization lists.

EXAMPLE 8.13 Initializing a Ragged Two-Dimensional Array

The array here is called a *ragged array* because the lengths of its rows vary.
```
class Test
{ public static void main(String args[])
  { int[][] a = { { 77, 33, 88 },
                  { 11, 55, 22, 99 },
                  { 66, 44 } };
    for (int i=0; i<a.length; i++)
    { for (int j=0; j<a[i].length; j++)
        System.out.print("\t" + a[i][j]);
      System.out.println();
    }
  }
}
```
The output is
```
        77      33      88
        11      55      22      99
        66      44
```

The initialization list could have been expressed as

```
int[][] a = { { 77, 33, 88 }, { 11, 55, 22, 99 }, { 66, 44 } };
```

(The compiler ignores all white space.) Arranging it as we did simply makes it more readable.

Note the use of nested `for` loops here. The outside loop is controlled by the row index `i`, and the inside loop is controlled by the column index `j`. The row index `i` increments until it reaches `a.length`, which is 3 in this example. For each value of `i`, the column index `j` increments until it reaches `a[i].length`, which in this example is 3 when `i` is 0, 4 when `i` is 1, and 2 when `i` is 2.

The control mechanism used above on the nested `for` loops is the standard way to process two-dimensional arrays. Processing three-dimensional arrays is similar:

```
for (int i=0; i<a.length; i++)
    for (int j=0; j<a[i].length; j++)
        for (int k=0; k<a[i][j].length; j++)
            // process a[i][j][k]...
```

Here we can imagine the element `a[i][j][k]` lying in plane `i`, row `j`, and column `k`. The element is analogous to a single letter on a line on a page in a book: `a[i][j][k]` would represent character number `k` on line number `j` on page number `i`., `a[i][j]` would represent line number `j` on page number `i`., and `a[i]` would represent page number `i`. The number of characters on line `j` on page `i` would be `a[i][j].length`, and the number of lines on page `i` would be `a[i].length`. So iteration `i` of the first loop would process page `a[i]`, iteration `j` of the second loop would process line `a[i][j]`, and iteration `k` of the third loop would process character `a[i][j][k]`.

Similarly, a four-dimensional array would be analogous to an encyclopedia consisting of a sequence of books. Element `a[9][281][36][54]` would represent a character number 54 on line number 36 on page number 281 in book number 9.

Review Questions

8.1 Trace by hand the execution of the invocation `strip("000121030012", '0')` of the `strip()` method in Example 8.3 on page 190.

8.2 How does determining the length of a character array differ from determining the length of a `String` object?

8.3 How does accessing an individual element of a character array differ from accessing the elements of a `String` object?

8.4 What happens if you use `w[5]` in an expression after allocating 5 elements to the array `w`?

8.5 What is the difference between a null array and an array of length zero?

8.6 What is the difference between an array of length zero and an array of four null references?

8.7 Why are arrays usually processed with `for` loops?

8.8 Why is an `Object[]` array called a universal array?

8.9 What is the difference between the `size` and the `capacity` of a `Vector` object?

8.10 What is the difference between a `Vector` object and an array of objects?

8.11 What is the difference between a `String` object and an array of `char` values?

8.12 What is the difference between a `StringBuffer` object and a `Vector` object of char values?

8.13 What does `int[]` represent?

8.14 What does `int[8]` represent?

8.15 What's wrong with this:
```
char[] name = "Boris Yeltsin";
```

8.16 Can an array store elements of different types?

Programming Problems

8.1 Implement the following method:
```
static double sum(double[] x)
{ // returns the sum of the elements in the array x
```

8.2 Implement the following method:
```
static double max(double[] x)
{ // returns the maximum of the elements in the array x
```

8.3 Implement the following method:
```
static double range(double[] x)
{ // returns the difference between the maximum and the minimum
  // of the elements in the array x
```

8.4 Implement the following modification of the `strip()` method defined in Example 8.3 on page 190:
```
static String strip(String s, char c, int p, int q)
{ // removes all occurrences c from the substring s[p:q-1]
```
Here, the notation `s[p:q-1]` means the substring of `s` that begins with `s[p]` and ends with `s[q-1]`. For example, if `s` is `"ABCDEFGHIJ"`, then `s[5:8}` would be `"FGH"`.

Supplementary Programming Problems

8.5 Modify the `strip()` method defined in Example 8.3 on page 190, using the following application of the `System.arraycopy()` method to shift all the remaining characters of `s[]` one position to the left each time the target character `c` is found in `s`:
```
System.arraycopy(s, i+1, s, i, n-i-1);
```

8.6 Modify the `strip()` method defined in Example 8.3 on page 190, using the following application of the `System.arraycopy()` method to shift all the remaining characters of `s[]` to the left `k` positions, where `k` is the number of consecutive occurrences of target character `c` found in `s`:
```
System.arraycopy(s, i+k, s, i, n-i-k);
```

8.7 Implement the following method:
```
static boolean areEqual(double[] x, double[] y)
{ // returns true iff each of the corresponding elements
  // of the two arrays match
```

8.8 Implement the following method:
```
static boolean areEqual(double[][] x, double[][] y)
{ // returns true iff each of the corresponding elements
  // of the two arrays match
```

8.9 Implement the following method for vectors:
```
static void swap(Vector v, int i, int j)
// Swaps the elements of v at positions i and j
// For example, if v represents the list {22,33,44,55,66,77},
// then swap(v,4,1) would change it to {22,66,44,55,33,77}
```

8.10 Implement the following method for vectors:
```
static void move(Vector v, int i, int j)
// Moves the element at position i to position j
// For example, if v represents the list {22,33,44,55,66,77},
// then swap(v,4,1) would change it to {22,66,33,44,55,77}
```

8.11 Define the subclass
```
class Vector1.2 extends Vector {}
```
and implement within it the following method:
```
boolean add(Object o)
// adds the object o to the end of the list
```

8.12 Define the subclass
```
class Vector1.2 extends Vector {}
```
and implement within it the following method:
```
boolean add(int i, Object o)
// adds the object o at position i in the list
```

8.13 Define the subclass
```
class Vector1.2 extends Vector {}
```
and implement within it the following method:
```
void clear()
// removes all the elements from the list
```

8.14 Define the subclass
```
class Vector1.2 extends Vector {}
```
and implement within it the following method:
```
Object get(int i)
// returns the object at position i in the list
```

8.15 Define the subclass
```
class Vector1.2 extends Vector {}
```
and implement within it the following method:
```
Object remove(int i)
// removes the object at position i in the list and returns it
```

8.16 Define the subclass
```
class Vector1.2 extends Vector {}
```
and implement within it the following method:
```
boolean remove(object o)
// removes the first occurrence of the object o in the list;
// returns true iff it was found
```

8.17 Define the subclass
```
class Vector1.2 extends Vector {}
```
and implement within it the following method:
```
void removeRange(int i, int j)
// removes all of the object o from position i to position j-1
```

8.18 Define the subclass
```
class Vector1.2 extends Vector {}
```
and implement within it the following method:
```
Object set(int i, Object o)
// reassigns the reference at position i to object o;
// returns a reference to the dereferenced object
```

8.19 Implement the following method for vectors:
```
int countDistinct()
// returns the number of objects referenced in the list
```

For example, the output from the code

```
Vector v = new Vector();
Point p = new Point(2,3);
Point q = new Point(2,3);
v.addElement(p);
v.addElement(p);
v.addElement(q);
System.out.println(v.size() + ", " + v.countDistinct());
```

would be

```
3, 2
```

because the list has three elements but they refer to two distinct objects.

8.20 Implement the following method for vectors:

```
int countUnique()
// returns the number of unique objects referenced in the list
```

For example, the output from the code

```
Vector v = new Vector();
Point p = new Point(8,5);
Point q = new Point(8,5);
v.addElement(p);
v.addElement(p);
v.addElement(q);
System.out.println(v.size() + ", " + v.countUnique());
```

would be

```
3, 1
```

because the list has three elements but they all represent the same point (8,5).

8.21 Implement the following method:

```
static double innerProduct(double[] x, double[] y)
{ // returns the inner product of x and y,
  // defined to be the sum of all x[i]*y[i]
```

8.22 Implement the following method:

```
static double[][] outerProduct(double[] x, double[] y)
{ // returns the outer product p of x and y,
  // defined by p[i][j]] = x[i]*y[j]
```

8.23 Implement the following method:

```
static void transpose(double[][] x)
{ // transposes the array x swapping each x[i][j] with x[j][i]
```

8.24 Implement the following method:

```
static int[][] pascalsTriangle(int n)
{ // returns Pascal's triangle with n+1 rows
```

8.25 Implement the following method:

```
static int[] fibonacci(int n)
{ // returns the first n+1 fibonacci numbers
```

8.26 Implement the following method:

```
static int[] prime(int n)
{ // returns the first n+1 prime numbers
```

Answers to Review Questions

8.1 The trace is shown at the top of the next page. The result of the invocation is the string `"121312"`.

8.2 The length of a character array (or any array type) is obtained from its `public length` field, whereas the length of a `String` object is obtained from its `length()` method. For example, in Example 8.2 on page 189, `a.length` produces the length of the array `a`, while `s.length()` produces the length of the string `s`.

8.3 The individual elements of a character array (or of any array type) are accessed by means of the subscript operator `[]`, whereas those of a `String` object are accessed from its `charAt()` method. For example, in Example 8.2 on page 189, `a[i]` produces the element at index `i` in the array `a`, while `s.charAt(i)` does the same for the string `s`.

8.4 If `w` has only 5 elements, then the expression `w[5]` will cause the program to fail because there is no such element. The 5 elements are `w[0]`, `w[1]`, `w[2]`, `w[3]`, and `w[4]`.

8.5 A null array is a naked array reference with no array object to which to refer. An array of length zero is an array object with zero element. For example:

```
int[] a;
int[] b = new int[0];
```

Here, `a` is a null array, and `b` is an array of length zero. One way that they differ is that `a.length` does not exist, while `b.length` exists and has the value 0. Of the two statements

```
int aLen = a.length;
int bLen = b.length;
```

the first will not compile, while the second will initialize `bLen` to 0.

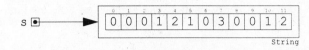

s →

String

i	j	i+j	sc	a[i]
0	0	0	0	
	1	1	0	
	2	2	0	
	3	3	1	1
1	4	4	2	2
2	5	5	1	1
3	6	6	0	
	4	7	3	3
4		8	0	
	5	9	0	
	6	10	0	
5		11	1	1
6		12	2	2

8.6 An array of length zero has length 0. An array of 4 references has length 4.

8.7 The real power of arrays comes from their facility of using an index variable to traverse the array, accessing each element with the same expression `a[i]`. All that is needed to make this work is a iterated statement in which the variable `i` serves as a counter, incrementing from 0 to `a.length-1`. That is exactly what a `for` loop does.

8.8 An array declared as `Object[]` is universal in the sense that its elements can refer to objects of any class.

8.9 The *size* of a `Vector` object is the actual number of `Object` references that it contains. The capacity is the number of spaces it has allocated for `Object` references.

8.10 A `Vector` object is an instance of the `Vector` class, so it can invoke its methods. An array of (references to) objects is quite similar, but it cannot use the methods defined in the `Vector` class.

8.11 A `String` object is an instance of the `String` class, so it can invoke its methods. An array of `char` also stores strings, but it has much less functionality.

8.12 Actually, you cannot really have a `Vector` objects of `char` values. The elements of a `Vector` object are references to instances of the `Object` class. But polymorphism allows those references to refer to instances of any class, including the `Character` class, whose objects encapsulate `char` values. In that case, the resulting vectors behave much like instances of the `StringBuffer` class. The major difference then is, of course, the difference in functionality of the two classes: the set of available methods.

8.13 The form `int[]` represents the type "array of `int`." It is used to declare array objects and array parameters, like this:

```
int[] a;
static sum(int[] a)
```

8.14 The form `int[8]` is used with the `new` operator to allocate an array of `int`s, like this:

```
int[] a = new int[8];
```

8.15 The reason that

```
char[] name = "Boris Yeltsin";
```

won't compile is that the expression `"Boris Yeltsin"` is a `String` literal, but `char[]` does not declare a `String` object.

8.16   An array cannot store elements of different types. However, it can store references which can refer to instances of different classes, provided that it is declared as

```
ClassX[] a;
```

where `ClassX` is an ancestor to all the classes involved.

Solutions to Programming Problems

8.1
```
static double sum(double[] x)
{ // returns the sum of the elements in the array x
  double s=0.0;
  for (int i=0; i<x.length; i++)
    s += x[i];
  return s;
}
```

8.2
```
static double max(double[] x)
{ // returns the maximum of the elements in the array x
  double m = x[0];
  for (int i=1; i<x.length; i++)
    if (x[i] > m) m = x[i];
  return m;
}
```

8.3
```
static double range(double[] x)
{ // returns the difference between the maximum and the minimum
  // of the elements in the array x
  double max = x[0];
  double min = x[0];
  for (int i=1; i<x.length; i++)
    if (x[i] < min) min = x[i];
    else if (x[i] > max) max = x[i];
  return (max - min);
}
```

8.4
```
class TestStripMethod
{ // Test driver for the strip() method
  static String strip(String s, char c, int p, int q)
  { // removes all occurrences c from s[p:q-1]
    int n = s.length();
    n = ( q<n ? q : n );                // n = min{ q, s.length() }
    char[] a = new char[n];
    int i=0;
    int j=0;
    while (p+i+j < n)                   // begin with s[p]
    { char sc = s.charAt(p+i+j); // p+i+j is the current index in s
      if (sc == c) j++;        // j is the number of characters removed
      else a[i++] = sc;        // i characters have been copied into a
    }
    return new String(a,0,i);    // duplicates a as a String object
  }
  public static void main(String args[])
  { String s = new String("ABCAAADEAFA");
    System.out.println(s);
    String ss = strip(s, 'A', 0,5);
    System.out.println(ss);
    ss = strip(s, 'A', 5, 8);
    System.out.println(ss);
    ss = strip(s, 'A', 5, 100);
    System.out.println(ss);
  }
}
```

Chapter 9

Graphics

A picture is worth 1024 words.

—Anonymous

9.1 THE AWT LIBRARIES

One of the main reasons that Java is such a popular programming language is that it makes it fairly easy to create programs with impressive graphics. This is managed by Java's vast graphics library, officially called the *Abstract Window Toolkit* (AWT).

The AWT (in Java 1.2) consists of over 25 packages which define hundreds of classes. The class hierarchy shown here lists some of most important graphics classes. The AWT packages are named `java.awt`, `java.awt.event`, `java.awt.font`, `java.awt.swing`, `java.awt.swing.event.`, *etc.* For example, the `java.awt.image` package defines a class named `PixelGrabber`. All of the classes listed in the hierarchy shown here are defined in the `java.awt` package.

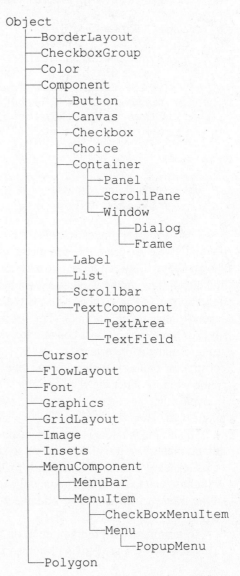

```
Object
  ├─BorderLayout
  ├─CheckboxGroup
  ├─Color
  ├─Component
  │   ├─Button
  │   ├─Canvas
  │   ├─Checkbox
  │   ├─Choice
  │   ├─Container
  │   │   ├─Panel
  │   │   ├─ScrollPane
  │   │   └─Window
  │   │       ├─Dialog
  │   │       └─Frame
  │   ├─Label
  │   ├─List
  │   ├─Scrollbar
  │   └─TextComponent
  │       ├─TextArea
  │       └─TextField
  ├─Cursor
  ├─FlowLayout
  ├─Font
  ├─Graphics
  ├─GridLayout
  ├─Image
  ├─Insets
  ├─MenuComponent
  │   ├─MenuBar
  │   └─MenuItem
  │       ├─CheckBoxMenuItem
  │       └─Menu
  │           └─PopupMenu
  └─Polygon
```

9.2 THE `Frame` CLASS

Most graphics are displayed within frames on a computer screen. As the class hierarchy shows here, a frame is a specialized window, which is a specialized container, which is a specialized component, which is a specialized object.

A *component* is an object that can be displayed on the screen and can interact with the user. For example, the close button in the upper right corner of a window (in Microsoft Windows) is a component. So are the scroll bar along the right edge of the window and the window itself. Components have special properties, including background color, cursor image, and font.

A *container* is a component that can contain other components. Windows are containers; buttons are not. Containers have special properties, including layout managers and insets.

A *window* is a container with some special properties, including a locale for managing various human languages, a toolkit for creating components, and a warning message for security purposes.

A *frame* is a window that has a title bar, a menu bar, a border, a cursor, and an icon image. Frame windows are the standard objects used for drawing graphics.

EXAMPLE 9.1 Creating a Simple Frame Window

This little program will be gradually enhanced in the examples that follow this one:

```
import java.awt.Frame;              // defines the Frame class

class TestFrame
{ public static void main(String[] args)
   { System.out.println("Creating a 250x100-pixel frame"
       + " with title \"Example 9.1\".");
     Frame frame = new Frame("Example 9.1");
     frame.setSize(250,100);       // 250 pixels wide and 100 pixels high
     frame.setVisible(true);       // displays the frame on the screen
     System.out.println("To quit, click on this window"
       + " and then press Ctrl+C.");
   }
}
```

The command line output is

```
Creating a 250x100-pixel frame with title "Example 9.1".
To quit, click on this window and then press Ctrl+C.
```

This program invokes the `println()` method twice to print the command line output shown above. Between those two actions, it creates and displays the frame window shown here. This is done by the `frame` object that is created in the second statement of `main()`. The `new` operator invokes the `Frame` class constructor, passing the string argument `"Example 9.1"` to it. The constructor copies that string to the title bar of the frame window. After the `frame` object is created, it invokes its `setSize()` method to set the size of the frame window to be 250 pixels wide and 100 pixels high. Then it invokes its `setVisible()` method to display the frame window.

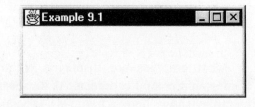

This frame window is not very responsive. If you click on the Java coffee cup icon, it will display its default menu. But it will not respond to any of the menu commands. Nor will it respond to a click on any of its standard buttons (Minimize, Maximize, and Close) in its upper right corner of the window. But it will allow you to resize and move the window. We won't be able to activate all the standard functionality of the frame window until we add event-handling code. This minimally functional frame is just the first step.

To terminate the program, click on the window that has the output message, and then press Ctrl+C. (This assumes you are running Microsoft Windows. In Unix, you have to `kill` the process.)

The `Frame` class is defined in the `java.awt` package. Besides the 11 methods that every class inherits from the `Object` class (`hashCode()`, `toString()`, *etc*.), the `Frame` class also inherits 125 members (fields and methods) from the `Component` class, 47 members from the `Container` class, and 16 members from the `Window` class. The `setSize()` and `setVisible()` methods used in Example 9.1 are both inherited from the `Component` class. The `setBackground()` method used in Example 9.2 is also inherited from the `Component` class.

EXAMPLE 9.2 Subclassing the `Frame` Class

This version of the program from Example 9.1 defines a subclass of the `Frame` class:

```java
import java.awt.Color;
import java.awt.Frame;

class MyFrame extends Frame
{ MyFrame(String s)
  { super(s);                      // passes s up to the Frame constructor
    setBackground(Color.blue);     // colors the frame bright blue
    setSize(250,100);              // 250 pixels wide and 100 pixels high
    setVisible(true);              // displays the frame on the screen
  }
}

class TestMyFrame
{ public static void main(String[] args)
  { System.out.println("Creating a 250x100-pixel frame"
      + " with title \"Example 9.2\".");
    new MyFrame("Example 9.2");  // creates the frame window
    System.out.println("To quit, click on this window"
      + " and then press Ctrl+C.");
  }
}
```

The `println()` methods have the same effect as in Example 9.1. In between them, the frame shown here is created. It appears bright blue on the screen.

The `MyFrame` class is defined as a subclass of the `Frame` class. In addition to the nearly 200 members that it inherits, it adds one more: the constructor:

  `MyFrame(String s)`

The first statement in this constructor is

  `super(s);`

This invokes the constructor of the parent superclass, which is the constructor

  `Frame(String s)`

This creates the frame window and copies the string `s` onto its title bar.

The remaining three lines in the `MyFrame` constructor set the attributes

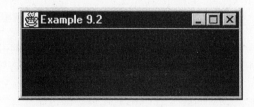

inherited from the `Frame` class: its background color, its size, and it visibility. These are standard mutator methods for the object's fields. Note that the color `blue` is a constant defined in the `java.awt.Color` class.

9.3 THE Color CLASS

Objects of the Color class are used to specify colors in graphics operations. One way to specify a color is to use the three-component *RGB code*. For example, the RGB code for the color orange is (255, 200, 0). The three numbers identify how much red, green, and blue is used to form the color. ("RGB" stands for "Red-Green-Blue.") Each number can range from 0 to 255. So the RGB code (255, 200, 0) for orange means that it has as much red as it can, it has about 80% of the green that it could have, and no blue. The Color class defines constants for the 13 special colors shown in the table below. But you can specify any one of the 16,777,216 different possible RGB codes. For example, (255, 215, 0) is gold, (127, 255, 212) is aquamarine, and (160, 32, 240) is purple.

Constants Defined in the Color Class

Object	RGB Code
Color.black	(0, 0, 0)
Color.blue	(0, 0, 255)
Color.cyan	(0, 255, 255)
Color.darkGray	(64, 64, 64)
Color.gray	(128, 128, 128)
Color.green	(0, 255, 0)
Color.lightGray	(192, 192, 192)
Color.magenta	(255, 0, 255)
Color.orange	(255, 200, 0)
Color.pink	(255, 175, 175)
Color.red	(255, 0, 0)
Color.white	(255, 255, 255)
Color.yellow	(255, 255, 0)

EXAMPLE 9.3 Different Colored Frames in Different Locations

This program modifies the one in Example 9.2. It defines another subclass of the Frame class to display two different colored frames in different locations:

```
import java.awt.Color;
import java.awt.Frame;

class ColoredFrame extends Frame
{ ColoredFrame(String s, Color color, int x, int y)
  { super(s + color.toString());
    setBackground(color);
    setSize(350,100);
    setLocation(x,y);   // puts upper left corner at (x,y)
    setVisible(true);
  }
}
```

```
class TestColoredFrame
{ public static void main(String[] args)
  { new ColoredFrame("Red: ", Color.red, 0, 0);
    new ColoredFrame("Green: ", Color.green, 0, 100);
  }
}
```

The constructor for the new `ColoredFrame()` subclass takes four arguments: a `String` object, a `Color` object, and two `ints`. The string is concatenated with the string representation of the `Color` object (produced by its `toString()` method) and passed along to the `Frame` constructor which creates the frame and copies that concatenated string to its title bar. The two integers are used as *x* and *y* coordinates to locate the position of the frame on the screen.

The `main()` method creates two `ColoredFrame` objects. The first is colored red and located at position (0,0), which is the upper left corner of the screen. The second is colored green and located at position (0,100). Since the heights of the frames are 100 pixels, the second frame is placed precisely at the bottom edge of the first, also at the left edge of the screen. They look like the picture here (except more colorful).

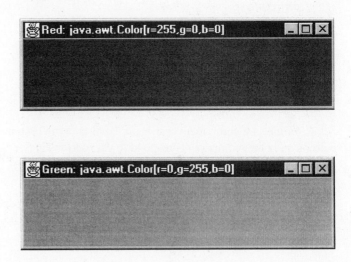

Notice the title bars. Each title was produced from the code

```
s + color.toString()
```

where `s` was the string passed to the `ColoredFrame` constructor, and color is the `Color` object passed. You can see how the `Color` class overrides the `toString()` method. It returns a string in the form `Color[r=rrr,g=ggg,b=bbb]` where (*rrr*, *ggg*, *bbb*) is the RGB code for the color.

9.4 COMPONENTS

Graphics programs get their functionality from the interactive components that are placed in the windows on the screen. These include buttons, scroll bars, text fields, menus, *etc*. These objects are instances of subclasses of the two abstract classes: `Component` and `MenuComponent`. In any user interface, the components are related by their containment hierarchy.

EXAMPLE 9.4 A Component Hierarchy

This user interface consists of 11 objects: three instances of the `Frame` class, two of the `TextField` class, one of the `Panel` class, one of the `Label` class, three of the `Button` class, and one of the `Scrollbar` class. The containers are `frame1`, `panel`, `frame2`, and `frame3`. The diagram at the top of the next page shows the containment hierarchy for these components. But the picture below gives a better visual description of the actual containment relationships among them.

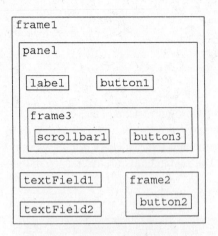

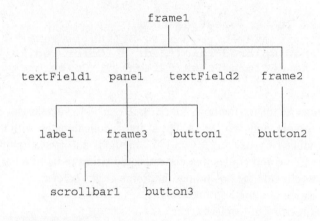

9.5 THE `Button` CLASS

A *button* is a component that has a label and can respond when pressed. We will see how buttons and other components respond to user actions in Section 9.7.

EXAMPLE 9.5 Adding a `Button` Component

This program creates a frame that contains a `Button` component.

```
import java.awt.Button;   // defines the Button class
import java.awt.Color;
import java.awt.Frame;

class ButtonFrame extends Frame
{ Button button;                          // declares button

  ButtonFrame(String s)
  { super(s);
    setBackground(Color.blue);
    setSize(200,100);
    setLocation(400,50);
    button = new Button("Click me!");  // creates button
    add(button);                       // makes button a component
    setVisible(true);
  }
}

class TestButtonFrame
{ public static void main(String[] args)
  { ButtonFrame buttonFrame = new ButtonFrame("Example 9.5");
  }
}
```

This program creates two component objects: buttonFrame and ButtonFrame.button. The latter is a component of the former, as indicated here.

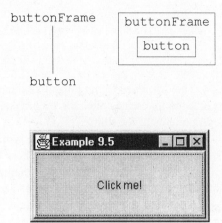

The statement in main() creates the object named buttonFrame as an instance of the ButtonFrame class. It passes the string literal "Example 9.5" to its constructor, which passes it on to the Frame constructor.

The ButtonFrame class declares one field: a Button object named button. (It inherits other fields from its ancestor classes, including those for color, size, and location.) It invokes the methods setBackground(), setSize(), and setLocation(), as in Example 9.3 on page 212. Then it instantiates its button component, passing the string literal "Click me!".

Every button has its own *label*, which is a String object that appears on the face of the button when it is displayed. You can set this label by invoking the button's setLabel() method, or you can pass the string to its constructor as was done here.

After the button is created, the ButtonFrame constructor must invoke the add() method to make the Button object a component of the ButtonFrame object. Then it invokes the setVisible() method to make the frame appear on the screen. Note that the button fills the entire frame.

Click on the button to see that it reacts visibly as you would expect.

9.6 MANAGING LAYOUTS

The arrangement of several components within a container is called their *layout*. Java defines the five layout classes FlowLayout, GridLayout, BorderLayout, CardLayout, and GridBagLayout. These are all subclasses of the LayoutManager class. You can set a container's layout by passing one of these LayoutManager objects to the container's setLayout() method.

The FlowLayout manager arranges the container's components in a left-to-right, top-to-bottom pattern, in the same flow that English words follow on a printed page.

EXAMPLE 9.6 Using the FlowLayout Manager

This program creates a ButtonFrame object named buttonFrame and six anonymous Button objects which are added to the frame as components. It passes an anonymous FlowLayout object to the frame's setLayout() method to arrange the buttons in a flow layout:

```
import java.awt.Button;
import java.awt.Frame;
import java.awt.FlowLayout;
class ButtonFrame extends Frame
{ ButtonFrame(String s)
  { super(s);
    setSize(200,100);
    setLayout(new FlowLayout());
    for (int i=0; i<6; i++)
      add(new Button("Button " + i));
    setVisible(true);
  }
}
```

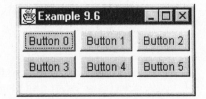

```
class TestButtonFrame
{ public static void main(String[] args)
  { ButtonFrame buttonFrame = new ButtonFrame("Example 9.6");
  }
}
```

The displayed frame looks like the picture here. The `for` loop creates the six buttons and makes them components of the frame.

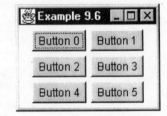

Drag on the edge of the frame window to resize it, making it taller and narrower. See how the buttons flow within the frame, rearranging themselves but still maintaining their "words-on-a-page" arrangement.

Note that the size of each button is set by default according to the size of its label.

EXAMPLE 9.7 Using the `GridLayout` Manager

This programs uses a `GridLayout` object to arrange 12 buttons in a 4-by-3 grid:

```
import java.awt.*;
class ButtonFrame extends Frame
{ ButtonFrame(String s)
  { super(s);
    setSize(300,200);
    setLayout(new GridLayout(4,3));
    for (int i=0; i<12; i++)
      add(new Button("Button " + i));
    setVisible(true);
  }
}

class TestButtonFrame
{ public static void main(String[] args)
  { new ButtonFrame("Example 9.7");
  }
}
```

The arguments 4 and 3 are passed to the `GridLayout` constructor, telling it to use 4 rows and 3 columns in the grid.

Note that we have switched to using the wild card character `*` in the import statement

```
import java.awt.*;
```

to avoid listing the AWT classes separately.

EXAMPLE 9.8 Using the `BorderLayout` Manager

This programs uses a `BorderLayout` object to arrange five buttons:

```
import java.awt.*;

class ButtonFrame extends Frame
{ ButtonFrame(String s)
  { super(s);
    setSize(150,100);
    setLayout(new BorderLayout());
    add(new Button("Superior"), BorderLayout.NORTH);
    add(new Button("Ontario"), BorderLayout.EAST);
    add(new Button("Erie"), BorderLayout.SOUTH);
    add(new Button("Michigan"), BorderLayout.WEST);
```

```
      add(new Button("Huron"), BorderLayout.CENTER);
      setVisible(true);
    }
}

class TestButtonFrame
{ public static void main(String[] args)
  { new ButtonFrame("Example 9.8");
  }
}
```

The `add()` method declared in the `Container` class has five versions. The one used in Example 9.8 is declared as

```
      public void add(Component component, Object constraint)
```

When the container's layout is a `BorderLayout` object, the `add()` method expects the constraint argument to be one of the five objects defined in the `BorderLayout` class: `NORTH`, `EAST`, `SOUTH`, `WEST`, or `CENTER`. These determine which of the five possible positions the component will be given.

9.7 EVENT-DRIVEN PROGRAMMING

To make components such as buttons and text fields functional, we have to implement the *listener interface* that gives their containers the power to "hear" them. This empowers the components to generate event objects in response to user actions upon them and provides the instructions for their containers to execute in response.

EXAMPLE 9.9 Handling the `Button` Click Event

The picture on the right shows how the `Button` and `ButtonFrame` objects would look without the code printed in boldface below. The `button` object has a label field containing the **"Click me!"** string, and the `buttonFrame` object has a field that refers to its `Button` component. By adding the code shown in boldface, we activate the button, allowing the frame to "hear" it and respond whenever it gets clicked.

```
      import java.awt.*;
      import java.awt.event.ActionEvent;
      import java.awt.event.ActionListener;

      class ButtonFrame extends Frame implements ActionListener
      { Button button;

        ButtonFrame(String s)
        { super(s);
          setBackground(Color.blue);
          setSize(200,100);
```

```
        setLayout(new FlowLayout());
        button = new Button("Click me!");
        add(button);
        button.addActionListener(this);
        setVisible(true);
    }

    public void actionPerformed(ActionEvent event)
    { if (event.getActionCommand().equals("Click me!"))
        System.out.println("Thank you!");
    }
}

class TestButtonFrame
{ public static void main(String[] args)
    { ButtonFrame buttonFrame =  new ButtonFrame("Example 9.9");
    }
}
```

To make instances of the `ButtonFrame` class responsive to actions on its components, we have to make it an *action listener*. That is done by (1) adding the "`implements ActionListener`" clause to its declaration, (2) implementing the `actionPerformed()` method, and (3) invoking the components' `addActionListener()` methods in its constructor. When this is done, the components to which it listens are called *source objects*, because this enables them to generate `ActionEvent` objects in response to the user actions upon them. In this example, the frame's `button` object is the source object.

By making the frame an action listener, it will automatically invoke its `actionPerformed()` method on any `ActionEvent` object that the button generates. The picture here shows how this is managed. The statement

   button.addActionListener(this);

assigns to the button's `actionListener` field a reference to the `ButtonFrame` object that contains it. Then whenever the button is clicked, it generates an `ActionEvent` object assigning the string in its label field to the `ActionEvent` object's `actionCommand` field. Then the run-time system invokes the `actionPerformed()` method on the listener object that is identified by `button.action-Listener`, passing that event object to it. In this case, that listener is the frame object, which finds that the event.actionCommand field does indeed equal the **"Click me!"** string, so it executes the `println()` statement.

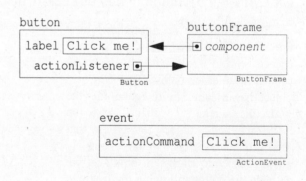

An *event-driven program* is simply a program that runs a main loop, called the *event loop*, that waits for input and then responds accordingly. This differs from our previous examples in that the input can come in a variety of forms, including *mouse events* (clicking and dragging). Such user actions are usually performed in a graphical context: clicking on a button, dragging an icon, *etc*. So the interactive context is called a *graphical user interface* (GUI). The objects that appear on the screen to prompt the user (windows, buttons, text fields, *etc*.) are called components. In Java, these objects are all instances of subclasses of the `Component` class.

EXAMPLE 9.10 Handling the `WindowClosing` Event

To handle the `WindowClosing` event, the frame must implement the `WindowListener` interface. This actually requires the implementation of seven more methods. But for this example, only the `windowClosing()` method needs to do anything. It would terminate the program when it "hears" the event:

```java
import java.awt.*;
import java.awt.event.*;

class ButtonFrame extends Frame
    implements ActionListener, WindowListener
{ Button button;

  ButtonFrame(String s)
  { super(s);
    setBackground(Color.blue);
    setSize(200,100);
    setLayout(new FlowLayout());
    addWindowListener(this);
    button = new Button("Click me!");
    add(button);
    button.addActionListener(this);
    setVisible(true);
  }

  public void windowClosed(WindowEvent event) {}
  public void windowDeiconified(WindowEvent event) {}
  public void windowIconified(WindowEvent event) {}
  public void windowActivated(WindowEvent event) {}
  public void windowDeactivated(WindowEvent event) {}
  public void windowOpened(WindowEvent event) {}

  public void windowClosing(WindowEvent event)
  { System.exit(0);
  }

  public void actionPerformed(ActionEvent event)
  { if (event.getActionCommand().equals("Click me!"))
      System.out.println("Thank you!");
  }
}
```

```
class TestButtonFrame
{ public static void main(String[] args)
  { ButtonFrame buttonFrame = new ButtonFrame("Example 9.10");
  }
}
```

Note that as an `ActionListener`, the frame listens for events generated by its button field. But as a `WindowListener`, it listens for events generated by itself. When you click on the close button, the window actually tells itself to close.

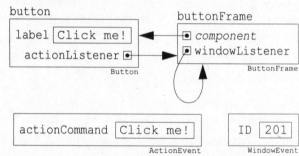

The picture here shows two event objects: an `ActionEvent` generated by `button` when the user clicked on the button, and a `WindowEvent` generated by `buttonFrame` when the user clicked on the window's close button (or selected the C̲lose command from the window's menu or pressed Alt + F4). Both of these event objects are handled by `buttonFrame` because it has been *registered* as both the `actionListener` for `button` and the `windowListener` for itself.

9.8 THE `TextField` CLASS

A *text field* is a text component that displays editable text. It provides a standard mechanism for input into graphics based applications.

EXAMPLE 9.11 A Temperature Conversion Object

```
import java.awt.*;
import java.awt.event.*;

class ConvertTemperatures extends Frame
   implements ActionListener, WindowListener
{ Label directions;
  TextField fahrenheit;
  Label celsius;

  ConvertTemperatures(String s)
  { super(s);
    setSize(250,100);
    setLayout(new FlowLayout());
    addWindowListener(this);
    directions = new Label("Enter temperature in Fahrenheit:");
    add(directions);
    fahrenheit = new TextField(2);
    add(fahrenheit);
    fahrenheit.addActionListener(this);
    celsius = new Label("                          ");
    celsius.setFont(new Font("TimesRoman 12 point bold.", 20, 20));
    add(celsius);
    setVisible(true);
  }

  public void windowClosed(WindowEvent event) {}
  public void windowDeiconified(WindowEvent event) {}
```

```
      public void windowIconified(WindowEvent event) {}
      public void windowActivated(WindowEvent event) {}
      public void windowDeactivated(WindowEvent event) {}
      public void windowOpened(WindowEvent event) {}
      public void windowClosing(WindowEvent event) { System.exit(0); }

      public void actionPerformed(ActionEvent event)
      { int f = Integer.parseInt(fahrenheit.getText());
        long c = Math.round(5.0*(f - 32)/9.0);
        fahrenheit.setText("");
        celsius.setText(f + "\u00B0F = " + c + "\u00B0C");
      }
  }

  class TestConvertTemperatures
  { public static void main(String[] args)
    { new ConvertTemperatures("Example 9.11");
    }
  }
```

Review Questions

9.1 What is the AWT?

9.2 What is the difference between a component and a container?

9.3 What is the purpose of the `add()` method?

Programming Problems

9.1 Modify Example 9.1 on page 210 so that it creates a frame 400 pixels wide and 200 pixels high and has the title "Problem 9.1".

9.2 Modify Example 9.2 on page 211 so that it paints the frame red instead of blue and has the title "Problem 9.2".

9.3 Modify Example 9.2 on page 211 so that it does the same without subclassing the `Frame` class and has the title "Problem 9.3".

9.4 Modify Example 9.3 on page 212 so that it displays 13 frame windows, one for each of the 13 predefined colors in the `Color` class. Arrange the frames in a tiled pattern using the `setLocation()` method as in Example 9.3.

9.5 Write a program similar to that in Example 9.3 on page 212 that prints an 8-by-8 grid of 64 tiled frames, each with a different background color. Use a pair of nested `for` loops.

Supplementary Programming Problems

9.6 Modify the program in Example 9.11 on page 220 so that it converts Fahrenheit to Kelvin. Use the fact that Kelvin = Celsius − 273.

9.7 Modify the program in Example 9.11 on page 220 so that it converts Celsius to Fahrenheit.

9.8 Write a program that draws six concentric circles, spaced 12 pixels apart.

9.9 Write a program that draws a spiral. Use the `drawArc()` method.

9.10 Write a program that draws characters of random size and random color at random locations.

9.11 Write a program that draws filled circles of random size and color at random locations.

9.12 Write a program that draws the two-coordinate position of the mouse when it is clicked.

9.13 Write a program that amortizes a loan. For a given loan amount, interest rate, and monthly payment, the display should list the schedule of monthly payments.

9.14 Write a program that implements a simple calculator with buttons for addition, subtraction, multiplication, and division.

Answers to Review Questions

9.1 The AWT is a library of Java packages that forms part of the Java API. It includes over 25 packages that define hundreds of classes used for graphical user interfaces (GUIs).

9.2 A *component* is an object, like a button or a scroll bar, that has a visual representation in a screen window. A *container* is a window-like component that can contain other components. Every component has a unique container that directly contains it.

9.3 The add() method makes a field a component. For example, in Example 9.5 on page 214, the Button object button is a field of the ButtonFrame object buttonFrame. But it doesn't become a component of that object until the line

        add(button);

executes.

Solutions to Programming Problems

9.1
```
import java.awt.Frame;
public class TestFrame extends Frame
{ public static void main(String[] args)
   { System.out.println("Creating a 400x200-pixel frame"
       + " with title \"Problem 9.1\".");
     Frame frame = new Frame("Problem 9.1");
     frame.setSize(400,200);
     frame.setVisible(true);
     System.out.println("To quit, click in this window"
       + " and then press Ctrl+C.");
   }
}
```

9.2
```
import java.awt.Color;
import java.awt.Frame;
class MyFrame extends Frame
{ MyFrame(String s)
   { super(s);
     setBackground(Color.red);
     setSize(250,100);
     setVisible(true);
   }
}
```

```
        class TestMyFrame
        { public static void main(String[] args)
          { System.out.println("Creating a 250x100-pixel frame"
               + " with title \"Problem 9.2\".");
            new MyFrame("Problem 9.2");
            System.out.println("To quit, click on this window"
               + " and then press Ctrl+C.");
          }
        }
```

9.3
```
        import java.awt.Color;
        import java.awt.Frame;
        class TestFrame
        { public static void main(String[] args)
          { Frame frame = new Frame("Problem 9.3");
            frame.setBackground(Color.blue);
            frame.setSize(250,100);
            frame.setVisible(true);
            System.out.println("To quit, click on this window"
               + " and then press Ctrl+C.");
          }
        }
```

9.4   Add the following lines to `main()`:
```
        new ColoredFrame("Blue: ", Color.blue, 700, 0);
        new ColoredFrame("Yellow: ", Color.yellow, 0, 100);
        new ColoredFrame("Magenta: ", Color.magenta, 350, 100);
        new ColoredFrame("Cyan: ", Color.cyan, 700, 100);
        new ColoredFrame("Orange: ", Color.orange, 0, 200);
        new ColoredFrame("Pink: ", Color.pink, 350, 200);
        new ColoredFrame("White: ", Color.white, 700, 200);
        new ColoredFrame("Light Gray: ", Color.lightGray, 0, 300);
        new ColoredFrame("Gray: ", Color.gray, 350, 300);
        new ColoredFrame("Dark Gray: ", Color.darkGray, 700, 300);
        new ColoredFrame("Black: ", Color.black, 0, 400);
```

9.5
```
        import java.awt.Color;
        import java.awt.Frame;
        class ColoredFrame extends Frame
        { ColoredFrame(Color color, int x, int y)
          { super();
            setBackground(color);
            setSize(100,100);
            setLocation(x,y);
            setVisible(true);
          }
        }

        class TestColoredFrame
        { public static void main(String[] args)
          { for (int i=0; i<8; i++)
              for (int j=0; j<8; j++)
              { Color color = new Color(32*i+31,32*j+31,4*i*j+3);
                new ColoredFrame(color,112*i,100*j);
              }
          }
        }
```

Chapter 10

Applets, Threads, and Exceptions

10.1 APPLETS

An *applet* is a Java program that must be run from another program, called its *host program*. Applets are usually run from Web browsers such as Netscape's Communicator or Microsoft's Internet Explorer. The word "applet" derives from the word "application," which means computer program.

EXAMPLE 10.1 The `HelloWorld` Applet

Here is our `HelloWorld` program from Chapter 1, written as an applet:

```
import java.applet.Applet;
import java.awt.Graphics;

public class Hello extends Applet
{ public void paint(Graphics g)
   { g.drawString("Hello, World!", 100, 50);
   }
}
```

Note that the applet has no `main()` method. Instead, it defines the `Hello` class as a subclass of the `Applet` class and overrides its `paint()` method.

To run your applet from a web page, you first have to create an HTML program. The acronym "HTML" stands for Hypertext Markup Language, which is the programming language used for web pages. Here is a minimal HTML program from which you can run your applet:

```
<applet code="Hello.class" width=300 height=100>
</applet>
```

Type this code, exactly as it appears here, into a separate text file named "Hello.html". Then execute the following two JDK commands at the DOS prompt:

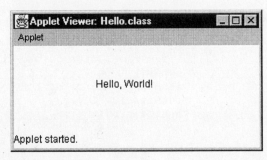

```
javac Hello.java
appletviewer Hello.html
```

The `javac` command compiles your applet just like a regular Java application program, producing the class file `Hello.class`. The `appletviewer` command launches a special program provided in the JDK that runs HTML programs just like a Web browser. In this case, the applet viewer runs the two-line HTML program that you created in the `Hello.html` file. The result is the panel shown here.

This HTML program simply tells the applet viewer to run the Java code contained in the `Hello.class` file, using a panel 100 pixels wide and 50 pixels high. Note the title bar on the panel lists the Java class.

An *HTML program* (also called an *HTML script*) is a sequence of three kinds of tokens: ordinary text characters, tags, and special symbols. The ordinary text is displayed as text. The tags (also called *elements*) are special instructions, like Java methods or C++ functions. Tags are identified by their names enclosed in angle brackets, like this: `<center>`. The special symbols (also called *entities*) are code punctuation marks such as the ampersand (`&`) and the quotation mark(`"`).

The HTML program in Example 10.1 consists of a single `applet` tag. This tag has three *attributes*: `code="Hello.class"`, `width=300`, and `height=100`. These are like arguments passed to a method or function, providing essential information about what is to be done. In this case, the action to be performed is the execution of a Java applet. To do that, the applet viewer needs to know the name of the applet (`code="Hello.class"`) and the size of the panel (`width=300 height=100`) to use. The code `</applet>` simply signals the end of the tag. For example, the tag `<img src="http://www.paris.org/Musees/Louvre/Treasures/gifs/Mona_Lisa.jpg">` would download and include a (186 KB) digital image of the Mona Lisa from the Louvre in Paris.

You can use your Web browser instead of the applet viewer to run your Java applet. Simply `Open` the `.html` file in your browser. For example, in Netscape's Navigator, select the `File > Open Page...` command from the menu and then select the file. The result looks like this:

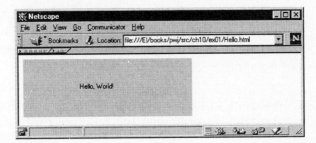

Similarly, in Microsoft's Internet Explorer, select the `File > Open` command from the menu and then select the file:

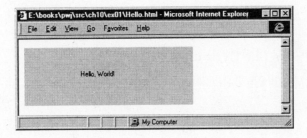

10.2 THE `Applet` CLASS

The `Applet` class is defined in the `java.applet` package. In fact, it is the only class defined in that package. It is a subclass of the `Panel` class, so applets are containers, similar to frames. In particular, events are handled by applets the same way they are handled by frames. (See Chapter 9.)

As an instance of a user-defined subclass of the `Applet` class, an applet normally overrides one or more of the following methods:

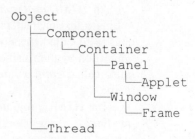

```
Applet.destroy()
Applet.init()
Applet.start()
Applet.stop()
Component.paint()
Component.repaint()
Component.update()
```

Of these, usually none of these except the `paint()` and `repaint()` methods are invoked explicitly by the applet.

The `init()` method is invoked automatically by the AWT run-time system when the applet is launched. Similar to a constructor, it is used for initializations.

The `start()` method is invoked automatically by the AWT whenever the HTML program is reloaded into the Web browser. That happens when you click on the Reload button in Netscape's Communicator or when you select View > Refresh from the menu (or press the F5 key) in Microsoft's Netscape Navigator.

The `stop()` method is invoked when the HTML page that contains the applet is left.

The `destroy()` method is automatically invoked by the AWT when the browser quits.

The `paint()` method is automatically invoked by the AWT run-time system whenever it detects that any part of the applet needs to be redrawn. It is similar to the `update()` method.

The `repaint()` method asks the AWT to redraw the frame. It calls `update()` which calls `paint()` to clear the panel by filling it with its background color and then to repaint it. This causes flickering in animation. To overcome flickering, override the `update()` method, as shown in Example 10.4.

The `repaint()` method has four forms:

```
public void repaint()
public void repaint(long ms)
public void repaint(int x, int y, int width, int height)
public void repaint(long ms, int x, int y, int width, int height)
```

EXAMPLE 10.2 The Life Cycle of an Applet

Run the following HTML script in Netscape's Communicator Web browser:

```
<applet code="LifeCycle.class" width=400 height=400>
</applet>
```

where `LifeCycle.class` is the compiled bytecode for the following Java source code:

```
import java.applet.Applet;
import java.awt.*;

public class LifeCycle extends Applet
{ int initCount=0;
  int startCount=0;
  int stopCount=0;
  int destroyCount=0;

  public void init()
  { ++initCount;
    System.out.println("init(): " + initCount);
  }
```

```
    public void start()
    { ++startCount;
      System.out.println("start() " + startCount);
    }

    public void stop()
    { ++stopCount;
      System.out.println("stop() " + stopCount);
    }

    public void destroy()
    { ++destroyCount;
      System.out.println("destroy() " + destroyCount);
    }
}
```

In Netscape, open the Java console window (use the menu item Communicator > Java Console in Netscape 4, Options > Show Java Console in Netscape 3). Load the HTML script to run the Java applet. Then click on the Reload button several times. The console looks like this.

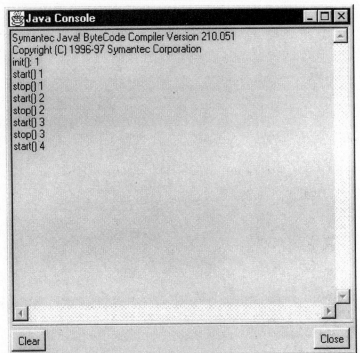

Each time any of the four explicit methods is invoked, the invocation is counted and that count is displayed. This example here shows that `init()` has been invoked once, `start()` has been invoked four times, `stop()` has been invoked three times, and `destroy()` has not yet been invoked.

10.3 THE Thread CLASS

A *thread* is an independent sequential flow of control within a process. Threads run within programs. A single application or applet can have many threads doing different things independently.

The `Thread` class is defined in java.lang as a subclass of the `Object` class. To use threads in your program, you need to define your own local subclass of the `Thread` class and therein override its `run()` method. Put the code that you want the threads of that subclass to execute in that `run()` method.

EXAMPLE 10.3 A Multithreaded Program

```
class MyThread extends Thread
{ int sleepTime;

  public MyThread(String s)
  { super(s);
    sleepTime = (int)(500*Math.random());
    System.out.println("Name: " + getName()
      + "\t Sleep: " + sleepTime);
  }

  public void run()
  { try { sleep(sleepTime); }
    catch(Exception e) {}
    System.out.println("Thread " + getName());
  }
}

public class TestThreads
{ public static void main(String[] args)
  { MyThread thread0, thread1, thread2, thread3;
    thread0 = new MyThread("0");
    thread1 = new MyThread("1");
    thread2 = new MyThread("2");
    thread3 = new MyThread("3");
    thread0.start();
    thread1.start();
    thread2.start();
    thread3.start();
    try { System.in.read(); }
    catch (Exception e) {}
  }
}
```

The output on the first run was

```
Name: 0 Sleep: 442
Name: 1 Sleep: 242
Name: 2 Sleep: 188
Name: 3 Sleep: 146
Thread 3
Thread 2
Thread 1
Thread 0
```

The output on the second run was

```
Name: 0 Sleep: 157
Name: 1 Sleep: 89
Name: 2 Sleep: 437
Name: 3 Sleep: 120
Thread 1
Thread 3
Thread 0
Thread 2
```

EXAMPLE 10.4 A Digital Clock Applet

Run the following HTML script in Netscape's Communicator Web browser:

```
<applet code="Clock.class" width=360 height=60>
</applet>
```

where `Clock.class` is the compiled bytecode for the following Java source code:

```java
import java.applet.Applet;
import java.awt.*;
import java.util.Calendar;

public class Clock extends Applet implements Runnable
{ Thread thread;
  Font font = new Font("Monospaced", Font.BOLD, 64);
  int hour, minute, second;

  public void init()
  { if (thread == null)
    { thread = new Thread(this);
      thread.start();
    }
  }

  public void run()
  { for (;;)   // forever
    { Calendar time=Calendar.getInstance();
      hour = time.get(Calendar.HOUR);
      minute = time.get(Calendar.MINUTE);
      second = time.get(Calendar.SECOND);
      repaint(5);   // requests re-drawing every 5 milliseconds
    }
  }

  public void destroy()
  { thread = null;
  }

  public void paint(Graphics g)
  { g.setFont(font);
    String time = String.valueOf(hour)
      + ":" + String.valueOf(minute)
      + ":" + String.valueOf(second);
    g.drawString(time, 50, 50);
  }
}
```

The running applet should look like this:

10.4 EXCEPTIONS

If anything can go wrong, it will.
—Murphy's Law

An *exception* is a run-time event that indicates that something has gone wrong. Exceptions are represented in Java by instances of the `Exception` class.

An exception is an event, like a mouse click on a window button. Except that, instead of being created by the user to achieve a specific result, exceptions are created by the system to alert the user of an event that might otherwise have gone undetected, or at least unrecognized. The inheritance hierarchy here suggests the variety of exceptions that can occur. The `FileNotFoundException` class and the `NullPointerException` class are common examples.

```
Object
  └─ Throwable
       ├─ Error
       │    ├─ LinkageError
       │    ├─ ThreadDeath
       │    └─ VirtualMachineError
       └─ Exception
            ├─ IOException
            │    ├─ EndOfFileException
            │    └─ FileNotFoundException
            ├─ NoSuchFieldException
            ├─ NoSuchMethodException
            └─ RuntimeException
                 ├─ ArithmeticException
                 ├─ IllegalArgumentException
                 ├─ IndexOutOfBoundsException
                 └─ NullPointerException
```

In Java, methods that can fail are declared with a `throws` clause. For example, the `read()` method in the `Reader` class is declared like this:

```
int read(char buf[], int offset, int count) throws IOException
```

The `throws IOException` clause means that this method can be invoked only within a `try` clause. That is what we did back in Example 1.2 on page 14, reproduced here:

EXAMPLE 10.5 The "HellAl" Program from Chapter 1

```
public class HelloAl
{ public static void main(String[] args)
  { final int LEN = 255;
    byte buffer[] = new byte[LEN];
    System.out.print("Enter your name: ");
    try { System.in.read(buffer, 0, LEN); }
    catch (Exception e) {}
    String name = new String(buffer);
    System.out.println("Hello, " + name.trim() + "!");
  }
}
```

The reason such methods must be used within `try` blocks is to guarantee that some provision is made to handle the exception; *i.e.*, the need for some alternative action is made explicit and easy for the programmer to use. The alternative action is written in the `catch` clause. No such alternative action was written in Example 10.5. But we could have done this instead:

```
try { System.in.read(buffer, 0, LEN); }
catch (Exception e) { System.out.println("ERROR: read() failed."); }
```

Like events, exceptions must be handled by specific software constructs. In Java, exception handling is managed by `try` blocks.

EXAMPLE 10.6 Testing Exceptions

```java
import java.io.*;

public class TestExceptions
{ static int getInt() throws IOException
  { BufferedReader input =
      new BufferedReader(new InputStreamReader(System.in));
    System.out.print("Enter an integer: ");
    String s = input.readLine();
    return Integer.parseInt(s);
  }

  public static void main(String[] args)
  { int n1=0, n2=1, n3=0;
    try
    { n1 = getInt();
      n2 = getInt();
      n3 = n1/n2;
    }
    catch (Exception e) { System.out.println("[" + e + "]"); }
    System.out.println(n1 + "/" + n2 + " = " + n3);
  }
}
```

The first sample run was
```
Enter an integer: 22
Enter an integer: 3
22/3 = 7
```

Everything worked normally here; no exceptions were thrown.

The second sample run was
```
Enter an integer: 22
Enter an integer: 0
[java.lang.ArithmeticException: / by zero]
22/0 = 0
```

Here, we intentionally tried to divide by zero to see what would happen. When the division `n1/n2` was attempted, an `ArithmeticException` object was thrown. It was caught by the exception handler
```
catch (Exception e) { System.out.println("[" + e + "]"); }
```
and processed by the `println()` method, which then invoked the method
```
ArithmeticException.toString()
```
to print the string "`java.lang.ArithmeticException: / by zero`".

The third sample run was
```
Enter an integer: 22
Enter an integer: w
[java.lang.NumberFormatException: w]
22/1 = 0
```

Here, we intentionally entered the letter `w` to see what would happen. In this case, the exception is thrown by the `readLine()` method within the `getInt()` method. But it is caught by the same exception handler
```
catch (Exception e) { System.out.println("[" + e + "]"); }
```

It invokes the `NumberFormatException.toString()` method to print the string "`java.lang.NumberFormatException: w`".

Review Questions

10.1   What is an applet?

10.2   What is the AppletViewer?

10.3   What is an HTML tag?

10.4   What is an `applet` tag?

10.5   How does the `Applet.init()` method get invoked?

10.6   How does the `Applet.destroy()` method get invoked?

10.7   How does the `Applet.start()` method get invoked?

10.8   How does the `Applet.stop()` method get invoked?

Programming Problems

10.1   Predict how the output from the program in Example 10.6 on page 231 will differ by moving the last line

```
System.out.println(n1 + "/" + n2 + " = " + n3);
```
up into the `try` clause, like this:
```
try
{ n1 = getInt();
  n2 = getInt();
  n3 = n1/n2;
  System.out.println(n1 + "/" + n2 + " = " + n3);
}
```
Then make the modification and see if your prediction was right. Explain the difference.

Supplementary Programming Problems

10.2   Re-write the "`Click me!`" program in Example 9.9 on page 217 as an applet.

10.3   Re-write the temperature conversion program in Example 9.11 on page 220 as an applet.

10.4   Write an applet that displays Pascal's Triangle (see Problem 5.7 on page 98), where the user selects the number of rows to be displayed.

10.5   Re-write the concentric circles program in Problem 9.8 on page 221 as an applet, where the user selects the distance between the circles.

10.6   Re-write the filled circles program in Problem 9.11 on page 221 as an applet, where the user selects the size the circles.

10.7   Re-write the amortization program in Problem 9.13 on page 221 as an applet.

10.8   Re-write the calculator program in Problem 9.14 on page 221 as an applet.

Answers to Review Questions

10.1   An *applet* is a Java program that has to be embedded in another program to be run. Applets are usually embedded in HTML scripts (Web pages).

10.2   The AppletViewer is a special program that comes with the Java Developer's Kit that allows you to run applets.

10.3   An HTML tag is a syntactical construct in the HTML language that abbreviates specific instructions to be executed when the HTML script is loaded into a Web browser. It is like a method in Java, a function in C++, a procedure in Pascal, or a subroutine in FORTRAN.

10.4   An `applet` tag is an HTML tag that runs a Java applet.

10.5   The `Applet.init()` method is invoked automatically by the Java run-time system when when the Web page in which it is embedded is loaded.

10.6   The `Applet.destroy()` method is invoked automatically by the Java run-time system when the Web page in which it is embedded is unloaded.

10.7   The `Applet.start()` method is invoked automatically by the Java run-time system when the Web page in which it is embedded is loaded or reloaded.

10.8   The `Applet.stop()` method is invoked automatically by the Java run-time system when the Web page in which it is embedded is reloaded.

Solutions to Programming Problems

10.1   The results are the same except that no erroneous ouput is printed; *i.e.* the ouput
```
22/0 = 0
22/1 = 0
```
does not occur. The reason is that the `try` block is exited as soon as an exception is thrown, in which case, the rest of the statements within the `try` block are never executed.

Appendix A

Acronyms

API	Application Programming Interface
AWT	Abstract Window Toolkit, or Abstract Windowing Toolkit
CGI	Common Gateway Interface
DLL	Dynamic Link Library
DOS	Disk Operating System
FTP	File Transfer Protocol
GIF	Graphics Interchange Format
GUI	Graphical User Interface
HTML	Hypertext Markup Language
HTTP	Hypertext Transfer Protocol
IDE	Integrated Development Environment, or Integrated Developer Environment
ISP	Internet Service Provider
JDK	Java Development Kit, or Java Developers' Kit
JIT	Just-In-Time (Java bytecode compiler)
JPEG	Joint Photography Engineering Group
JVM	Java Virtual Machine
MIME	Multipurpose Internet Mail Extension
POP	Post Office Protocol
SMTP	Simple Mail Transfer Protocol
TCP/IP	Transmission Control Protocol/Internet Protocol
URL	Uniform Resource Locator
WWW	World-Wide Web
Y2K	Year 2 Thousand

Appendix B

The JBuilder IDE

JBuilder is an integrated development environment (IDE) for programming in Java, produced by Borland International, now called "Inprise." It is popular among professional Java programmers. This appendix describes some of its features. For more information, check the following Web page:

http://www.inprise.com/jbuilder/

Its brief description of their product is

> JBuilder 2 is the most comprehensive set of visual development tools for creating Pure Java business and database applications. Simplify development with JDK Switching, CodeInsight, Beans Express, and BeanInsight, plus: Pure Java DataExpress components, complete JDBC connectivity, 200+ JBCL and JFC/Swing beans with source, and more!

Like other IDE, JBuilder includes the usual features:

1. a powerful built-in editor;
2. an automatic means for managing multi-file projects;
3. a debugger;
4. a compiler;
5. an on-line reference library.

It also comes with two manuals that are easy to use.

JBuilder2, released in May 1998, uses Java 1.1.5. It's on-line reference includes the Java API:

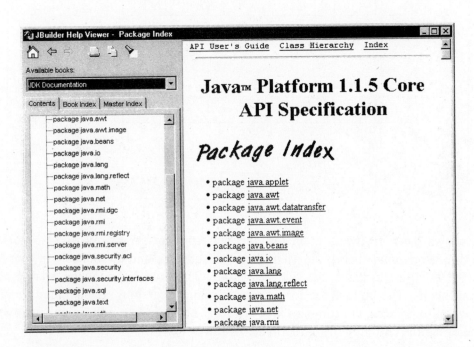

JBuilder's main window looks like this:

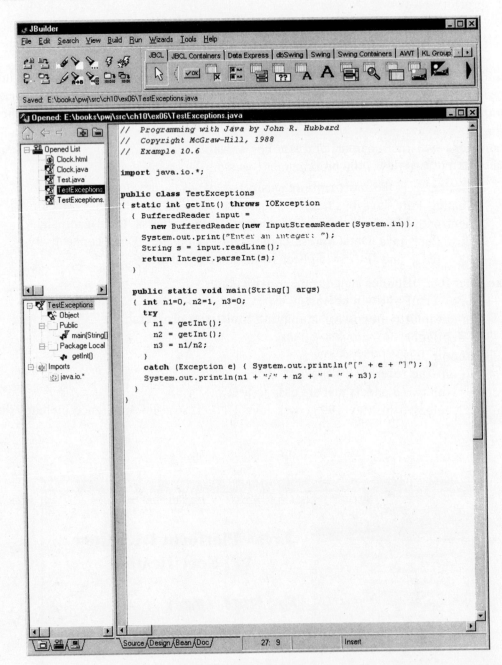

This shows the main window on top and the AppBrowser below it. The main window contains three horizontal "bars": the Menu bar, the Tool bar, and the Status bar. The Menu bar contains the usual menu items: File, Edit, Search, *etc*. The Tool bar contains a large number of buttons and icons. The buttons are for quick compiling, searching, debugging, *etc*. The icons allow drag-and-drop access to common Java classes. The status bar in this picture shows the path and name of the file currently displayed in the AppBrowser

```
E:\book\pwj\src\ch10\ex06\TestExceptions.java.
```

The AppBrowser includes a number of very useful and well-engineered features: a powerful editor, directory browsers, class browsers, *etc.* For example, in the picture here, the lower left window gives a hierarchical listing of all the parts of the displayed class file: the class heading, each class member, the packages, the imports, *etc.* If you click on any of these listings, the corresponding part in the source code file is immediately located in the editor.

The editor itself uses color-coding for the various syntactical parts of the Java language. For example, comments are shown in blue, string literals are in red, *etc.* This feature is very helpful in locating syntax errors such as a misplaced quotation mark.

One particularly nice feature of the editor is its provision of pop-up lists of the Java library class methods and their parameter lists. For example, the screen capture here shows what happened immediately after the programmer typed the dot on the line

```
    String s = input.
```
The pop-up scroll list shows all the methods of the `String` class. When the programmer typed `r` next, the system immediately highlighted the listing

```
    read : int
```
in the scroll list. Then all the programmer needed to do was to press the down arrow key once to select the listing

```
    readLine : String
```
and then press Return to have that method name inserted into the edited file at the cursor.

A similar feature is provided for method parameters. For example, when the programmer typed the left parenthesis on the next line

```
    return Integer.parseInt(
```
another pop-up scroll list appeared, like this, showing the possible parameter lists for this method. This shows immediately that there are two versions of the `Integer.parseInt()` method: one that takes a single `String` argument, and one that takes a `String` argument followed by an `int` argument. It also indicates that the `int` represents the radix of the string being converted.

This kind of instantaneous information is invaluable, especially with the Java language with over 1500 classes and over 10,000 methods. No programmer can remember even a small part of that information. JBuilder saves the programmer from the time-consuming task of searching the reference manuals.

Appendix C

The CodeWarrior IDE

CodeWarrior is an integrated development environment (IDE) for programming in Java, C++, C, and Pascal. Produced by Metrowerks, it is popular among students. This appendix describes some of its features. For more information, check the web page

```
http://www.metrowerks.com/
```

Like other IDE, CodeWarrior includes the usual features:

1. a powerful built-in editor;

2. an automatic means for managing multi-file projects;

3. a debugger;

4. a compiler;

5. an on-line reference library.

Although CodeWarrior does not come with any printed manuals, the book by **[Trudeau]** (see Appendix F) is of some help.

A special version of the IDE, called CodeWarrior Lite, can be downloaded for free from their website.

CodeWarrior3 was released in March 1998. Its main window looks like this:

Appendix D

Computer Numbers

The numbers that computers use are similar to the numbers of theoretical mathematics. But there are some important differences. This appendix summarizes them.

D.1 THE FINITE AND THE INFINITE

The biggest differences between computer numbers and mathematical numbers are the direct result of the inescapable fact that computer storage is finite. The consequences are:

1. The range of possible values for any number type is finite.
2. The precision of any floating-point number is limited.

D.2 NUMBER TYPES

Mathematical number types: integer, rational, real, complex, hypercomplex, and transfinite.
Computer number types: integer, floating-point.
Java number types: `byte`, `short`, `int`, `long`, `float`, `double`, `BigInteger`, `BigDecimal`

D.3 RANGES OF INTEGER TYPES

`byte`: −128 to 127
`short`: −32,768 to 32,767
`int`: −2,146,473,648 to 2,147,483,647
`long`: −9,223,372,036,854,775,808 to 9,223,372,036,854,775,807 (See Example D.2 below.)
`BigInteger`: unlimited by the Java language

D.4 INTEGER OVERFLOW

Integer values "wraparound" when they overflow.

EXAMPLE D.1 Overflow of `byte` Integers

```
class Test
{ // Tests integer overflow
  public static void main(String args[])
  { byte n=1;
```

```
      for (int i=1; i<=8; i++)
      { n *= 2;
         System.out.println("2^" + i + " = " + n);
      }
   }
}
```

The output is
```
2^1 = 2
2^2 = 4
2^3 = 8
2^4 = 16
2^5 = 32
2^6 = 64
2^7 = -128
2^8 = 0
```
The product $2 \cdot 64$ was computed to be -128, and the product $2 \cdot (-128)$ was computed to be 0!
Similar errors occur for the other three primitive integer types.

EXAMPLE D.2 The `BigInteger` Class

The `BigInteger` class is defined in the `java.math` package. It provides integers of "arbitrary precision."
```
import java.math.*;
class Test
{ // Tests integer overflow for BigInteger objects
   public static void main(String args[])
   { long p = Integer.parseInt(args[0]);  // from the command line
      final BigInteger two = BigInteger.valueOf(2);
      BigInteger n = BigInteger.valueOf(1);
      for (int i=0; i<p; i++)
        n = n.multiply(two);
      System.out.println("2^" + p + " = " + n);
   }
}
```
This program assumes an integer is typed on the command line. The first line of `main()` extracts that integer value (received by `main()` through the string `args[0]`) and initializes `p` with it.

The first sample run was
```
E:\books\pwj\src\appD\ex02>java Test 7
2^7 = 128
```
The power 2^7 was computed to be 128.

The second sample run was
```
E:\books\pwj\src\appD\ex02>java Test 63
2^63 = 9223372036854775808
```
The power 2^7 was computed to be 128.

The third sample run was
```
E:\books\pwj\src\appD\ex02>java Test 1000
2^1000 = 10715086071862673209484250490600018105614048117055336074
43750388370351051124936122493198378815695858127594672917553146825
18714528569231404359845775746985748039345677748242309854210746050
62371141877954182153046474983581941267398767559165543946077062914
5711964776865421676604298316526243868372056680693 76
```

D.5 RANGES OF FLOATING-POINT TYPES

`float`: $\pm 1.40129846432481707 \times 10^{-45}$ to $\pm 3.40282346638528860 \times 10^{-38}$

`double`: $\pm 4.94065645841246544 \times 10^{-324}$ to $\pm 1.79769313486231570 \times 10^{-308}$

`BigDecimal`: unlimited by the Java language

D.6 THE `INFINITY` AND `NaN` CONSTANTS

Recall (Section 6.10 on page 133) that the constants `POSITIVE_INFINITY` and `NEGATIVE_INFINITY` are defined in the `Double` wrapper class. They represent the mathematical symbols ∞ and $-\infty$, which have the property that $-\infty < x < \infty$ for all real numbers x.

The name `NaN` means "not a number." That is a bit misleading because infinity and minus infinity are also not numbers. In mathematics, `NaN` is called an *indeterminate form*.

EXAMPLE D.3 Testing Transfinite Arithmetic

```
class Test
{ // Tests transfinite arithmetic

  public static void main(String args[])
  { final double PInf = Double.POSITIVE_INFINITY;
    final double NInf = Double.NEGATIVE_INFINITY;
    System.out.println("1.0/0.0 = " + 1.0/0.0);
    System.out.println("-1.0/0.0 = " + -1.0/0.0);
    System.out.println("0.0/0.0 = " + 0.0/0.0);
    System.out.println("0.0*Infinity = " + 0.0*PInf );
    System.out.println("Infinity*Infinity = " + PInf*PInf );
    System.out.println("Infinity*(-Infinity) = " + PInf*NInf );
    System.out.println("0.0*(-Infinity) = " + 0.0*NInf );
    System.out.println("0.0*NaN = " + 0.0*Double.NaN);
  }
}
```

The output is

```
1.0/0.0 = Infinity
-1.0/0.0 = -Infinity
0.0/0.0 = NaN
0.0*Infinity = NaN
Infinity*Infinity = Infinity
Infinity*(-Infinity) = -Infinity
0.0*(-Infinity) = NaN
0.0*NaN = NaN
```

The following tables summarize transfinite arithmetic. They assume that $0 < c < \infty$.

Addition

+	0	$-c$	c	$-\infty$	∞	NaN
0	0	$-c$	c	$-\infty$	∞	NaN
$-c$	$-c$	$-2c$	0	$-\infty$	∞	NaN
c	c	0	$2c$	$-\infty$	∞	NaN
$-\infty$	$-\infty$	$-\infty$	$-\infty$	$-\infty$	NaN	NaN
∞	∞	∞	∞	NaN	∞	NaN
NaN	NaN	NaN	NaN	NaN	NaN	NaN

Subtraction

$-$	0	$-c$	c	$-\infty$	∞	NaN
0	0	c	$-c$	∞	$-\infty$	NaN
$-c$	$-c$	0	$-2c$	∞	$-\infty$	NaN
c	c	$2c$	0	∞	$-\infty$	NaN
$-\infty$	$-\infty$	$-\infty$	$-\infty$	NaN	$-\infty$	NaN
∞	∞	∞	∞	∞	NaN	NaN
NaN	NaN	NaN	NaN	NaN	NaN	NaN

Multiplication

*	0	$-c$	c	$-\infty$	∞	NaN
0	0	0	0	NaN	NaN	NaN
$-c$	0	c^2	$-c^2$	∞	$-\infty$	NaN
c	0	$-c^2$	c^2	$-\infty$	∞	NaN
$-\infty$	NaN	∞	$-\infty$	∞	∞	NaN
∞	NaN	$-\infty$	∞	$-\infty$	∞	NaN
NaN	NaN	NaN	NaN	NaN	NaN	NaN

Division

/	0+	$-c$	c	$-\infty$	∞	NaN
0	NaN	0	0	0	0	NaN
$-c$	$-\infty$	1	-1	0	0	NaN
c	∞	-1	1	0	0	NaN
$-\infty$	$-\infty$	∞	$-\infty$	NaN	NaN	NaN
∞	∞	$-\infty$	∞	NaN	NaN	NaN
NaN	NaN	NaN	NaN	NaN	NaN	NaN

EXAMPLE D.4 Testing Transfinite Comparisons

```
class Test
{ // Tests transfinite comparisons

  public static void main(String args[])
  { final double PIN = Double.POSITIVE_INFINITY;
    final double NIN = Double.NEGATIVE_INFINITY;
    final double NAN = Double.NaN;
    System.out.println("(4.0 < Infinity) = " + (4.0 < PIN));
    System.out.println("(4.0 < -Infinity) = " + (4.0 < NIN));
    System.out.println("(4.0 < NaN) = " + (4.0 < NAN));
    System.out.println("(Infinity == Infinity) = " + (PIN == PIN));
    System.out.println("(-Infinity == -Infinity) = " + (NIN == NIN));
    System.out.println("(NaN == NaN) = " + (NAN == NAN));
  }
}
```

The output is

```
(4.0 < Infinity) = true
(4.0 < -Infinity) = false
(4.0 < NaN) = false
(Infinity == Infinity) = true
(-Infinity == -Infinity) = true
(NaN == NaN) = false
```

The following tables summarize transfinite comparisons.

Less Than

<	0	−c	c	−∞	∞	NaN
0	false	false	true	false	true	false
−c	true	false	true	false	true	false
c	false	false	false	false	true	false
−∞	true	true	true	false	true	false
∞	false	false	false	false	false	false
NaN	false	false	false	false	false	false

Equality

==	0	−c	c	−∞	∞	NaN
0	true	false	false	false	false	false
−c	false	true	false	false	false	false
c	false	false	true	false	false	false
−∞	false	false	false	true	false	false
∞	false	false	false	false	true	false
NaN	false	false	false	false	false	false

Appendix E

Unicode

Unicode is the international standardized character set that Java uses for its `String` and `StringBuffer` classes. Each code is a 16-bit integer with unique value in the range 0 to 65,535. These values are usually expressed in hexadecimal form. For example, the infinity symbol ∞ has the Unicode value 8734, which is 221E in hexadecimal.

In Java, the character whose Unicode is *hhhh* in hexadecimal is expressed as `\uhhhh`. For example, the infinity symbol is expressed as `\u221E`.

The first 127 values are the same as the ASCII Code (American Standard Code for Information Interchange).The following table summarizes the various alphabets and their Unicodes.

You can obtain more information from the Unicode Consortium website
`http://www.unicode.org/`
Also, see the book **[Unicode]** listed in Appendix F.

Unicode	Alphabet
\u0000 - \u024F	Latin Alphabets
\u0370 - \u03FF	Greek
\u0400 - \u04FF	Cyrillic
\u0530 - \u058F	Armenian
\u0590 - \u05FF	Hebrew
\u0600 - \u06FF	Arabic
\u0900 - \u097F	Devanagari
\u0980 - \u09FF	Bengali
\u0A00 - \u0A7F	Gurmukhi
\u0A80 - \u0AFF	Gujarati
\u0B00 - \u0B7F	Oriya
\u0B80 - \u0BFF	Tamil
\u0C00 - \u0C7F	Teluga
\u0C80 - \u0CFF	Kannada
\u0D00 - \u0D7F	Malayam
\u0E00 - \u0E7F	Thai
\u0E80 - \u0EFF	Lao
\u0F00 - \u0FBF	Tibetan
\u10A0 - \u10FF	Georgian
\u1100 - \u11FF	Hangul Jamo
\u2000 - \u206F	Punctuation
\u2070 - \u209F	Superscripts and subscripts

Unicode	Alphabet
\u20A0 - \u20CF	Currency symbols
\u20D0 - \u20FF	Diacritical marks
\u2100 - \u214F	Letterlike symbols
\u2150 - \u218F	Numeral forms
\u2190 - \u21FF	Arrows
\u2200 - \u22FF	Mathematical symbols
\u2300 - \u23FF	Miscellaneous technical symbols
\u2400 - \u243F	Control pictures
\u2440 - \u245F	Optical Character Recognition symbols
\u2460 - \u24FF	Enclosed alphanumerics
\u2500 - \u257F	Box drawing
\u2580 - \u259F	Block elements
\u25A0 - \u25FF	Geometric shapes
\u2700 - \u27BF	Dingbats
\u3040 - \u309F	Hiragana
\u30A0 - \u30FF	Katakana
\u3100 - \u312F	Bopomofo
\u3130 - \u318F	Jamo
\u3190 - \u319F	Kanbun
\u3200 - \u32FF	Enclosed CJK letters and months
\u4E00 - \u9FFF	CJK Ideographs

Appendix F

References

[Arnold]

The Java Programming Language, by Ken Arnold and James Gosling.
Addison-Wesley, Reading, MA (http://www2.awl.com/corp/), 1996, 0-201-63455-4.

[Bell]

Java for Students, by Douglas Bell and Mike Parr.
Prentice Hall, Englewood Cliffs, NJ, 1998 (http://www.prenticehall.com/), 0-13-858440-0.

[Boone]

Java Essentials for C and C++ Programmers, by Barry Boone.
Addison-Wesley, Reading, MA (http://www.aw.com/devpress/), 1998, 0-201-47946-X.

[Campione]

The Java Tutorial, by Mary Campione and Kathy Walrath.
Addison-Wesley, Reading, MA (http://www2.awl.com/corp/), 1998, 0-201-63454-6.

[Chan1]

The Java Class Libraries, Second Edition, Volume 1, by Patrick Chan, Rosanna Lee, and D. Kramer.
Addison-Wesley, Reading, MA (http://www2.awl.com/corp/), 1998, 0-201-31002-3.

[Chan2]

The Java Class Libraries, Second Edition, Volume 2, by Patrick Chan and Rosanna Lee.
Addison-Wesley, Reading, MA (http://www2.awl.com/corp/), 1998, 0-201-31003-1.

[Chan3]

The Java Developers ALMANAC, by Patrick Chan.
Addison-Wesley, Reading, MA, 1998 (http://www2.awl.com/corp/), 0-201-37967-8.

[Daconta]

Java for C/C++ Programmers, by Michael C. Daconta.
John Wiley & Sons, New York, NY (http://www.wiley.com/), 1996, 0-471-15324-9.

[Deitel]

Java How to Program, by H. M. Deitel and P. J. Deitel.
Prentice Hall, Englewood Cliffs, NJ, 1997 (http://www.prenticehall.com/), 0-13-263401-5.

[Grand1]

Java Language Reference, by Mark Grand.
O'Reilly & Associates, Sebastopol, CA (http://www.oreilly.com/), 1997, 1-56592-326-X.

[Grand2]

Java Fundamental Classes Reference, by Mark Grand and Jonathan Knudsen.
O'Reilly & Associates, Sebastopol, CA (http://www.oreilly.com/), 1997, 1-56592-241-7.

[Heller]

Java 1.1 Developer's Handbook, by Philip Heller and Simon Roberts.
SYBEX, Alameda, CA (http://www.sybex.com/), 1997, 0-7821-1919-0.

[Holmes]

Programming with Java, by Barry Holmes.
Jones and Bartlett, Sudbury, MA 01776 (http://www.jbpub.com), 0-7637-0707-4.

[Holzner]

Java 1.1, No Experience Required, by Steven Holzner.
SYBEX, Alameda, CA (http://www.sybex.com/), 1997, 0-7821-2083-0.

[Horstmann1]

Core Java 1.1, Volume I - Fundamentals, by Cay S. Horstmann and Gary Cornell.
Prentice Hall, Englewood Cliffs, NJ (http://www.prenticehall.com/), 0-13-766957-7.

[Horstmann2]

Computing Concepts with Java Essentials, by Cay S. Horstmann.
John Wiley & Sons, New York, NY (http://www.wiley.com/), 1998, 0-471-17223-5.

[Kamin]

An Introduction to Computer Science Using Java, by S. N. Kamin, M. D. Mickunas, and E. M. Reingold.
WCB/McGraw-Hill, New York, NY (http://www.pbg.mcgraw-hill.com/), 1998,
0-07-034224-5.

[Lewis]

Java Software Solutions, Foundations of Program Design, by John Lewis and William Loftus.
Addison-Wesley, Reading, MA, 1998 (http://www2.awl.com/corp/), 0-57164-1.

[Liang]

An Introduction to Java Programming, by Y. Daniel Liang.
Que Education & Training (http://www.mcp.com/resources/education/queet/),
Indianapolis, IN, 1998, 1-57576-548-9.

[Trudeau]

Mastering CodeWarrior for Windows 95/NT, The Official Guide, by Jim Trudeau.
SYBEX, Alameda, CA (http://www.sybex.com/), 1997, 1-7821-2057-1.

[Unicode]

The Unicode Standard, Version 2.0, by The Unicode Consortium.
Addison-Wesley, Reading, MA (http://www2.awl.com/corp/), 1996, 0-201-48345-9.

[Vanhelsuwe]

Mastering Java 1.1, Second Edition, by Laurence Vanhelsuwe.
SYBEX, Alameda, CA (http://www.sybex.com/), 1997, 0-7821-2070-9.

[Zukowski]

Java AWT Reference, by John Zukowski.
O'Reilly & Associates, Sebastopol, CA (http://www.oreilly.com/), 1997, 1-56592-240-9.

Index